Typographic Specimens:

The Great Typefaces

Typographic Specimens:

The Great Typefaces

Philip Meggs
Rob Carter

A VNR book

JOHN WILEY & SONS, INC.
New York   Chichester   Weinheim   Brisbane   Singapore   Toronto

Published by John Wiley & Sons, Inc.

Published simultaneously in Canada.

Library of Congress Cataloging-in-Publication Data:

Typographic specimens: the great typefaces/[compiled by] Philip Meggs, Rob Carter.
p.   cm.
ISBN 0-471-28429-7
1. Printing—Specimens.   2. Type and type-founding.   I. Meggs, Philip B.
II. Carter, Rob.
Z250.T97 1993   93-29588
686.2'24—dc20

Printed in the United States of America

10   9

Acknowledgments

The contributions of many people are deeply appreciated. More than one hundred designers responded to the survey questionnaire used to select the typefaces included in this book; their thoughtful participation and collective judgement made an invaluable contribution.

The graphic designers who created the design interpretations for each typeface are identified on the contents page and opposite their page designs. We deeply appreciate their participation in this project.

Martin Antoinetti, Librarian of the Grolier Club, and Bill Davis of The Monotype Corporation provided generous assistance.

At Van Nostrand Reinhold, Acquisitions Editor Amanda Miller, Executive Editor Wendy Lochner, Production Editor Anthony Calcara, Production Manager Sandra Cohen, and Editorial Assistant Kelly Francis assisted in the production of this book.

At Virginia Commonwealth University, Jerry Bates, Jeff Price, Richard Schuessler, and Karen White provided advice and logistical help. Diana Lively and Harriet Turner provided invaluable assistance. Dr. Murry N. DePillars and John DeMao have offered continued support.

Libby Phillips Meggs and Sally Plumb Carter offered unending encouragement and good humor during frantic efforts to meet editorial and design deadlines.

We thank these individuals for their help.

Introduction

Typographic specimens have been an important design tool since the first specimen sheets were produced in the early decades of typography following Johann Gutenberg's invention of movable type around 1450. Early printers and typefounders used specimen sheets to attract customers for their graphic services. Printed specimens provide an opportunity to study and learn about typefaces, to select and plan typography, and to increase one's understanding of letterforms. Specimens aid in the selection of fonts to be purchased for the font library used by a designer. Even though contemporary technology enables one to view typography on screen and study printed sample proofs in planning a design, specimen books introduce unfamiliar typefaces in printed form and aid in the development of connoisseurship. Comparative analysis of similar faces in printed form becomes possible.

There has been a phenomenal growth in the number of typefaces available over the past two decades, introducing many weeds into the typographic garden. The motivation for this book was a desire to combine in one resource the finest typeface designs. The criterion for design excellence in a typeface includes a harmony of form achieved by unifying diverse letters within the alphabet; this creates a rhythmic quality satisfying to the reader or viewer. This combination of unity and diversity creates legibility. Originality, the introduction of new forms into the typographic landscape, is often a hallmark of a significant typeface; however, even subtle innovations within a tradition can create an important typeface. A typeface gains distinction through unique proportions, characters, and shapes, but when these identifying properties are too exaggerated or pronounced, they intrude upon the integrity of the typeface.

First, the authors selected over one hundred type families whose properties seemed to satisfy these criteria. To minimize the influence of personal subjective judgement upon the final selection, over one hundred prominent designers and design educators were sent a ballot listing these typefaces and were asked to vote for the type families that best fulfilled their personal criteria for typographic excellence. They were also asked to write in any typefaces they felt should have been included on the list. This jury provided remarkably consistent viewpoints when selecting fonts they regarded as great typefaces. The typefaces contained in this book represent the results of this poll without alteration; certainly, each of the authors would have compiled a somewhat different selection, as would have each participant in the poll.

Originally it was our intent to select experimental or applied designs to open the section for each type family in the book. A number of designers returned ballots with a note expressing interest in developing an experimental page or submitting an existing design for one of the type families. We began asking designers if they would like to design a page and quickly found enough interest to cover the type families represented in this book. The diversity and originality of these design interpretations add a lively dimension to the book.

Traditional standard type sizes have become somewhat irrelevant since contemporary computer software enables type sizes and spaces to be altered in thousandths of a point, and the wide availability of enlarging and reducing copier machines lessens the need for a variety of specimen sizes. Three display sizes are shown of most fonts, and the point size appears in small flags adjacent to the specimens.

Researching the origins of each type family increased our awareness of the forces shaping the evolution of typeface design. These include handwriting, technology, the cultural milieu, marketing, and the original visions of creative type designers. Early in the evolution of typography, written forms provided models for typefaces; this influence continues today.

Technology and typeface design

Technological advances alter typeface design, and these influences are not always positive. Hand-set metal type was cast from matrices which were made by stamping hand-carved punches into a softer metal. Typeface design was dependent upon the skill and artistry of the punchcutter, while the limitations of this handcraft process ultimately determined the quality and nature of letterform designs.

The industrial revolution brought technical advances including more precise carving, making possible such refinements as thinner strokes and sharper serifs. Mechanical routers enabled the manufacture of wood type for large display purposes, while mechanical punchcutters permitted very precise metal type based on the designer's drawings rather than carved punches. Expanded use of display advertising and posters led to the development of whole new categories of typeface design to satisfy the new applications.

The invention of Linotype and Monotype keyboard typesetting machines in the 1880s made text type far more economical and efficient than hand-set metal type. This reduced the cost of books, magazines, and newspapers. Typefaces were designed specifically for the !imitations of these machines; for example, a Linotype machine held two fonts in its magazine, and they had to have the exact same set width. Regular, italic, and bold fonts mixed on the same line required identical set widths. Ironically, as machine-set type replaced hand-set type for text, an expanded need developed for new handset typefaces used in advertising headlines and editorial display type.

During the 1960s, photographic typesetting processes rapidly replaced hand- and machine-set metal type. The low cost of developing new photographic fonts created a new explosion in typeface design. Metal typefaces were redesigned for different sizes, because the thinner stroke weights had to be heavier in smaller sizes to appear optically correct. But phototype used one master font for all sizes, often causing thick strokes to appear too heavy in large sizes, while thin strokes would drop out in very small sizes.

Phototype yielded to digital type during the 1980s. Letterforms were generated by pixels, so the resolution of the output device became an important factor influencing typeface design. The digital type revolution brought great flexibility to typographic design, but this was a two-edged sword, permitting subtle design nuance as well as extreme distortion of letterforms that often violated the integrity of the typeface designer's work.

The revivals
The Arts and Crafts Movement of the late 19th century looked back to historical eras of printing and designed typefaces modeled after early printed books. This inspired a period of revivals during the first three decades of the 20th century, when new versions of rarely attainable typefaces such as Garamond, Baskerville, and Bodoni were created. Metal type foundries – including Berthold, Stempel, and Bauer in Germany, Deberny & Peignot in France, and with American Type Founders in the United States – and typesetting machine manufacturers, such as Linotype, Monotype, and Ludlow, developed their versions of the classical typefaces. This proliferation of variations continued unabated when phototype, rub-down lettering, and digital type companies drew their own variations, altered existing designs, or pirated type designer's work.

By 1990, a staggering range of originals, revivals, adaptations, and copies created a confusing number of variations. Controversies erupted over the relative merits of a bewildering number of variations of traditional typefaces such as Garamond. Often the original font is not necessarily the best version, because later versions sometimes incorporate design refinements or exploit the superior capabilities of new technology. In other cases, some revivals or copies violate the design integrity of the original. The versions chosen for this book are based on often competing considerations: fidelity to the original design; subtle visual refinements or improvements incorporated in the redrawn version; and availability for contemporary electronic-page design. Versions that depart significantly from the original font by exaggerating distinguishing features such as serifs and proportions have been avoided.

The cultural milieu
Visual forms dominant during each epoch often had a pronounced influence upon the development of typefaces. This can be seen in the Victorian Era, when the same ornate gingerbread decorating houses and porches found its way into typeface design. These exaggerated designs have survived, not as typographic masterpieces, but as nostalgic artifacts evoking a historical period. On the other hand, geometric typefaces were designed during the 1920s and 1930s based on elemental forms such as the circle, square, and triangle. This paralleled similar forms in fine art as well as architectural, product, and graphic design of this period; however, these geometric typefaces including Futura and Kabel have survived the passage of time as important members of the typographic lexicon.

Typefaces have been designed during each era that capture the spirit and sensibilities of that time. Extensive use by many designers creates a market for specific typefaces and the equipment used to set them. This has led competing companies to develop copies and variations. For example, the popularity of Futura spawned a host of imitations including Metro and Spartan. Font manufacturers have used extensive promotion to generate markets for their latest typeface designs. Typography often experiences cyclical changes not unlike the fashion industry. Typefaces become wildly popular, then after periods of extensive use, they are no longer used. Designers move on to the next innovation or revival.

Effective typographic design is dependent upon a broad perceptual and conceptual understanding of typefaces and their potential for communication and expression. One method of achieving this understanding is comparative study of well-designed fonts. We hope this book will be a useful resource for everyone who works with type.

Contents

12 1976 Typografische Monatsblätter

TM

Schweizer Grafische Mitteilungen

SGM

Revue suisse de l'imprimerie
Edition spéciale Décembre 1976

RSI

TM SGM RSI 12.1976 (vertical, left margin)

Eine Auswahl bestimmter Arbeiten Weingarts von 1969 bis 1976. Gedanken und Beobachtungen eines Freundes. Und persönliche Bemerkungen von ihm.

Ist diese Typografie noch zu retten?
Oder leben wir auf dem Mond? Is This Typography Worth Supporting, Or Do We Live On The Moon? A special selection from the works of Weingart, from 1969-1976. Thoughts and observations of a friend. And personal comments from the author.

0001
0094

Die Typografie ist noch nicht tot! Sie wirkt zwar heute ein bisschen
Typography is not dead, yet! But its effect is undoubtedly
blutarm und unentschlossen. Doch im grossen und ganzen ist sie in Ordnung.
anemic and vague. But by and large, it is intact. It is definitely less than ever

0002
0095

Sie ist zwar weniger denn je eine Gebrauchskunst. Dafür aber steht ihr
a practical skill. Instead, it endures as an intrinsic necessity.
Gebrauchswert hoch im Kurs.

Typography lives! It is not regarded today with the primacy of
Die Typografie lebt! Sie nimmt sich heute vielleicht nicht mehr so
perhaps 10 or 20 years ago, and is comprehended less as a "picture", but

0003
0096

wichtig wie vor 10 oder 20 Jahren, versteht sich weniger als Bild, tritt
rather, more as a "text". Nevertheless, it remains a prominent element of "visual
hinter den Text zurück. Trotzdem ist sie noch immer ein wichtiger Teil ‹visueller
communication": indispensable, and occasionally fresh, even original.
Kommunikation›: überall gefördert, ansehnlich und mitunter sogar noch

Currently: typography is still typography, although less
überraschend originell.

0097 complacent, conceited, and self-confident, than in the late fifties. And,
0004
Kurzum: die Typografie heute ist noch immer Typografie. Weniger
correspondingly, more functional, in that it has become completely adjusted
selbstgefällig, selbstbewusst und selbstsicher zwar als noch Ende der
to the rapid methods of mass communication.
fünfziger Jahre. Dafür aber ‹funktionaler›: in den schnellen Verwertungsprozess

0098 This connotes "adapted": adapted to the developments
0005 der Massenkommunikation voll eingepasst.

within the composing and print technologies; to the stipulations of an unstable
Das heisst: angepasst. Angepasst an die Erfordernisse neuerer Satz-
market; to the supposedly effective usage by the design profession; and
und Drucktechniken. An die Bedingungen schnell sich verändernder
0099 also adapted to a particularly unpleasant phenomenon of our profession: to design

Fortsetzung des Textes: Seite 4/Innenteil
Continuation of text: Inside/page 14

::

Sondernummer Dezember 1976 Special Edition December 1976

Sondernummer Dezember 1976 Ist diese Typografie noch zu retten? Oder leben wir auf dem Mond? (vertical, left margin)

Design: **Wolfgang Weingart**

Akzidenz-Grotesk, distributed under the name Standard in England and the United States, was first issued in 1898 by the Berthold type foundry of Berlin. The original type family consisted of ten fonts whose design was carefully coordinated. Berthold issued the family in light, regular, medium and bold stroke weights, plus three extended and three condensed versions. There were no italic fonts in the original family. As additional variations were cast and released, Akzidenz-Grotesk was an early example of a type family promoted to printers and designers as a complete range. The Bauer type foundry, one of Berthold's leading German competitors, countered in 1906 with the similar Venus type family in light, medium, and bold weights, plus three condensed and two extended versions. During the first decade of the century, American advertising designers used Standard and Venus with great frequency. Competitive sans-serif display fonts, such as Franklin Gothic and News Gothic from American Type Founders, were developed.

Akzidenz-Grotesk has little discernable variation in stroke weight. The top of the **A** is flat, and the **G** has a spur. The a and t have a curved serif at the foot. The x-height is larger than most typefaces from the turn of the century, and ascenders and descenders are rather short.

Specimens are set in
Berthold Akzidenz-Grotesk

Akzidenz-Grotesk fell from favor as designers embraced geometric sans-serif fonts such as Futura during the 1930s and 1940s; it became widely used again during the 1950s under the influence of the Swiss design movement that advocated asymmetrical organization of Akzidenz-Grotesk on grid systems. It inspired important new sans serifs, including Univers and Helvetica.

ABCDEF
GHIJKLM
NOPQRS
TUVWXY
Z&(.,""; :)

abcdefgh
ijklmnopq
rstuvwxyz
$123456
7890!?

abcdefghijklmnopqrstuvwxyz
ABCDEFGHIJKLMNOPQRSTUVWXYZ
$&1234567890(.,"";:!?)

72

abcdefghijklmnop
qrstuvwxyzABC
DEFGHIJKLMNO
PQRSTUVWXYZ
$&1234567890
(.,"";:!?)

36

abcdefghijklmnopqrstuvwxyz
ABCDEFGHIJKLMNOPQRSTUW
XYZ$&1234567890(.,"";:!?)

Akzidenz-Grotesk Bold

abcdefghijklmnopqrstuvwxyz
ABCDEFGHIJKLMNOPQRSTUVWXYZ
$&1234567890(.,"";:!?)

abcdefghijklmno
pqrstuvwxyzABC
DEFGHIJKLMNO
PQRSTUVWXYZ
$&1234567890
(.,"";:!?)

abcdefghijklmnopqrstuvwxyz
ABCDEFGHIJKLMNOPQRSTUWX
YZ$&1234567890(.,"";:!?)

abcdefghijklmnopqrstuvwxyz
ABCDEFGHIJKLMNOPQRSTUVWXYZ
$&1234567890(.,"";:!?)

72

abcdefghijklmno
pqrstuvwxyzABC
DEFGHIJKLMNO
PQRSTUVWXYZ
$&1234567890
(.,"";:!?)

36

abcdefghijklmnopqrstuvwxyz
ABCDEFGHIJKLMNOPQRSTUWX
YZ$&1234567890(.,"";:!?)

abcdefghijklmnopqrstuvwxyz
ABCDEFGHIJKLMNOPQRSTUVWXYZ
$&1234567890(.,"";:!?)

18

72

abcdefghijklm
nopqrstuvwxyz
ABCDEFGHIJK
LMNOPQRSTU
VWXYZ$&1234
567890(.,"";:!?)

36

abcdefghijklmnopqrstuvwxyz
ABCDEFGHIJKLMNOPQRSTU
WXYZ$&1234567890(.,"";:!?)

Akzidenz-Grotesk Regular

abcdefghijklmnopqrstuvwxyz
ABCDEFGHIJKLMNOPQRSTUVWXYZ
$1234567890&(.,"";:!?)

abcdefghijklmnopqrstuvwxyz
ABCDEFGHIJKLMNOPQRSTUVWXYZ
$1234567890&(.,"";:!?)

Typography, the major communications advance between the invention of writing and the age of electronic mass communications in the twentieth century, played a pivotal role in the social, economic, and religious uph eavals that occurred during the fifteenth and sixteenth centuries. The mod ern nation developed as a result of the vigorous spirit of nationalism that swept over Europe and led to the American and French revolutions of the late eighteenth century. In addition to being a powerful vehicle for spre ading ideas about human rights and the sovereignty of the people, typo graphic printing stabilized and unified languages. Illiteracy, the inability to read and write, began a long, steady decline. Typography radically altered education. The medieval classroom had been a scriptorium of sorts, whe re each student penned his own book. Learning became an increasingly private, rather than communal, process. Human dialog, extended by type, began to take place on a global scale that bridged time and space. Gutenberg's invention was the first mechanization of a skilled handicraft.

Typography, the major communications advance between the in vention of writing and the age of electronic mass communications in the twentieth century, played a pivotal role in the social, eco nomic, and religious upheavals that occurred during the fifteenth and sixteenth centuries. The modern nation developed as a result of the vigorous spirit of nationalism that swept over Europe and led to the American and French revolutions of the late eighteenth century. In addition to being a powerful vehicle for spreading ide as about human rights and the sovereignty of the people, typogra phic printing stabilized and unified languages. Illiteracy, the inabi lity to read and write, began a long, steady decline. Typography radically altered education. The medieval classroom had been a scriptorium of sorts, where each student penned his own book.

Typography, the major communications advance between the invention of writing and the age of electronic mass communications in the twentieth century, played a pivotal role in the social, economic, and religious uph eavals that occurred during the fifteenth and sixteenth centuries. The mod ern nation developed as a result of the vigorous spirit of nationalism that swept over Europe and led to the American and French revolutions of the late eighteenth century. In addition to being a powerful vehicle for spre ading ideas about human rights and the sovereignty of the people, typo graphic printing stabilized and unified languages. Illiteracy, the inability to read and write, began a long, steady decline. Typography radically altered education. The medieval classroom had been a scriptorium of sorts, whe re each student penned his own book. Learning became an increasingly private, rather than communal, process. Human dialog, extended by type,

Typography, the major communications advance between the in vention of writing and the age of electronic mass communications in the twentieth century, played a pivotal role in the social, eco nomic, and religious upheavals that occurred during the fifteenth and sixteenth centuries. The modern nation developed as a result of the vigorous spirit of nationalism that swept over Europe and led to the American and French revolutions of the late eighteenth century. In addition to being a powerful vehicle for spreading ide as about human rights and the sovereignty of the people, typogra phic printing stabilized and unified languages. Illiteracy, the inabi lity to read and write, began a long, steady decline. Typography radically altered education. The medieval classroom had been a

Typography, the major communications advance between the invention of writing and the age of electronic mass communications in the twentieth century, played a pivotal role in the social, economic, and religious uph eavals that occurred during the fifteenth and sixteenth centuries. The mod ern nation developed as a result of the vigorous spirit of nationalism that swept over Europe and led to the American and French revolutions of the late eighteenth century. In addition to being a powerful vehicle for spre ading ideas about human rights and the sovereignty of the people, typo graphic printing stabilized and unified languages. Illiteracy, the inability to read and write, began a long, steady decline. Typography radically altered education. The medieval classroom had been a scriptorium of sorts, whe re each student penned his own book. Learning became an increasingly

Typography, the major communications advance between the in vention of writing and the age of electronic mass communications in the twentieth century, played a pivotal role in the social, eco nomic, and religious upheavals that occurred during the fifteenth and sixteenth centuries. The modern nation developed as a result of the vigorous spirit of nationalism that swept over Europe and led to the American and French revolutions of the late eighteenth century. In addition to being a powerful vehicle for spreading ide as about human rights and the sovereignty of the people, typogra phic printing stabilized and unified languages. Illiteracy, the inabi lity to read and write, began a long, steady decline. Typography

Typography, the major communications advance between the invention of writing and the age of electronic mass communications in the twentieth century, played a pivotal role in the social, economic, and religious uph eavals that occurred during the fifteenth and sixteenth centuries. The mod ern nation developed as a result of the vigorous spirit of nationalism that swept over Europe and led to the American and French revolutions of the late eighteenth century. In addition to being a powerful vehicle for spre ading ideas about human rights and the sovereignty of the people, typo graphic printing stabilized and unified languages. Illiteracy, the inability to read and write, began a long, steady decline. Typography radically altered education. The medieval classroom had been a scriptorium of sorts, whe

Typography, the major communications advance between the in vention of writing and the age of electronic mass communications in the twentieth century, played a pivotal role in the social, eco nomic, and religious upheavals that occurred during the fifteenth and sixteenth centuries. The modern nation developed as a result of the vigorous spirit of nationalism that swept over Europe and led to the American and French revolutions of the late eighteenth century. In addition to being a powerful vehicle for spreading ide as about human rights and the sovereignty of the people, typogra phic printing stabilized and unified languages. Illiteracy, the inabi

abcdefghijklmnopqrstuvwxyz
ABCDEFGHIJKLMNOPQRSTUVWXYZ
$1234567890&(.,"";:!?)

abcdefghijklmnopqrstuvwxyz
ABCDEFGHIJKLMNOPQRSTUVWXYZ
$1234567890&(.,"";:!?)

10/10

Typography, the major communications advance between the invention of writing and the age of electronic mass com munications in the twentieth century, played a pivotal role in the social, economic, and religious upheavals that occurred during the fifteenth and sixteenth centuries. The modern na tion developed as a result of the vigorous spirit of nation alism that swept over Europe and led to the American and French revolutions of the late eighteenth century. In add ition to being a powerful vehicle for spreading ideas about human rights and the sovereignty of the people, typo graphic printing stabilized and unified lan guages. Illiteracy, the inability to read and write, began a long, steady decline.

12/12

Typography, the major communications advance between the invention of writing and the age of el ectronic mass communications in the twentieth century, played a pivotal role in the social, econ omic, and religious upheavals that occurred dur ing the fifteenth and sixteenth centuries. The mod ern nation developed as a result of the vigorous spirit of nationalism that swept over Europe and led to the American and French revolutions of the late eighteenth century. In addition to being a po

10/11

Typography, the major communications advance between the invention of writing and the age of electronic mass com munications in the twentieth century, played a pivotal role in the social, economic, and religious upheavals that occurred during the fifteenth and sixteenth centuries. The modern na tion developed as a result of the vigorous spirit of nation alism that swept over Europe and led to the American and French revolutions of the late eighteenth century. In add ition to being a powerful vehicle for spreading ideas about human rights and the sovereignty of the people, typo graphic printing stabilized and unified lan guages. Illiteracy,

12/13

Typography, the major communications advance between the invention of writing and the age of el ectronic mass communications in the twentieth century, played a pivotal role in the social, econ omic, and religious upheavals that occurred dur ing the fifteenth and sixteenth centuries. The mod ern nation developed as a result of the vigorous spirit of nationalism that swept over Europe and led to the American and French revolutions of the

10/12

Typography, the major communications advance between the invention of writing and the age of electronic mass com munications in the twentieth century, played a pivotal role in the social, economic, and religious upheavals that occurred during the fifteenth and sixteenth centuries. The modern na tion developed as a result of the vigorous spirit of nation alism that swept over Europe and led to the American and French revolutions of the late eighteenth century. In add ition to being a powerful vehicle for spreading ideas about

12/14

Typography, the major communications advance between the invention of writing and the age of el ectronic mass communications in the twentieth century, played a pivotal role in the social, econ omic, and religious upheavals that occurred dur ing the fifteenth and sixteenth centuries. The mod ern nation developed as a result of the vigorous spirit of nationalism that swept over Europe and

10/13

Typography, the major communications advance between the invention of writing and the age of electronic mass com munications in the twentieth century, played a pivotal role in the social, economic, and religious upheavals that occurred during the fifteenth and sixteenth centuries. The modern na tion developed as a result of the vigorous spirit of nation alism that swept over Europe and led to the American and French revolutions of the late eighteenth century. In add ition to being a powerful vehicle for spreading ideas about

12/15

Typography, the major communications advance between the invention of writing and the age of el ectronic mass communications in the twentieth century, played a pivotal role in the social, econ omic, and religious upheavals that occurred dur ing the fifteenth and sixteenth centuries. The mod ·ern nation developed as a result of the vigorous spirit of nationalism that swept over Europe and

The quick brown fox jumps over the l**A**zy dog.

The quick **B**rown fox jumps over the lazy dog.

The qui**C**k brown fox jumps over the lazy dog.

The quick brown fox jumps over the lazy **D**og.

The quick brown fox jumps ov**E**r the lazy dog.

The quick brown **F**ox jumps over the lazy dog.

The quick brown fox jumps over the lazy do**G**.

T**H**e quick brown fox jumps over the lazy dog.

The qu**I**ck brown fox jumps over the lazy dog.

The quick brown fox **J**umps over the lazy dog.

The quic**K** brown fox jumps over the lazy dog.

The quick brown fox jumps over the **L**azy dog.

The quick brown fox ju**M**ps over the lazy dog.

The quick brow**N** fox jumps over the lazy dog.

The quick brown fox jumps over the lazy d**O**g.

The quick brown fox jum**P**s over the lazy dog.

The **Q**uick brown fox jumps over the lazy dog.

The quick b**R**own fox jumps over the lazy dog.

The quick brown fox jump**S** over the lazy dog.

The quick brown fox jumps over **T**he lazy dog.

The q**U**ick brown fox jumps over the lazy dog.

The quick brown fox jumps o**V**er the lazy dog.

The quick bro**W**n fox jumps over the lazy dog.

The quick brown fo**X** jumps over the lazy dog.

The quick brown fox jumps over the laz**Y** dog.

The quick brown fox jumps over the la**Z**y dog.

Design: **Philip Meggs**

Specimens are set in
ITC American Typewriter

The first commercially produced keyboard typing machine was invented by Christopher Sholes and James Densmore in Milwaukee. The machine was encased in wood and the keys were in alphabetical order. In 1876, the Remington #1 typewriter was released. It was encased in metal and the organization of the keys resembled a type case. It is documented that Mark Twain was the first author to type a manuscript – *The Adventures of Tom Sawyer* – on the machine. As the typewriter developed into a standard writing tool, its ubiquitous letters became commonplace, and hence a classic.

Although typewriters mechanically position all letters with the same amount of space, American Typewriter has proportional set widths. Joel Kadan designed American Typewriter for the International Typeface Corporation in 1974. It was an update of earlier typewriter faces including Remington. Kadan designed the light and medium fonts; Tony Stan and Ed Benguiat developed other variants.

American Typewriter is an open face with concave, rounded serifs, and no contrast between the strokes within the letters. The typeface has exaggerated, curvilinear features that are apparent in the capital letters **J**, **Q**, and **R**, and in the lowercase letters **a**, **g**, and **r**. The **E** and **F** have very long serifs, and the **G** has a spur.

This typeface is widely used in advertising and in corporate applications where an informal yet business-like quality is desired. The even texture of the face provides text that is very readable.

ABCDEF
GHIJKLM
NOPQRST
UVWXYZ
&(.,""..;)

abcdefghi
jklmnopq
rstuvwx
yz$1234
567890!?

abcdefghijklmnopqrstuvwxyz
ABCDEFGHIJKLMNOPQRSTUVWXYZ
$&1234567890(.,"";:!?)

72

abcdefghijklmn
opqrstuvwxyz
ABCDEFGHIJK
LMNOPQRSTU
VWXYZ$&123
4567890(.,"";:!?)

36

abcdefghijklmnopqrstuvwxyz
ABCDEFGHIJKLMNOPQRSTU
VWXYZ$&1234567890(.,"";:!?)

American Typewriter Medium Italic

abcdefghijklmnopqrstuvwxyz
ABCDEFGHIJKLMNOPQRSTUVWXYZ
$&1234567890(.,""::!?)

18

72

abcdefghijklmn
opqrstuvwxyz
ABCDEFGHIJK
LMNOPQRSTU
VWXYZ$&123
4567890(.,"";:!?)

36

abcdefghijklmnopqrstuvwxyz
ABCDEFGHIJKLMNOPQRSTU
VWXYZ$&1234567890(.,"";:!?)

abcdefghijklmnopqrstuvwxyz
ABCDEFGHIJKLMNOPQRSTUVWXY
Z$&1234567890(.,"";:!?)

60

abcdefghijklmn
opqrstuvwxyzA
BCDEFGHIJKL
MNOPQRSTUV
WXYZ$&123456
7890(.,"";:!?)

32

abcdefghijklmnopqrstuvwxyz
ABCDEFGHIJKLMNOPQRSTUV
WXYZ$&1234567890(.,"";:!?)

abcdefghijklmnopqrstuvwxyz
ABCDEFGHIJKLMNOPQRSTUVWX
YZ$&1234567890(.,"";:!?)

18

60

abcdefghijklmn
opqrstuvwxyzA
BCDEFGHIJKL
MNOPQRSTUV
WXYZ$&123456
7890(.,"";:!?)

32

abcdefghijklmnopqrstuvwxyz
ABCDEFGHIJKLMNOPRSTUV
WXYZ$&1234567890(.,"";:!?)

American Typewriter

abcdefghijklmnopqrstuvwxyz
ABCDEFGHIJKLMNOPQRSTUVWXYZ
$1234567890&(.,"";:!?

abcdefghijklmnopqrstuvwxyz
ABCDEFGHIJKLMNOPQRSTUVWXYZ
$1234567890&(.,"";:!?)

Typography, the major communications advance between the invention of writing and the age of electronic mass communic ations in the twentieth century, *played a pivotal role* in the s ocial, economic, and religious upheavals that occurred during the fifteenth and sixteenth centuries. The modern nation dev eloped as a result of the vigorous spirit of nationalism that s wept over Europe and led to the American and French revolu tions of the late eighteenth century. In addition to being a po werful vehicle for spreading ideas about human rights and th e sovereignty of the people, typographic printing stabilized a nd unified languages. Illiteracy, the inability to read and writ e, began a long, steady decline. Typography radically altered education. The medieval classroom had been a scriptorium of sorts, where each student penned his own book. Learning bec ame an increasingly private, rather than communal, process.

Typography, the major communications advance betw een the invention of writing and the age of electronic mass communications in the twentieth century, *played a pivotal role* in the social, economic, and religious up heavals that occurred during the fifteenth and sixteen th centuries. The modern nation developed as a result of the vigorous spirit of nationalism that swept over E urope and led to the American and French revolutions of the late eighteenth century. In addition to being a p owerful vehicle for spreading ideas about human righ ts and the sovereignty of the people, typographic print ing stabilized and unified languages. Illiteracy, the ina bility to read and write, began a long, steady decline.

Typography, the major communications advance between the invention of writing and the age of electronic mass communic ations in the twentieth century, *played a pivotal role* in the s ocial, economic, and religious upheavals that occurred during the fifteenth and sixteenth centuries. The modern nation dev eloped as a result of the vigorous spirit of nationalism that s wept over Europe and led to the American and French revolu tions of the late eighteenth century. In addition to being a po werful vehicle for spreading ideas about human rights and th e sovereignty of the people, typographic printing stabilized a nd unified languages. Illiteracy, the inability to read and writ e, began a long, steady decline. Typography radically altered education. The medieval classroom had been a scriptorium of

Typography, the major communications advance betw een the invention of writing and the age of electronic mass communications in the twentieth century, *played a pivotal role* in the social, economic, and religious up heavals that occurred during the fifteenth and sixteen th centuries. The modern nation developed as a result of the vigorous spirit of nationalism that swept over E urope and led to the American and French revolutions of the late eighteenth century. In addition to being a p owerful vehicle for spreading ideas about human righ ts and the sovereignty of the people, typographic print ing stabilized and unified languages. Illiteracy, the ina

Typography, the major communications advance between the invention of writing and the age of electronic mass communic ations in the twentieth century, *played a pivotal role* in the s ocial, economic, and religious upheavals that occurred during the fifteenth and sixteenth centuries. The modern nation dev eloped as a result of the vigorous spirit of nationalism that s wept over Europe and led to the American and French revolu tions of the late eighteenth century. In addition to being a po werful vehicle for spreading ideas about human rights and th e sovereignty of the people, typographic printing stabilized a nd unified languages. Illiteracy, the inability to read and writ e, began a long, steady decline. Typography radically altered

Typography, the major communications advance betw een the invention of writing and the age of electronic mass communications in the twentieth century, *played a pivotal role* in the social, economic, and religious up heavals that occurred during the fifteenth and sixteen th centuries. The modern nation developed as a result of the vigorous spirit of nationalism that swept over E urope and led to the American and French revolutions of the late eighteenth century. In addition to being a p owerful vehicle for spreading ideas about human righ ts and the sovereignty of the people, typographic print

Typography, the major communications advance between the invention of writing and the age of electronic mass communic ations in the twentieth century, *played a pivotal role* in the s ocial, economic, and religious upheavals that occurred during the fifteenth and sixteenth centuries. The modern nation dev eloped as a result of the vigorous spirit of nationalism that s wept over Europe and led to the American and French revolu tions of the late eighteenth century. In addition to being a po werful vehicle for spreading ideas about human rights and th e sovereignty of the people, typographic printing stabilized a nd unified languages. Illiteracy, the inability to read and writ

Typography, the major communications advance betw een the invention of writing and the age of electronic mass communications in the twentieth century, *played a pivotal role* in the social, economic, and religious up heavals that occurred during the fifteenth and sixteen th centuries. The modern nation developed as a result of the vigorous spirit of nationalism that swept over E urope and led to the American and French revolutions of the late eighteenth century. In addition to being a p owerful vehicle for spreading ideas about human righ

abcdefghijklmnopqrstuvwxyz
ABCDEFGHIJKLMNOPQRSTUVWXYZ
$1234567890&(.,""";:!?)

abcdefghijklmnopqrstuvwxyz
ABCDEFGHIJKLMNOPQRSTUVWXYZ
$1234567890&(.,""";:!?)

10/10

Typography, the major communications advance between the invention of writing and the age of electronic mass communications in the twentieth century, *played a pivotal role* in the social, economic, and religious upheavals that occurred during the fifteenth and sixteenth centuries. The modern nation developed as a result of the vigorous spirit of nationalism that swept over Europe and led to the American and French revolutions of the late eighteenth century. In addition to being a powerful vehicle for spreading ideas about human rights and the sovereignty of the people, typo

10/11

Typography, the major communications advance between the invention of writing and the age of electronic mass communications in the twentieth century, *played a pivotal role* in the social, economic, and religious upheavals that occurred during the fifteenth and sixteenth centuries. The modern nation developed as a result of the vigorous spirit of nationalism that swept over Europe and led to the American and French revolutions of the late eighteenth century. In addition to being a powerful vehicle for spreading ideas about hum

10/12

Typography, the major communications advance between the invention of writing and the age of electronic mass communications in the twentieth century, *played a pivotal role* in the social, economic, and religious upheavals that occurred during the fifteenth and sixteenth centuries. The modern nation developed as a result of the vigorous spirit of nationalism that swept over Europe and led to the American and French revolutions of the late eighteenth century. In addition to being a

10/13

Typography, the major communications advance between the invention of writing and the age of electronic mass communications in the twentieth century, *played a pivotal role* in the social, economic, and religious upheavals that occurred during the fifteenth and sixteenth centuries. The modern nation developed as a result of the vigorous spirit of nationalism that swept over Europe and led to the American and French revolutions of th

12/12

Typography, the major communications advance between the invention of writing and the age of electronic mass communications in the twentieth century, *played a pivotal role* in the social, economic, and religious upheavals that occurred during the fifteenth and sixteenth centuries. The modern nation developed as a result of the vigorous spirit of nationalism that swept over Europe and led to the Americ

12/13

Typography, the major communications advance between the invention of writing and the age of electronic mass communications in the twentieth century, *played a pivotal role* in the social, economic, and religious upheavals that occurred during the fifteenth and sixteenth centuries. The modern nation developed as a result of the vigorous spirit of nationalism that

12/14

Typography, the major communications advance between the invention of writing and the age of electronic mass communications in the twentieth century, *played a pivotal role* in the social, economic, and religious upheavals that occurred during the fifteenth and sixteenth centuries. The modern nation developed as a result

12/15

Typography, the major communications advance between the invention of writing and the age of electronic mass communications in the twentieth century, *played a pivotal role* in the social, economic, and religious upheavals that occurred during the fifteenth and sixteenth centuries. The modern nation developed as a result

A mongst the several mechanic Arts that have engaged my attention, there is no one which I have pursued with so much steadiness and pleasure, as that of *Letter-Founding*.

Baskerville

H aving been an early admirer of the beauty of Letters, I became insensibly desirous of contributing to the perfection of them.

I formed to my self Ideas of greater accuracy than had yet appeared, and have endeavoured to produce a *Sett* of *Types* according to what I conceived to be their true proportion.

—*John Baskerville, 1758*

Design: **Keith Jones**

Specimens are set in
Monotype Baskerville

John Baskerville of Birmingham, England, sought excellence by improving type, the printing press, and paper when he established his press in the 1750s; he wrote that his early admiration of the beauty of letters inspired a desire to contribute to their perfection. The 18th century saw a gradual evolution in typeface design. As the century opened, old-style typefaces (Bembo, Garamond) were dominant; by the end of the century the modern styles of Giambattista Bodoni and Firmin Didot prevailed. Baskerville fonts from the middle of this transformation are called Transitional type.

Baskerville tried to improve upon Caslon Old Style by increasing the contrast between thick-and-thin strokes, making serifs sharper and more tapered, and shifting the axis of rounded letters to a more vertical position. Some letters became wider, and curved strokes became more circular in shape. Characters are more regular and consistent in size and form. Baskerville's background as a writing master inspired a calligraphic swash tail on the **Q** and cursive serifs in *Baskerville Italic*. His types were an important inspiration for Bodoni and Didot, who pushed their designs toward even greater contrast and geometric refinement.

American book designer Bruce Rogers admired Baskerville's type in 1917 and arranged for their use by Harvard University Press. As part of its program of revivals, the British Monotype Company released its Baskerville in 1923; Linotype issued its version in 1931. The harmony and beauty of Baskerville have inspired its use in books and magazines; its elegance and refinement make it an excellent typeface to convey dignity and tradition.

abcdefghij
klmnopqrs
tuvwxyz
$12345678
90!?

abcdefghijklmnopqrstuvwxyz
ABCDEFGHIJKLMNOPQRSTU
VWXYZ$&1234567890(.,"";:!?)

72

abcdefghijklmnop
qrstuvwxyzABCD
EFGHIJKLMNO
PQRSTUVWXY
Z$&1234567890
(.,"";:!?)

36

abcdefghijklmnopqrstuvwxyz
ABCDEFGHIJKLMNOPQRSTU
VWXYZ$&1234567890(.,"";:!?)

Baskerville Italic

abcdefghijklmnopqrstuvwxyz
ABCDEFGHIJKLMNOPQRSTU
VWXYZ$&1234567890(.,""";:!?)

18

72

abcdefghijklmnopqr
stuvwxyzABCDEF
GHIJKLMNOPQ
RSTUVWXYZ
$&1234567890
(.,"";:!?)

36

abcdefghijklmnopqrstuvwxyz
ABCDEFGHIJKLMNOPQRSTU
VWXYZ$&1234567890(.,""";:!?)

abcdefghijklmnopqrstuvwxyz
ABCDEFGHIJKLMNOPQRSTU
VWXYZ$&1234567890(.,""";:!?)

abcdefghijklm
nopqrstuvwxyz
ABCDEFGHIJK
LMNOPQRSTU
VWXYZ$&12345
67890(.,"""";:!?)

abcdefghijklmnopqrstuvwxyz
ABCDEFGHIJKLMNOPQRSTU
VWXYZ$&1234567890(.,""";:!?)

abcdefghijklmnopqrstuvwxyz
ABCDEFGHIJKLMNOPQRSTU
VWXYZ$&1234567890(.,""";:!?)

18

72

abcdefghijklm
nopqrstuvwxyz
ABCDEFGHIJKL
MNOPQRSTUV
WXYZ$&1234567
890(.,"""";:!?)

36

abcdefghijklmnopqrstuvwxyz
ABCDEFGHIJKLMNOPQRSTU
VWXYZ$&1234567890(.,""";:!?)

Baskerville

abcdefghijklmnopqrstuvwxyz
ABCDEFGHIJKLMNOPQRSTUVWXYZ
$1234567890&(.,"";:!?)

abcdefghijklmnopqrstuvwxyz
ABCDEFGHIJKLMNOPQRSTUVWXYZ
$1234567890&(.,"";:!?)

8/8

Typography, the major communications advance between the invention of writing and the age of electronic mass communications in the twentieth cen tury, *played a pivotal role* in the social, economic, and religious upheavals that occ urred during the fifteenth and sixteenth centuries. The modern nation devlo ped as a result of the vigorous spirit of nationalism that swept over Europe and led to the American and French revolutions of the late eighteenth century. In addition to being a powerful vehicle for spreading ideas about human rights and the sovereignty of the people, typographic printing stabilized and unified la nguages. Illiteracy, the inability to read and write, began a long, steady decline. Ty pography radically altered education. The medieval classroom had been a script orium of sorts, where each student penned his own book. Learning became an increasingly private, rather than communal, process. Human dialog, extended by type, began to take place on a global scale that bridged time and space. Gu tenberg's invention was the first mechanization of a skilled handicraft. As such, it set into motion, over the next three hundred years, the machinations that wo

9/9

Typography, the major communications advance between the inven tion of writing and the age of electronic mass communications in the twe ntieth century, *played a pivotal role* in the social, economic, and religious upheavals that occurred during the fifteenth and sixteenth centuries. The modern nation developed as a result of the vigorous spirit of nation alism that swept over Europe and led to the American and French revo lutions of the late eighteenth century. In addition to being a powerful ve hicle for spreading ideas about human rights and the sovereignty of the pe ople, typographic printing stabilized and unified languages. Illiteracy, the inability to read and write, began a long, steady decline. Typography rad ically altered education. The medieval classroom had been a scriptorium of sorts, where each student penned his own book. Learning became an increasingly private, rather than communal, process. Human dialog, ex

8/9

Typography, the major communications advance between the invention of writing and the age of electronic mass communications in the twentieth cen tury, *played a pivotal role* in the social, economic, and religious upheavals that occ urred during the fifteenth and sixteenth centuries. The modern nation devlo ped as a result of the vigorous spirit of nationalism that swept over Europe and led to the American and French revolutions of the late eighteenth century. In addition to being a powerful vehicle for spreading ideas about human rights and the sovereignty of the people, typographic printing stabilized and unified la nguages. Illiteracy, the inability to read and write, began a long, steady decline. Ty pography radically altered education. The medieval classroom had been a script orium of sorts, where each student penned his own book. Learning became an increasingly private, rather than communal, process. Human dialog, extended by type, began to take place on a global scale that bridged time and space. Gu

9/10

Typography, the major communications advance between the inven tion of writing and the age of electronic mass communications in the twe ntieth century, *played a pivotal role* in the social, economic, and religious upheavals that occurred during the fifteenth and sixteenth centuries. The modern nation developed as a result of the vigorous spirit of nation alism that swept over Europe and led to the American and French revo lutions of the late eighteenth century. In addition to being a powerful ve hicle for spreading ideas about human rights and the sovereignty of the pe ople, typographic printing stabilized and unified languages. Illiteracy, the inability to read and write, began a long, steady decline. Typography rad ically altered education. The medieval classroom had been a scriptorium of sorts, where each student penned his own book. Learning became an

8/10

Typography, the major communications advance between the invention of writing and the age of electronic mass communications in the twentieth cen tury, *played a pivotal role* in the social, economic, and religious upheavals that occ urred during the fifteenth and sixteenth centuries. The modern nation devlo ped as a result of the vigorous spirit of nationalism that swept over Europe and led to the American and French revolutions of the late eighteenth century. In addition to being a powerful vehicle for spreading ideas about human rights and the sovereignty of the people, typographic printing stabilized and unified la nguages. Illiteracy, the inability to read and write, began a long, steady decline. Ty pography radically altered education. The medieval classroom had been a script orium of sorts, where each student penned his own book. Learning became an increasingly private, rather than communal, process. Human dialog, extended

9/11

Typography, the major communications advance between the inven tion of writing and the age of electronic mass communications in the twe ntieth century, *played a pivotal role* in the social, economic, and religious upheavals that occurred during the fifteenth and sixteenth centuries. The modern nation developed as a result of the vigorous spirit of nation alism that swept over Europe and led to the American and French revo lutions of the late eighteenth century. In addition to being a powerful ve hicle for spreading ideas about human rights and the sovereignty of the pe ople, typographic printing stabilized and unified languages. Illiteracy, the inability to read and write, began a long, steady decline. Typography rad ically altered education. The medieval classroom had been a scriptorium

8/11

Typography, the major communications advance between the invention of writing and the age of electronic mass communications in the twentieth cen tury, *played a pivotal role* in the social, economic, and religious upheavals that occ urred during the fifteenth and sixteenth centuries. The modern nation devlo ped as a result of the vigorous spirit of nationalism that swept over Europe and led to the American and French revolutions of the late eighteenth century. In addition to being a powerful vehicle for spreading ideas about human rights and the sovereignty of the people, typographic printing stabilized and unified la nguages. Illiteracy, the inability to read and write, began a long, steady decline. Ty pography radically altered education. The medieval classroom had been a script orium of sorts, where each student penned his own book. Learning became an

9/12

Typography, the major communications advance between the inven tion of writing and the age of electronic mass communications in the twe ntieth century, *played a pivotal role* in the social, economic, and religious upheavals that occurred during the fifteenth and sixteenth centuries. The modern nation developed as a result of the vigorous spirit of nation alism that swept over Europe and led to the American and French revo lutions of the late eighteenth century. In addition to being a powerful ve hicle for spreading ideas about human rights and the sovereignty of the pe ople, typographic printing stabilized and unified languages. Illiteracy, the inability to read and write, began a long, steady decline. Typography rad

abcdefghijklmnopqrstuvwxyz
ABCDEFGHIJKLMNOPQRSTUVWXYZ
$1234567890&(.,"";:!?)

abcdefghijklmnopqrstuvwxyz
ABCDEFGHIJKLMNOPQRSTUVWXYZ
$1234567890&(.,"";:!?)

10/10

Typography, the major communications advance between the invention of writing and the age of electronic mass communi cations in the twentieth century, *played a pivotal role* in the social, eco nomic, and religious upheavals that occurred during the fifteenth and sixteenth centuries. The modern nation developed as a result of the vigorous spirit of nationalism that swept over Europe and led to the American and French revolutions of the late eighteenth century. In addition to being a powerful vehicle for spreading id eas about human rights and the sovereignty of the people, typo graphic printing stabilized and unified languages. Illiteracy, the in ability to read and write, began a long, steady decline. Typography

12/12

Typography, the major communications advance bet ween the invention of writing and the age of electronic mass communications in the twentieth century, *played a pivotal role* in the social, economic, and religious uphea vals that occurred during the fifteenth and sixteenth cen turies. The modern nation developed as a result of the vi gorous spirit of nationalism that swept over Europe and led to the American and French revolutions of the late eighteenth century. In addition to being a powerful

10/11

Typography, the major communications advance between the invention of writing and the age of electronic mass communi cations in the twentieth century, *played a pivotal role* in the social, eco nomic, and religious upheavals that occurred during the fifteenth and sixteenth centuries. The modern nation developed as a result of the vigorous spirit of nationalism that swept over Europe and led to the American and French revolutions of the late eighteenth century. In addition to being a powerful vehicle for spreading id eas about human rights and the sovereignty of the people, typo graphic printing stabilized and unified languages. Illiteracy, the in ability to read and write, began a long, steady decline. Typography

12/13

Typography, the major communications advance bet ween the invention of writing and the age of electronic mass communications in the twentieth century, *played a pivotal role* in the social, economic, and religious uphea vals that occurred during the fifteenth and sixteenth cen turies. The modern nation developed as a result of the vi gorous spirit of nationalism that swept over Europe and led to the American and French revolutions of the late eighteenth century. In addition to being a powerful

10/12

Typography, the major communications advance between the invention of writing and the age of electronic mass communi cations in the twentieth century, *played a pivotal role* in the social, eco nomic, and religious upheavals that occurred during the fifteenth and sixteenth centuries. The modern nation developed as a result of the vigorous spirit of nationalism that swept over Europe and led to the American and French revolutions of the late eighteenth century. In addition to being a powerful vehicle for spreading id eas about human rights and the sovereignty of the people, typo

12/14

Typography, the major communications advance bet ween the invention of writing and the age of electronic mass communications in the twentieth century, *played a pivotal role* in the social, economic, and religious uphea vals that occurred during the fifteenth and sixteenth cen turies. The modern nation developed as a result of the vi gorous spirit of nationalism that swept over Europe and led to the American and French revolutions of the

10/13

Typography, the major communications advance between the invention of writing and the age of electronic mass communi cations in the twentieth century, *played a pivotal role* in the social, eco nomic, and religious upheavals that occurred during the fifteenth and sixteenth centuries. The modern nation developed as a result of the vigorous spirit of nationalism that swept over Europe and led to the American and French revolutions of the late eighteenth century. In addition to being a powerful vehicle for spreading id eas about human rights and the sovereignty of the people, typo

12/15

Typography, the major communications advance bet ween the invention of writing and the age of electronic mass communications in the twentieth century, *played a pivotal role* in the social, economic, and religious uphea vals that occurred during the fifteenth and sixteenth cen turies. The modern nation developed as a result of the vi gorous spirit of nationalism that swept over Europe and led to the American and French revolutions of the

nuſpiam eſſe libenti

ripae, tum arbor

nisamo nitat :neq

uid nobis frigus ho

n tanto aeſtatis ardor

idem pérbene; qui m

us reuocaſti;

abiicio, cum

úc quidem n

5

Ego uero fili

q̃ in hac cum

etiam fluminis amoe

uereare, nequid nobis

praeſertim in tanto a

feciſti tu quidem pér

cogitationibus reuoca

ſime ſemper abiicio t

uenitur; et núc quid

pacto furtim irrepſ

fi

P S s &

B O B E M B E

B b

Design: **Jeff Price**

Specimens are set in
Monotype Bembo

Initiated by Stanley Morison, Bembo was revived in 1929 by the Lanston Monotype Corporation. The model for this classic face was De Aetna, cut in 1495 by Francesco Griffo. Under the direction of the Venetian printer and publisher Aldus Manutius. Later, Claude Garamond was influenced by Griffo's types for his designs. As a result, De Aetna became the forerunner of the most ubiquitous types in Europe during the following two centuries.

Griffo was perhaps the first type designer to depart from the strong influences of the humanist manuscript hand. Utilizing the capabilities of engraving tools and craft skills, his types were more precise and the serifs more refined than earlier Roman letters. Griffo based his designs on Roman inscriptions, just as Nicolas Jenson had done in 1470. However, a major characteristic that distinguishes Griffo's types from earlier Venetian forms is the way in which the ascenders of the lowercase letters stand taller than the capitals.

Bembo does its best to represent the inherent proportions and visual characteristics of Griffo's types, but of course relied upon modern production methods which resulted in a more consistent and refined revival. The stress of the letterforms is angled, and the serifs in the lowercase characters are oblique. More specific earmarks include a **W** with crossed stems, a **K** with a bowed arm and leg, and an **M** and **n** with inclined stems. The **G** does not have a spur; the **a** possesses a small bowl, and the **f** has an extended terminal.

The proportions of Bembo provide a text that is extremely consistent in color and texture. It is this quality that has enabled the face to remain one of the most popular book types since its release.

Bembo Regular

ABCDEF
GHIJKLM
NOPQRS
TUVWX
YZ&(,""";)

abcdefghij
klmnopqrs
tuvwxyz$1
23456789
0!?

abcdefghijklmnopqrstuvwxyz
ABCDEFGHIJKLMNOPQRSTUVWXYZ
$&1234567890(.,""";:!?)

72

abcdefghijklmno
pqrstuvwxyzABC
DEFGHIJKLMN
OPQRSTUVW
XYZ$&12345678
90(.,""";..!?)

36

abcdefghijklmnopqrstuvwxyz
ABCDEFGHIJKLMNOPQRSTU
VWXYZ$&1234567890(.,""";:!?)

Bembo Regular Italic

abcdefghijklmnopqrstuvwxyz
ABCDEFGHIJKLMNOPQRSTUVWXYZ
$&1234567890(.,"";:!?)

18

72

abcdefghijklmnopqrst
uvwxyzABCDEF
GHIJKLMNOPQ
RSTUVWXYZ$&
1234567890(.,"";:!?)

36

abcdefghijklmnopqrstuvwxyz
ABCDEFGHIJKLMNOPQRSTU
VWXYZ$&1234567890(.,"";:!?)

abcdefghijklmnopqrstuvwxyz
ABCDEFGHIJKLMNOPQRSTUVWXYZ
$&1234567890(.,""'';:!?)

72

abcdefghijklmn
opqrstuvwxyzA
BCDEFGHIJKL
MNOPQRSTU
VWXYZ$&1234
567890(.,"'';:!?)

36

abcdefghijklmnopqrstuvwxyz
ABCDEFGHIJKLMNOPQRSTU
VWXYZ$&1234567890(.,"'';:!?)

Bembo Bold Italic

abcdefghijklmnopqrstuvwxyz
ABCDEFGHIJKLMNOPQRSTUVWXYZ
$&1234567890(.,"";:!?)

18

72

abcdefghijklmnopq
rstuvwxyzABCD
EFGHIJKLMN
OPQRSTUVW
XYZ$&123456789
0(., "";:!?)

36

abcdefghijklmnopqrstuvwxyz
ABCDEFGHIJKLMNOPRSTUV
WXYZ$&1234567890(.,"";:!?)

Bembo Regular

abcdefghijklmnopqrstuvwxyz
ABCDEFGHIJKLMNOPQRSTUVWXYZ
$1234567890&(.,"";:!?)

abcdefghijklmnopqrstuvwxyz
ABCDEFGHIJKLMNOPQRSTUVWXYZ
$1234567890&(.,"";:!?)

8/8

Typography, the major communications advance between the invention of writing and the age of electronic mass communications in the twentieth century, *played a pivotal role* in the social, economic, and religious upheavals that occurred during the fifteenth and sixteenth centuries. The modern nation developed as a result of the vigorous spirit of nationalism that swept over Europe and led to the American and French revolutions of the late eighteenth century. In addition to being a powerful vehicle for spreading ideas about human rights and the sovereignty of the people, typographic printing stabilized and unified languages. Illiteracy, the inability to read and write, began a long, steady decline. Typography radically altered education. The medieval classroom had been a scriptorium of sorts, where each student penned his own book. Learning became an increasingly private, rather than communal, process. Human dialog, extended by type, began to take place on a global scale that bridged time and space. Gutenberg's invention was the first mechanization of a skilled handicraft. As such, it set into motion, over the next three hundred years, the machinations that

8/9

Typography, the major communications advance between the invention of writing and the age of electronic mass communications in the twentieth century, *played a pivotal role* in the social, economic, and religious upheavals that occurred during the fifteenth and sixteenth centuries. The modern nation developed as a result of the vigorous spirit of nationalism that swept over Europe and led to the American and French revolutions of the late eighteenth century. In addition to being a powerful vehicle for spreading ideas about human rights and the sovereignty of the people, typographic printing stabilized and unified languages. Illiteracy, the inability to read and write, began a long, steady decline. Typography radically altered education. The medieval classroom had been a scriptorium of sorts, where each student penned his own book. Learning became an increasingly private, rather than communal, process. Human dialog, extended by type, began to take place on a global scale that bridged time and space. G

8/10

Typography, the major communications advance between the invention of writing and the age of electronic mass communications in the twentieth century, *played a pivotal role* in the social, economic, and religious upheavals that occurred during the fifteenth and sixteenth centuries. The modern nation developed as a result of the vigorous spirit of nationalism that swept over Europe and led to the American and French revolutions of the late eighteenth century. In addition to being a powerful vehicle for spreading ideas about human rights and the sovereignty of the people, typographic printing stabilized and unified languages. Illiteracy, the inability to read and write, began a long, steady decline. Typography radically altered education. The medieval classroom had been a scriptorium of sorts, where each student penned his own book. Learning became an increasingly private, rather than communal, process. Human dialog, extended

8/11

Typography, the major communications advance between the invention of writing and the age of electronic mass communications in the twentieth century, *played a pivotal role* in the social, economic, and religious upheavals that occurred during the fifteenth and sixteenth centuries. The modern nation developed as a result of the vigorous spirit of nationalism that swept over Europe and led to the American and French revolutions of the late eighteenth century. In addition to being a powerful vehicle for spreading ideas about human rights and the sovereignty of the people, typographic printing stabilized and unified languages. Illiteracy, the inability to read and write, began a long, steady decline. Typography radically altered education. The medieval classroom had been a scriptorium of sorts, where each student penned his own book. Learning became

9/9

Typography, the major communications advance between the invention of writing and the age of electronic mass communications in the twentieth century, *played a pivotal role* in the social, economic, and religious upheavals that occurred during the fifteenth and sixteenth centuries. The modern nation developed as a result of the vigorous spirit of nationalism that swept over Europe and led to the American and French revolutions of the late eighteenth century. In addition to being a powerful vehicle for spreading ideas about human rights and the sovereignty of the people, typographic printing stabilized and unified languages. Illiteracy, the inability to read and write, began a long, steady decline. Typography radically altered education. The medieval classroom had been a scriptorium of sorts, where each student penned his own book. Learning became an increasingly private, rather than comm

9/10

Typography, the major communications advance between the invention of writing and the age of electronic mass communications in the twentieth century, *played a pivotal role* in the social, economic, and religious upheavals that occurred during the fifteenth and sixteenth centuries. The modern nation developed as a result of the vigorous spirit of nationalism that swept over Europe and led to the American and French revolutions of the late eighteenth century. In addition to being a powerful vehicle for spreading ideas about human rights and the sovereignty of the people, typographic printing stabilized and unified languages. Illiteracy, the inability to read and write, began a long, steady decline. Typography radically altered education. The medieval classroom had been a scriptorium of sorts, where each student penned his o

9/11

Typography, the major communications advance between the invention of writing and the age of electronic mass communications in the twentieth century, *played a pivotal role* in the social, economic, and religious upheavals that occurred during the fifteenth and sixteenth centuries. The modern nation developed as a result of the vigorous spirit of nationalism that swept over Europe and led to the American and French revolutions of the late eighteenth century. In addition to being a powerful vehicle for spreading ideas about human rights and the sovereignty of the people, typographic printing stabilized and unified languages. Illiteracy, the inability to read and write, began a long, steady decline. Typography radically altered education. The medieval classroom

9/12

Typography, the major communications advance between the invention of writing and the age of electronic mass communications in the twentieth century, *played a pivotal role* in the social, economic, and religious upheavals that occurred during the fifteenth and sixteenth centuries. The modern nation developed as a result of the vigorous spirit of nationalism that swept over Europe and led to the American and French revolutions of the late eighteenth century. In addition to being a powerful vehicle for spreading ideas about human rights and the sovereignty of the people, typographic printing stabilized and unified languages. Illiteracy, the inability to read and write, began a long, steady

abcdefghijklmnopqrstuvwxyz
ABCDEFGHIJKLMNOPQRSTUVWXYZ
$1234567890&(.,"";:!?)

abcdefghijklmnopqrstuvwxyz
ABCDEFGHIJKLMNOPQRSTUVWXYZ
$1234567890&(.,"";:!?)

10/10

Typography, the major communications advance between th
e invention of writing and the age of electronic mass communi
cations in the twentieth century, *played a pivotal role* in the socia
l, economic, and religious upheavals that occurred during the f
ifteenth and sixteenth centuries. The modern nation developed
as a result of the vigorous spirit of nationalism that swept over
Europe and led to the American and French revolutions of the
late eighteenth century. In addition to being a powerful vehicle
for spreading ideas about human rights and the sovereignty of
the people, typographic printing stabilized and unified language
s. Illiteracy, the inability to read and write, began a long, steady
decline. Typography radically altered education. The medieval

---

12/12

Typography, the major communications advance b
etween the invention of writing and the age of electr
onic mass communications in the twentieth century,
played a pivotal role in the social, economic, and relig
ious upheavals that occurred during the fifteenth and
sixteenth centuries. The modern nation developed as
a result of the vigorous spirit of nationalism that sw
ept over Europe and led to the American and Frenc
h revolutions of the late eighteenth century. In additi
on to being a powerful vehicle for spreading ideas ab

10/11

Typography, the major communications advance between th
e invention of writing and the age of electronic mass communi
cations in the twentieth century, *played a pivotal role* in the socia
l, economic, and religious upheavals that occurred during the f
ifteenth and sixteenth centuries. The modern nation developed
as a result of the vigorous spirit of nationalism that swept over
Europe and led to the American and French revolutions of the
late eighteenth century. In addition to being a powerful vehicle
for spreading ideas about human rights and the sovereignty of
the people, typographic printing stabilized and unified language
s. Illiteracy, the inability to read and write, began a long, steady

---

12/13

Typography, the major communications advance b
etween the invention of writing and the age of electr
onic mass communications in the twentieth century,
played a pivotal role in the social, economic, and relig
ious upheavals that occurred during the fifteenth and
sixteenth centuries. The modern nation developed as
a result of the vigorous spirit of nationalism that sw
ept over Europe and led to the American and Frenc
h revolutions of the late eighteenth century. In additi

10/12

Typography, the major communications advance between th
e invention of writing and the age of electronic mass communi
cations in the twentieth century, *played a pivotal role* in the socia
l, economic, and religious upheavals that occurred during the f
ifteenth and sixteenth centuries. The modern nation developed
as a result of the vigorous spirit of nationalism that swept over
Europe and led to the American and French revolutions of the
late eighteenth century. In addition to being a powerful vehicle
for spreading ideas about human rights and the sovereignty of
the people, typographic printing stabilized and unified language

---

12/14

Typography, the major communications advance b
etween the invention of writing and the age of electr
onic mass communications in the twentieth century,
played a pivotal role in the social, economic, and relig
ious upheavals that occurred during the fifteenth and
sixteenth centuries. The modern nation developed as
a result of the vigorous spirit of nationalism that sw
ept over Europe and led to the American and Frenc
h revolutions of the late eighteenth century. In additi

10/13

Typography, the major communications advance between th
e invention of writing and the age of electronic mass communi
cations in the twentieth century, *played a pivotal role* in the socia
l, economic, and religious upheavals that occurred during the f
ifteenth and sixteenth centuries. The modern nation developed
as a result of the vigorous spirit of nationalism that swept over
Europe and led to the American and French revolutions of the
late eighteenth century. In addition to being a powerful vehicle
for spreading ideas about human rights and the sovereignty of

---

12/15

Typography, the major communications advance b
etween the invention of writing and the age of electr
onic mass communications in the twentieth century,
played a pivotal role in the social, economic, and relig
ious upheavals that occurred during the fifteenth and
sixteenth centuries. The modern nation developed as
a result of the vigorous spirit of nationalism that sw
ept over Europe and led to the American and Frenc

Macaroni

Spaghetti

Rigatoni

Scallopini

Tortellini

Linguini

Bodoni

Fettuccini

Ravioli

Spumoni

Design: **Rob Carter**

Giambattista Bodoni of Parma is remembered as a type designer whose unadorned letters completely broke from past traditions. During the early part of his career he copied the types and ornaments of Pierre Simone Fournier. Fournier's types in turn were modeled after the Romaine du Roi, which in 1692 had been ordered by Louis XIV. In 1768, Bodoni became the Director of the Duke of Parma's Stamperia Reale, and around 1790 during his stewardship there, he designed his first roman types that were more geometric in appearance.

Bodoni types are visually luminescent due to the extreme contrasts between thick and thin strokes. The original forms are characterized by subtly bracketed serifs, although most copies ignore this feature. The mathematical precision of the letters provides a vertical stress, and the ascenders and descenders appear long in relation to the x-height. The **M** and **W** are narrow, the **R** features a curved leg, and the **Q** has a low tail that extends vertically. The **G** possesses a low bar and serif, and the **C** and **G** have vertical serifs.

The most important revival of Bodoni is the 1911 version by Morris Benton for American Type Founders. Monotype and Haas also produced reasonable versions. Bauer produced what is perhaps the closest in spirit to Bodoni's original types, with their bracketed serifs, crisp contrasts, and delicate thick-thin transitions.

The many typefaces that bear Bodoni's name continue to be widely used. In advertising and newspapers they commonly function as display typography. For publication designers, the sturdy texture of the letterforms provide distinctive text pages.

Specimens are set in
Bauer Bodoni

abcdefghij
klmnopqr
stuvwxyz$
1234567 8
90!?

abcdefghijklmnopqrstuvwxyz
ABCDEFGHIJKLMNOPQRSTUVWXYZ
$&1234567890(.,""",:!?)

72

abcdefghijklmno
pqrstuvwxyzABC
DEFGHIJKLMN
OPQRSTUVW
XYZ$&12345678
90(.,"",:!?)

36

abcdefghijklmnopqrstuvwxyz
ABCDEFGHIJKLMNOPQRSTU
VWXYZ$&1234567890(.,"",:!?)

abcdefghijklmnopqrstuvwxyz
ABCDEFGHIJKLMNOPQRSTUVWXYZ
$&1234567890(.,"";:!?)

abcdefghijklmnopqrstuvwxyzAB
CDEFGHIJKLM
NOPQRSTUVWX
YZ$&123456789
0(.,"";:!?)

abcdefghijklmnopqrstuvwxyz
ABCDEFGHIJKLMNOPQRSTU
VWXYZ$&1234567890(.,"";:!?)

abcdefghijklmnopqrstuvwxyz
ABCDEFGHIJKLMNOPQRSTUVWXYZ
$&1234567890(.,""",;:!?)

72

abcdefghijklmn
opqrstuvwxyzA
BCDEFGHIJKL
MNOPQRSTUV
WXYZ$&12345
67890(.,"""";:!?)

36

abcdefghijklmnopqrstuvwxyz
ABCDEFGHIJKLMNOPQRSTU
VWXYZ$&1234567890(.,"""";:!?)

abcdefghijklmnopqrstuvwxyz
ABCDEFGHIJKLMNOPQRSTUVWXYZ
$&1234567890(.,""::!?)

18

72

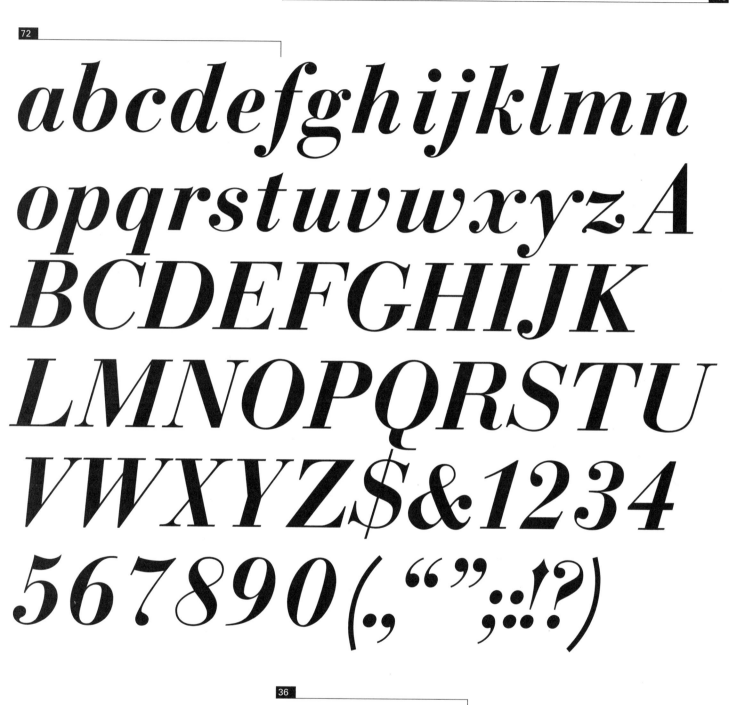

abcdefghijklmn
opqrstuvwxyzA
BCDEFGHIJK
LMNOPQRSTU
VWXYZ$&1234
567890(.,"";:!?)

36

abcdefghijklmnopqrstuvwxyz
ABCDEFGHIJKLMNOPQRSTUV
WXYZ$&1234567890(.,"";:!?)

Bodoni Roman

abcdefghijklmnopqrstuvwxyz
ABCDEFGHIJKLMNOPQRSTUVWXYZ
$1234567890&(.,"";:!?)

abcdefghijklmnopqrstuvwxyz
ABCDEFGHIJKLMNOPQRSTUVWXYZ
$1234567890&(.,"";:!?)

Typography, the major communications advance between the invention of writing and the age of electronic mass communications in the twentieth century, *played a pivotal role* in the social, economic, and religious upheavals that occurred during the fifteenth and sixteenth centuries. The modern nation developed as a result of the vigorous spirit of nationalism that swept over Europe and led to the American and French revolutions of the late eighteenth century. In addition to being a powerful vehicle for spreading ideas about human rights and the sovereignty of the people, typographic printing stabilized and unified languages. Illiteracy, the inability to read and write, began a long, steady decline. Typography radically altered education. The medieval classroom had been a scriptorium of sorts, where each student penned his own book. Learning became an increasingly private, rather than communal, process. Human dialog, extended by type, began to take place on a global scale that bridged time and space. Gu

Typography, the major communications advance between the invention of writing and the age of electronic mass communications in the twentieth century, *played a pivotal role* in the social, economic, and religious upheavals that occurred during the fifteenth and sixteenth centuries. The modern nation developed as a result of the vigorous spirit of nationalism that swept over Europe and led to the American and French revolutions of the late eighteenth century. In addition to being a powerful vehicle for spreading ideas about human rights and the sovereignty of the people, typographic printing stabilized and unified languages. Illiteracy, the inability to read and write, began a long, steady decline. Typography radically altered education. The medieval classroom had been a scriptorium of sorts, where each student penned his own book. L

Typography, the major communications advance between the invention of writing and the age of electronic mass communications in the twentieth century, *played a pivotal role* in the social, economic, and religious upheavals that occurred during the fifteenth and sixteenth centuries. The modern nation developed as a result of the vigorous spirit of nationalism that swept over Europe and led to the American and French revolutions of the late eighteenth century. In addition to being a powerful vehicle for spreading ideas about human rights and the sovereignty of the people, typographic printing stabilized and unified languages. Illiteracy, the inability to read and write, began a long, steady decline. Typography radically altered education. The medieval classroom had been a scriptorium of sorts, where each student penned his own book. Learning became an increasingly private, rather than communal, process. Human dialog, extended by ty

Typography, the major communications advance between the invention of writing and the age of electronic mass communications in the twentieth century, *played a pivotal role* in the social, economic, and religious upheavals that occurred during the fifteenth and sixteenth centuries. The modern nation developed as a result of the vigorous spirit of nationalism that swept over Europe and led to the American and French revolutions of the late eighteenth century. In addition to being a powerful vehicle for spreading ideas about human rights and the sovereignty of the people, typographic printing stabilized and unified languages. Illiteracy, the inability to read and write, began a long, steady decline. Typography radically altered education. The medieval classroom had been a

Typography, the major communications advance between the invention of writing and the age of electronic mass communications in the twentieth century, *played a pivotal role* in the social, economic, and religious upheavals that occurred during the fifteenth and sixteenth centuries. The modern nation developed as a result of the vigorous spirit of nationalism that swept over Europe and led to the American and French revolutions of the late eighteenth century. In addition to being a powerful vehicle for spreading ideas about human rights and the sovereignty of the people, typographic printing stabilized and unified languages. Illiteracy, the inability to read and write, began a long, steady decline. Typography radically altered education. The medieval classroom had been a scriptorium of sorts, where each student penned his own book. Learning became an increasing

Typography, the major communications advance between the invention of writing and the age of electronic mass communications in the twentieth century, *played a pivotal role* in the social, economic, and religious upheavals that occurred during the fifteenth and sixteenth centuries. The modern nation developed as a result of the vigorous spirit of nationalism that swept over Europe and led to the American and French revolutions of the late eighteenth century. In addition to being a powerful vehicle for spreading ideas about human rights and the sovereignty of the people, typographic printing stabilized and unified languages. Illiteracy, the inability to read and write, began a long, steady decline. Typograph

Typography, the major communications advance between the invention of writing and the age of electronic mass communications in the twentieth century, *played a pivotal role* in the social, economic, and religious upheavals that occurred during the fifteenth and sixteenth centuries. The modern nation developed as a result of the vigorous spirit of nationalism that swept over Europe and led to the American and French revolutions of the late eighteenth century. In addition to being a powerful vehicle for spreading ideas about human rights and the sovereignty of the people, typographic printing stabilized and unified languages. Illiteracy, the inability to read and write, began a long, steady decline. Typography radically altered education. The medieval classroom had been a scriptorium of sorts,

Typography, the major communications advance between the invention of writing and the age of electronic mass communications in the twentieth century, *played a pivotal role* in the social, economic, and religious upheavals that occurred during the fifteenth and sixteenth centuries. The modern nation developed as a result of the vigorous spirit of nationalism that swept over Europe and led to the American and French revolutions of the late eighteenth century. In addition to being a powerful vehicle for spreading ideas about human rights and the sovereignty of the people, typographic printing stabilized and unified languages. Illiteracy, the ina

abcdefghijklmnopqrstuvwxyz
ABCDEFGHIJKLMNOPQRSTUVWXYZ
$1234567890&(.,"";:!?)

10/10

Typography, the major communications advance between the invention of writing and the age of electronic mass co mmunications in the twentieth century, *played a pivotal r ole* in the social, economic, and religious upheavals that oc curred during the fifteenth and sixteenth centuries. The m odern nation developed as a result of the vigorous spirit of nationalism that swept over Europe and led to the Americ an and French revolutions of the late eighteenth century. I n addition to being a powerful vehicle for spreading ideas about human rights and the sovereignty of the people, typ ographic printing stabilized and unified languages. Illitera cy, the inability to read and write, began a long, steady

10/11

Typography, the major communications advance between the invention of writing and the age of electronic mass co mmunications in the twentieth century, *played a pivotal r ole* in the social, economic, and religious upheavals that oc curred during the fifteenth and sixteenth centuries. The m odern nation developed as a result of the vigorous spirit of nationalism that swept over Europe and led to the Americ an and French revolutions of the late eighteenth century. I n addition to being a powerful vehicle for spreading ideas about human rights and the sovereignty of the people, typ ographic printing stabilized and unified languages. Illitera

10/12

Typography, the major communications advance between the invention of writing and the age of electronic mass co mmunications in the twentieth century, *played a pivotal r ole* in the social, economic, and religious upheavals that oc curred during the fifteenth and sixteenth centuries. The m odern nation developed as a result of the vigorous spirit of nationalism that swept over Europe and led to the Americ an and French revolutions of the late eighteenth century. I n addition to being a powerful vehicle for spreading ideas about human rights and the sovereignty of the people, typ

10/13

Typography, the major communications advance between the invention of writing and the age of electronic mass co mmunications in the twentieth century, *played a pivotal r ole* in the social, economic, and religious upheavals that oc curred during the fifteenth and sixteenth centuries. The m odern nation developed as a result of the vigorous spirit of nationalism that swept over Europe and led to the Americ an and French revolutions of the late eighteenth century. I n addition to being a powerful vehicle for spreading ideas

abcdefghijklmnopqrstuvwxyz
ABCDEFGHIJKLMNOPQRSTUVWXYZ
$1234567890&(.,"";:!?)

12/12

Typography, the major communications advanc e between the invention of writing and the age of electronic mass communications in the twentieth century, *played a pivotal role* in the social, econo mic, and religious upheavals that occurred durin g the fifteenth and sixteenth centuries. The mode rn nation developed as a result of the vigorous sp irit of nationalism that swept over Europe and le d to the American and French revolutions of the late eighteenth century. In addition to being a po

12/13

Typography, the major communications advanc e between the invention of writing and the age of electronic mass communications in the twentieth century, *played a pivotal role* in the social, econo mic, and religious upheavals that occurred durin g the fifteenth and sixteenth centuries. The mode rn nation developed as a result of the vigorous sp irit of nationalism that swept over Europe and le d to the American and French revolutions of the

12/14

Typography, the major communications advanc e between the invention of writing and the age of electronic mass communications in the twentieth century, *played a pivotal role* in the social, econo mic, and religious upheavals that occurred durin g the fifteenth and sixteenth centuries. The mode rn nation developed as a result of the vigorous sp irit of nationalism that swept over Europe and le d to the American and French revolutions of the

12/15

Typography, the major communications advanc e between the invention of writing and the age of electronic mass communications in the twentieth century, *played a pivotal role* in the social, econo mic, and religious upheavals that occurred durin g the fifteenth and sixteenth centuries. The mode rn nation developed as a result of the vigorous sp irit of nationalism that swept over Europe and le

You say **ee**ther   And I say **eye**ther

You say **nee**ther   And I say **ny**ther

You like po**ta**to   And I like po**tah**to

You like to**ma**to   And I like to**mah**to

You say **laugh**ter   And I say **lawf**ter

You say **aft**er   And I say **awf**ter

You like van**illa**   And I like van**ella**

Let's Call the Whole Thing Off

Design: **Rob Carter**

Specimens are set in
ITC Bookman

Wadsworth A. Parker, responsible for issuing new types at the Bruce Foundry and later at the American Type Founders, is thought to have named Bookman around 1900. It was adapted by ATF from the Bruce Foundry's Old Style Antique No. 310. Subsequently, several other manufacturers have adapted versions of Bookman, including Ludlow, Linotype, Monotype, and ITC.

It is fair to say that Bookman has always been a subject of controversy among typographic designers. Some consider it a face of great distinction; others hold it in contempt. Despite any misgivings about the face, Bookman has been widely used throughout the century in advertising and in books. Its popularity in advertising is partly due to the many swash variants of the letters which appeal to some art directors. Book designers sensitive to the visual attributes and spacing requirements of Bookman have created masterful pages with this typeface.

Bookman was first designed as a primer or book face. It has a very heavy but open appearance, with generous counters and subtle contrasts between the different parts of the letters. The ascenders and descenders are very short. The transitional serifs, as in the **E** and **F**, are large, and the **C** terminates without a bottom serif. The **T** has oblique serifs; the **M** has parallel stems, and the **W** possesses center strokes that join at cap height.

Bookman continues today to be used primarily in advertising. Given current trends in book design, Bookman is less often the typeface of choice. Considering the fickleness of typographic taste, perhaps this classic face will again in the future curve upward on the acceptance scale.

ABCDEF
GHIJKL
MNOPQR
STUVWX
YZ&(,"",;;)

abcdefgh
ijklmnop
qrstuvwx
yz$1234
567890!?

abcdefghijklmnopqrstuvwxyz
ABCDEFGHIJKLMNOPQRSTUVWXYZ
$&1234567890(.,""";:!?)

72

abcdefghijklm
nopqrstuvwxyz
ABCDEFGHIJ
KLMNOPQRST
UVWXYZ$&123
4567890(.,"""';:!?)

36

abcdefghijklmnopqrstuvwxyz
ABCDEFGHIJKLMNOPQRSTU
VWXYZ$&1234567890(.,""";:!?)

Bookman Medium Italic

abcdefghijklmnopqrstuvwxyz
ABCDEFGHIJKLMNOPQRSTUVWXZ
$&1234567890(.,"";:!?)

18

72

abcdefghijklm
nopqrstuvwxy
zABCDEFGHIJ
KLMNOPQRST
UVWXYZ$&12
34567890(.,"";:!?)

36

abcdefghijklmnopqrstuvwxyz
ABCDEFGHIJKLMNOPQRSTU
VWXYZ$&1234567890(.,"";:!?)

abcdefghijklmnopqrstuvwxyz
ABCDEFGHIJKLMNOPQRSTUVWXY
$&1234567890(.,""";:!?)

63

abcdefghijklmn
opqrstuvwxyzA
BCDEFGHIJKL
MNOPQRSTUV
WXYZ$&12345
67890(.,"""";:!?)

32

abcdefghijklmnopqrstuvwxyz
ABCDEFGHIJKLMNOPQRSTU
VWXYZ$&1234567890(.,"""";:!?)

Bookman Bold Italic

abcdefghijklmnopqrstuvwxyz
ABCDEFGHIJKLMNOPQRSTUVW
XYZ$&1234567890(.,""";:!?)

abcdefghijklm
nopqrstuvwxyz
ABCDEFGHIJK
LMNOPQRSTUV
WXYZ$&12345
67890(.,""";:!?)

abcdefghijklmnopqrstuvwx
yzABCDEFGHIJKLMNOPRSTU
VWXYZ$&1234567890(.,""";:!?)

Bookman Medium

abcdefghijklmnopqrstuvwxyz
ABCDEFGHIJKLMNOPQRSTUVWXYZ
$1234567890&(.,"";:!?)

abcdefghijklmnopqrstuvwxyz
ABCDEFGHIJKLMNOPQRSTUVWXYZ
$1234567890&(.,"";:!?)

8/8

Typography, the major communications advance between the invention of writing and the age of electronic mass communications in the twentieth century, *played a pivotal role* in the social, economic, and religious upheavals that occurred during the fifteenth and sixteenth centuries. The modern nation developed as a result of the vigorous spirit of nationalism that swept over Europe and led to the American and French revolutions of the late eighteenth century. In addition to being a powerful vehicle for spreading ideas about human rights and the sovereignty of the people, typographic printing stabilized and unified languages. Illiteracy, the inability to read and write, began a long, steady decline. Typography radically altered education. The medieval classroom had been a scriptorium of sorts, where each student penned his own book. Learning became an increasingly private, rather than communal, process. Human dialog, extend

9/9

Typography, the major communications advance between the invention of writing and the age of electronic mass communications in the twentieth century, *played a pivotal role* in the social, economic, and religious upheavals that occurred during the fifteenth and sixteenth centuries. The modern nation developed as a result of the vigorous spirit of nationalism that swept over Europe and led to the American and French revolutions of the late eighteenth century. In addition to being a powerful vehicle for spreading ideas about human rights and the sovereignty of the people, typographic printing stabilized and unified languages. Illiteracy, the inability to read and write, began a long, steady decline. Typography radi

8/9

Typography, the major communications advance between the invention of writing and the age of electronic mass communications in the twentieth century, *played a pivotal role* in the social, economic, and religious upheavals that occurred during the fifteenth and sixteenth centuries. The modern nation developed as a result of the vigorous spirit of nationalism that swept over Europe and led to the American and French revolutions of the late eighteenth century. In addition to being a powerful vehicle for spreading ideas about human rights and the sovereignty of the people, typographic printing stabilized and unified languages. Illiteracy, the inability to read and write, began a long, steady decline. Typography radically altered education. The medieval classroom had been a scriptorium of sorts, where each s

9/10

Typography, the major communications advance between the invention of writing and the age of electronic mass communications in the twentieth century, *played a pivotal role* in the social, economic, and religious upheavals that occurred during the fifteenth and sixteenth centuries. The modern nation developed as a result of the vigorous spirit of nationalism that swept over Europe and led to the American and French revolutions of the late eighteenth century. In addition to being a powerful vehicle for spreading ideas about human rights and the sovereignty of the people, typographic printing stabilized and unified languages. Illiteracy, the inability to read

8/10

Typography, the major communications advance between the invention of writing and the age of electronic mass communications in the twentieth century, *played a pivotal role* in the social, economic, and religious upheavals that occurred during the fifteenth and sixteenth centuries. The modern nation developed as a result of the vigorous spirit of nationalism that swept over Europe and led to the American and French revolutions of the late eighteenth century. In addition to being a powerful vehicle for spreading ideas about human rights and the sovereignty of the people, typographic printing stabilized and unified languages. Illiteracy, the inability to read and write, began a long, steady decline. Typography radically altered education. The me

9/11

Typography, the major communications advance between the invention of writing and the age of electronic mass communications in the twentieth century, *played a pivotal role* in the social, economic, and religious upheavals that occurred during the fifteenth and sixteenth centuries. The modern nation developed as a result of the vigorous spirit of nationalism that swept over Europe and led to the American and French revolutions of the late eighteenth century. In addition to being a powerful vehicle for spreading ideas about human rights and the sovereignty of the people, typographic printing stabilize

8/11

Typography, the major communications advance between the invention of writing and the age of electronic mass communications in the twentieth century, *played a pivotal role* in the social, economic, and religious upheavals that occurred during the fifteenth and sixteenth centuries. The modern nation developed as a result of the vigorous spirit of nationalism that swept over Europe and led to the American and French revolutions of the late eighteenth century. In addition to being a powerful vehicle for spreading ideas about human rights and the sovereignty of the people, typographic printing stabilized and unified languages. Illiteracy, the inability to read and write, began a long,

9/12

Typography, the major communications advance between the invention of writing and the age of electronic mass communications in the twentieth century, *played a pivotal role* in the social, economic, and religious upheavals that occurred during the fifteenth and sixteenth centuries. The modern nation developed as a result of the vigorous spirit of nationalism that swept over Europe and led to the American and French revolutions of the late eighteenth century. In addition to being a powerful vehicle for spreading ideas about human rights and the

Bookman Medium

abcdefghijklmnopqrstuvwxyz
ABCDEFGHIJKLMNOPQRSTUVWXYZ
$1234567890&(.,"";:!?)

abcdefghijklmnopqrstuvwxyz
ABCDEFGHIJKLMNOPQRSTUVWXYZ
$1234567890&(.,"";:!?)

10/10

Typography, the major communications advance between the invention of writing and the age of ele ctronic mass communications in the twentieth ce ntury, *played a pivotal role* in the social, economic, and religious upheavals that occurred during the fifteenth and sixteenth centuries. The modern nat ion developed as a result of the vigorous spirit of nationalism that swept over Europe and led to the American and French revolutions of the late eig hteenth century. In addition to being a powerful vehicle for spreading ideas about human rights and the sovereignty of the people, typographic printi

10/11

Typography, the major communications advance between the invention of writing and the age of ele ctronic mass communications in the twentieth ce ntury, *played a pivotal role* in the social, economic, and religious upheavals that occurred during the fifteenth and sixteenth centuries. The modern nat ion developed as a result of the vigorous spirit of nationalism that swept over Europe and led to the American and French revolutions of the late eig hteenth century. In addition to being a powerful vehicle for spreading ideas about human rights and

10/12

Typography, the major communications advance between the invention of writing and the age of ele ctronic mass communications in the twentieth ce ntury, *played a pivotal role* in the social, economic, and religious upheavals that occurred during the fifteenth and sixteenth centuries. The modern nat ion developed as a result of the vigorous spirit of nationalism that swept over Europe and led to the American and French revolutions of the late eig hteenth century. In addition to being a powerful

10/13

Typography, the major communications advance between the invention of writing and the age of ele ctronic mass communications in the twentieth ce ntury, *played a pivotal role* in the social, economic, and religious upheavals that occurred during the fifteenth and sixteenth centuries. The modern nat ion developed as a result of the vigorous spirit of nationalism that swept over Europe and led to the American and French revolutions of the late eig

12/12

Typography, the major communications advance between the invention of writing and the age of electronic mass communi cations in the twentieth century, *played a pivotal role* in the social, economic, and rel igious upheavals that occurred during the fifteenth and sixteenth centuries. The modern nation developed as a result of the vigorous spirit of nationalism that swept over Europe and led to the American and

12/13

Typography, the major communications advance between the invention of writing and the age of electronic mass communi cations in the twentieth century, *played a pivotal role* in the social, economic, and rel igious upheavals that occurred during the fifteenth and sixteenth centuries. The modern nation developed as a result of the vigorous spirit of nationalism that swept

12/14

Typography, the major communications advance between the invention of writing and the age of electronic mass communi cations in the twentieth century, *played a pivotal role* in the social, economic, and rel igious upheavals that occurred during the fifteenth and sixteenth centuries. The modern nation developed as a result of the

12/15

Typography, the major communications advance between the invention of writing and the age of electronic mass communi cations in the twentieth century, *played a pivotal role* in the social, economic, and rel igious upheavals that occurred during the fifteenth and sixteenth centuries. The modern nation developed as a result of the

1939

The effort that matured into CALEDONIA started with a strong liking for the Scotch Modern face. But why modify Scotch? Well, there was a kind of wooden heaviness about the modeling of some of the original Wilson letters that didn't seem to need to be there. Why couldn't you go back to the feeling about printing types that inspired the Wilson punch-cutter and then just liven up a few of his curves without changing the action and color of the face? The attack along that line did not turn out very well. It appears that Scotch is Scotch, and doesn't stay Scotch if you sweat the fat off it. The next effort was to look at Baskerville and Bodoni and Didot, and all the designers who were working in that general direction. We turned to one of the types that Bulmer used, cut for him by William Martin around 1790-and here seemed a good place to start again. The result of this last effort was most promising; so we went on and finished the alphabets and christened it CALEDONIA because the project was inspired in the first instance by the work of Scotch typefounders ●

Dwiggins, William Addison, Typographer and Carpenter-Artist; Black and White-Smith. b. Martinsville, Ohio, 1880; Rich-mond, Ind., Cambridge, Ohio; Chicago, Ill., Boston, Mass. res. Hingham, Mass. Mem. Boston Art Club, Boston Society of Water color Painters, the Society of Printers. No School. Secretary, the Society of Calligraphers ...that is all.

About the "liveliness of action" that one sees in the Martin letters, and to a less degree (one modestly says) in Caledonia; that quality is in the curves – the way they get away from the straight stems with a calligraphic flick, and in the nervous angle on the under side of the arches as they descend to the right. The finishing strokes at the bottoms of letters, cut straight across without "brackets", making sharp angles with the upright stems, add "snap" to many of the old "modern face" designs – and why not to Caledonia?

The Romans referred to ancient Scotland as Caledonia.

"Caledonia has the ease of good clear speech, with just a hint of a pleasant Scotch accent."

Design: **Clifford A. Harvey**

Specimens are set in
Linotype New Caledonia

Caledonia (also called Cornelia) is a modified Scotch Roman that was designed for the Mergenthaler Linotype Company by W.A. Dwiggins in 1938. In his assignment to revise Scotch Roman, which is a cross between a modern and old style roman, Dwiggins found in Bulmer the inspiration for the task. By applying the essence of Bulmer to the basic structure of Scotch Roman, Dwiggins hit upon a combination that became one of the most admired and used typefaces ever produced in the United States.

The basic anatomical features of Caledonia are capitals that are shorter than the ascenders of the lowercase letters for a blending between the capitals and the lowercase, a medium x-height, a vertical stress, and a distinct contrast in the strokes of the letters. More specifically, the serifs are slightly concave; the **t** does not have a serif; the dots of the **i** and **j** are offset to the right; the **a**, **c**, and **f** have large tears; the **g** has a square ear, and the italic capitals feature truncated serifs. The proportional harmony and detailing of Caledonia provide optimum readability; it is a functional face with no affected characters. It is available in regular, bold, and italic variations. In 1979, Linotype released an updated version called New Caledonia, adding weights such as semi-bold and black.

Caledonia is one of the most used text faces for books. In the area of mass-market publications such as paperback books, Caledonia is the choice of many designers, for even in printing conditions where quality impressions and paper are not major concerns, it maintains its integrity.

Caledonia Regular

ABCDEF
GHIJKL
MNOPQ
RSTUVW
XYZ&(""",";")

125

abcdefghi
jklmnopqr
stuvwxyz$
12345678
90!?

abcdefghijklmnopqrstuvwxyz
ABCDEFGHIJKLMNOPQRSTUVWXYZ
$&1234567890(.,""";:!?)

72

abcdefghijklmno
pqrstuvwxyzABC
DEFGHIJKLMN
OPQRSTUVW
XYZ$&12345678
90(.,"""";:!?)

36

abcdefghijklmnopqrstuvwxyz
ABCDEFGHIJKLMNOPQRSTU
VWXYZ$&1234567890(.,""";:!?)

abcdefghijklmnopqrstuvwxyz
ABCDEFGHIJKLMNOPQRSTUVWXYZ
$&1234567890(.,""'';:!?)

18

72

abcdefghijklmnop
qrstuvwxyzABC
DEFGHIJKLMN
OPQRSTUVWXY
Z$&1234567890
(.,""'';:!?)

36

abcdefghijklmnopqrstuvwxyz
ABCDEFGHIJKLMNOPQRSTU
VWXYZ$&1234567890(.,""'';:!?)

abcdefghijklmnopqrstuvwxyz
ABCDEFGHIJKLMNOPQRSTUVWXYZ
$&1234567890(,"";:!?)

72

abcdefghijklmn
opqrstuvwxyzA
BCDEFGHIJK
LMNOPQRSTU
VWXYZ$&1234
567890(,"";:!?)

36

abcdefghijklmnopqrstuvwxyz
ABCDEFGHIJKLMNOPQRSTU
VWXYZ$&1234567890(,"";:!?)

abcdefghijklmnopqrstuvwxyz
ABCDEFGHIJKLMNOPQRSTUVWXYZ
$&1234567890(.,""";:!?)

18

72

abcdefghijklmn
opqrstuvwxyzA
BCDEFGHIJK
LMNOPQRSTU
VWXYZ$&1234
567890(.,"";:!?)

36

abcdefghijklmnopqrstuvwxyz
ABCDEFGHIJKLMNOPRSTUV
WXYZ$&1234567890(.,"";:!?)

Caledonia Regular

abcdefghijklmnopqrstuvwxyz
ABCDEFGHIJKLMNOPQRSTUVWXYZ
$1234567890&(.,"";:!?)

abcdefghijklmnopqrstuvwxyz
ABCDEFGHIJKLMNOPQRSTUVWXYZ
$1234567890&(.,"";:!?)

8/8

Typography, the major communications advance between the invention of writing and the age of electronic mass communications in the twentieth cent ury, *played a pivotal role* in the social, economic, and religious upheavals tha t occurred during the fifteenth and sixteenth centuries. The modern nation developed as a result of the vigorous spirit of nationalism that swept over Eu rope and led to the American and French revolutions of the late eighteenth century. In addition to being a powerful vehicle for spreading ideas about h uman rights and the sovereignty of the people, typographic printing stabilize d and unified languages. Illiteracy, the inability to read and write, began a lo ng, steady decline. Typography radically altered education. The medieval cla ssroom had been a scriptorium of sorts, where each student penned his own book. Learning became an increasingly private, rather than communal, proc ess. Human dialog, extended by type, began to take place on a global scale t hat bridged time and space. Gutenberg's invention was the first mechanizati

9/9

Typography, the major communications advance between the inve ntion of writing and the age of electronic mass communications in t he twentieth century, *played a pivotal role* in the social, economic, and religious upheavals that occurred during the fifteenth and sixte enth centuries. The modern nation developed as a result of the vigo rous spirit of nationalism that swept over Europe and led to the Am erican and French revolutions of the late eighteenth century. In ad dition to being a powerful vehicle for spreading ideas about human rights and the sovereignty of the people, typographic printing stabili zed and unified languages. Illiteracy, the inability to read and write, began a long, steady decline. Typography radically altered educatio n. The medieval classroom had been a scriptorium of sorts, where e ach student penned his own book. Learning became an increasingly

8/9

Typography, the major communications advance between the invention of writing and the age of electronic mass communications in the twentieth cent ury, *played a pivotal role* in the social, economic, and religious upheavals tha t occurred during the fifteenth and sixteenth centuries. The modern nation developed as a result of the vigorous spirit of nationalism that swept over Eu rope and led to the American and French revolutions of the late eighteenth century. In addition to being a powerful vehicle for spreading ideas about h uman rights and the sovereignty of the people, typographic printing stabilize d and unified languages. Illiteracy, the inability to read and write, began a lo ng, steady decline. Typography radically altered education. The medieval cla ssroom had been a scriptorium of sorts, where each student penned his own book. Learning became an increasingly private, rather than communal, proc ess. Human dialog, extended by type, began to take place on a global scale t

9/10

Typography, the major communications advance between the inve ntion of writing and the age of electronic mass communications in t he twentieth century, *played a pivotal role* in the social, economic, and religious upheavals that occurred during the fifteenth and sixte enth centuries. The modern nation developed as a result of the vigo rous spirit of nationalism that swept over Europe and led to the Am erican and French revolutions of the late eighteenth century. In ad dition to being a powerful vehicle for spreading ideas about human rights and the sovereignty of the people, typographic printing stabili zed and unified languages. Illiteracy, the inability to read and write, began a long, steady decline. Typography radically altered educatio n. The medieval classroom had been a scriptorium of sorts, where e

8/10

Typography, the major communications advance between the invention of writing and the age of electronic mass communications in the twentieth cent ury, *played a pivotal role* in the social, economic, and religious upheavals tha t occurred during the fifteenth and sixteenth centuries. The modern nation developed as a result of the vigorous spirit of nationalism that swept over Eu rope and led to the American and French revolutions of the late eighteenth century. In addition to being a powerful vehicle for spreading ideas about h uman rights and the sovereignty of the people, typographic printing stabilize d and unified languages. Illiteracy, the inability to read and write, began a lo ng, steady decline. Typography radically altered education. The medieval cla ssroom had been a scriptorium of sorts, where each student penned his own book. Learning became an increasingly private, rather than communal, proc

9/11

Typography, the major communications advance between the inve ntion of writing and the age of electronic mass communications in t he twentieth century, *played a pivotal role* in the social, economic, and religious upheavals that occurred during the fifteenth and sixte enth centuries. The modern nation developed as a result of the vigo rous spirit of nationalism that swept over Europe and led to the Am erican and French revolutions of the late eighteenth century. In ad dition to being a powerful vehicle for spreading ideas about human rights and the sovereignty of the people, typographic printing stabili zed and unified languages. Illiteracy, the inability to read and write, began a long, steady decline. Typography radically altered educatio

8/11

Typography, the major communications advance between the invention of writing and the age of electronic mass communications in the twentieth cent ury, *played a pivotal role* in the social, economic, and religious upheavals tha t occurred during the fifteenth and sixteenth centuries. The modern nation developed as a result of the vigorous spirit of nationalism that swept over Eu rope and led to the American and French revolutions of the late eighteenth century. In addition to being a powerful vehicle for spreading ideas about h uman rights and the sovereignty of the people, typographic printing stabilize d and unified languages. Illiteracy, the inability to read and write, began a lo ng, steady decline. Typography radically altered education. The medieval cla ssroom had been a scriptorium of sorts, where each student penned his own

9/12

Typography, the major communications advance between the inve ntion of writing and the age of electronic mass communications in t he twentieth century, *played a pivotal role* in the social, economic, and religious upheavals that occurred during the fifteenth and sixte enth centuries. The modern nation developed as a result of the vigo rous spirit of nationalism that swept over Europe and led to the Am erican and French revolutions of the late eighteenth century. In ad dition to being a powerful vehicle for spreading ideas about human rights and the sovereignty of the people, typographic printing stabili zed and unified languages. Illiteracy, the inability to read and write,

abcdefghijklmnopqrstuvwxyz
ABCDEFGHIJKLMNOPQRSTUVWXYZ
$1234567890&(.,"";:!?)

abcdefghijklmnopqrstuvwxyz
ABCDEFGHIJKLMNOPQRSTUVWXYZ
$1234567890&(.,"";:!?)

10/10

Typography, the major communications advance between t he invention of writing and the age of electronic mass comm unications in the twentieth century, *played a pivotal role* in t he social, economic, and religious upheavals that occurred d uring the fifteenth and sixteenth centuries. The modern nati on developed as a result of the vigorous spirit of nationalism that swept over Europe and led to the American and French revolutions of the late eighteenth century. In addition to bei ng a powerful vehicle for spreading ideas about human right s and the sovereignty of the people, typographic printing stab ilized and unified languages. Illiteracy, the inability to read a nd write, began a long, steady decline. Typography radically

12/12

Typography, the major communications advance between the invention of writing and the age of ele ctronic mass communications in the twentieth cent ury, *played a pivotal role* in the social, economic, a nd religious upheavals that occurred during the fifteenth and sixteenth centuries. The modern nati on developed as a result of the vigorous spirit of na tionalism that swept over Europe and led to the A merican and French revolutions of the late eightee nth century. In addition to being a powerful vehicl

10/11

Typography, the major communications advance between t he invention of writing and the age of electronic mass comm unications in the twentieth century, *played a pivotal role* in t he social, economic, and religious upheavals that occurred d uring the fifteenth and sixteenth centuries. The modern nati on developed as a result of the vigorous spirit of nationalism that swept over Europe and led to the American and French revolutions of the late eighteenth century. In addition to bei ng a powerful vehicle for spreading ideas about human right s and the sovereignty of the people, typographic printing stab ilized and unified languages. Illiteracy, the inability to read a

12/13

Typography, the major communications advance between the invention of writing and the age of ele ctronic mass communications in the twentieth cent ury, *played a pivotal role* in the social, economic, a nd religious upheavals that occurred during the fifteenth and sixteenth centuries. The modern nati on developed as a result of the vigorous spirit of na tionalism that swept over Europe and led to the A merican and French revolutions of the late eightee

10/12

Typography, the major communications advance between t he invention of writing and the age of electronic mass comm unications in the twentieth century, *played a pivotal role* in t he social, economic, and religious upheavals that occurred d uring the fifteenth and sixteenth centuries. The modern nati on developed as a result of the vigorous spirit of nationalism that swept over Europe and led to the American and French revolutions of the late eighteenth century. In addition to bei ng a powerful vehicle for spreading ideas about human right s and the sovereignty of the people, typographic printing stab

12/14

Typography, the major communications advance between the invention of writing and the age of ele ctronic mass communications in the twentieth cent ury, *played a pivotal role* in the social, economic, a nd religious upheavals that occurred during the fifteenth and sixteenth centuries. The modern nati on developed as a result of the vigorous spirit of na tionalism that swept over Europe and led to the A merican and French revolutions of the late eightee

10/13

Typography, the major communications advance between t he invention of writing and the age of electronic mass comm unications in the twentieth century, *played a pivotal role* in t he social, economic, and religious upheavals that occurred d uring the fifteenth and sixteenth centuries. The modern nati on developed as a result of the vigorous spirit of nationalism that swept over Europe and led to the American and French revolutions of the late eighteenth century. In addition to bei ng a powerful vehicle for spreading ideas about human right

12/15

Typography, the major communications advance between the invention of writing and the age of ele ctronic mass communications in the twentieth cent ury, *played a pivotal role* in the social, economic, a nd religious upheavals that occurred during the fifteenth and sixteenth centuries. The modern nati on developed as a result of the vigorous spirit of na tionalism that swept over Europe and led to the A

Paul Rand

Design
Form
and
Chaos

Yale University Press
New Haven and London
1993

Design: **Paul Rand**

Specimens are set in
Adobe Caslon

The first Caslon old face types were designed in 1725 by the English typefounder William Caslon. Before turning to typeface design, he was an engraver of ornate designs and images on metal objects such as guns. Caslon's types were influenced by Dutch typefaces of the late eighteenth century, but his artistic skills enabled him to improve upon these models, bringing a variety of form and subtlety of detail not characteristic in the types being imported from the Netherlands.

Caslon types are considered "warm and friendly" and "comfortable to the eye;" they have a robust texture, sturdy forms, and a wide variety of shapes. Some of Caslon's letters lack refinement and perfection; yet the overall effect of a text set in Caslon is legible and aesthetically appealing. The strokes in Caslon fonts are somewhat heavier than many earlier Old Style fonts; the serifs are thicker and a bit stubby. The **A** has a concave hollow at its apex, and the **G** does not have a foot serif. The Caslon italic ampersand, *&*, is much admired for its flowing *C* and *S* curves, which evoke the flamboyant Rococo designs of its epoch, while echoing Caslon's early ornamental engraving. In Caslon italic, an irregular rhythm is created by captials that slant at different angles; for example, *A, V*, and *W* have a very pronounced slant. Some modern versions depart from Caslon's original designs by making the letters more uniform.

Caslon fonts are used by book and magazine designers, for the readability and textural vitality prized by printers and readers in Caslon's era continue to enhance texts over two-and-a-half centuries after the first Caslon fonts were designed.

ABCDEF
GHIJKLM
NOPQRS
TUVWX
YZ&(,"",";:)

abcdefghijk
lmnopqrst
uvwxyz$12
34567890!?

abcdefghijklmnopqrstuvwxyz
ABCDEFGHIJKLMNOPQRSTU
VWXYZ$&1234567890(.,"";:!?)

72

abcdefghijklmnopq
rstuvwxyzABCD
EFGHIJKLMNO
PQRSTUVWXY
Z$&1234567890
(.,"";:!?)

36

abcdefghijklmnopqrstuvwxyz
ABCDEFGHIJKLMNOPQRSTU
VWXYZ$&1234567890(.,"";:!?)

Caslon Italic

abcdefghijklmnopqrstuvwxyz
ABCDEFGHIJKLMNOPQRSTU
VWXYZ$&1234567890(.,"";:!?)

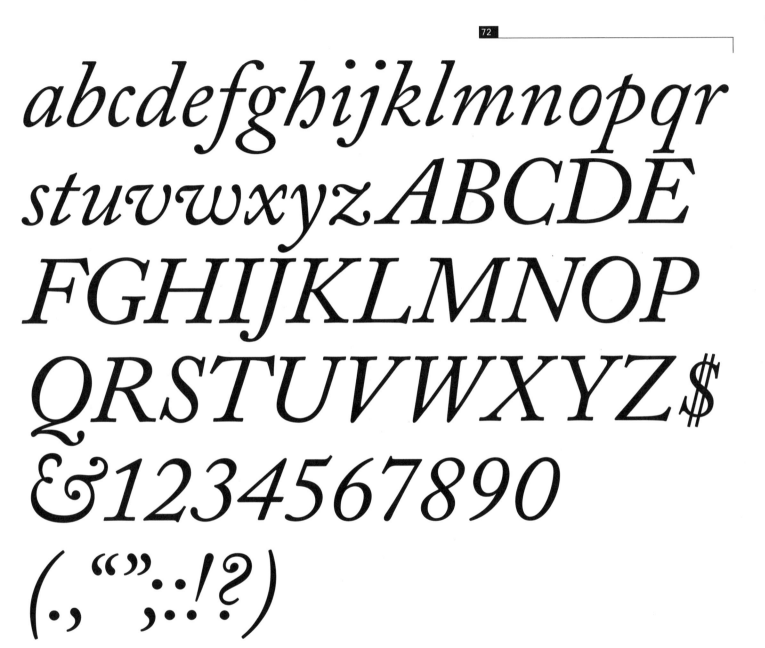

abcdefghijklmnopqr
stuvwxyzABCDE
FGHIJKLMNOP
QRSTUVWXYZ$
&1234567890
(.,"";:!?)

abcdefghijklmnopqrstuvwxyz
ABCDEFGHIJKLMNOPQRSTU
VWXYZ$&1234567890(.,"";:!?)

abcdefghijklmnopqrstuvwxyz
ABCDEFGHIJKLMNOPQRSTU
VWXYZ$&1234567890(.,"";:!?)

72

abcdefghijklmno
pqrstuvwxyz
ABCDEFGHIJ
KLMNOPQRS
TUVWXYZ$&1
234567890(.,"";:!?)

36

abcdefghijklmnopqrstuvwxyz
ABCDEFGHIJKLMNOPQRST
UVWXYZ$&1234567890(.,"";:!?)

*abcdefghijklmnopqrstuvwxyz
ABCDEFGHIJKLMNOPQRSTU
VWXYZ$&1234567890(.,"";:!?)*

18

72

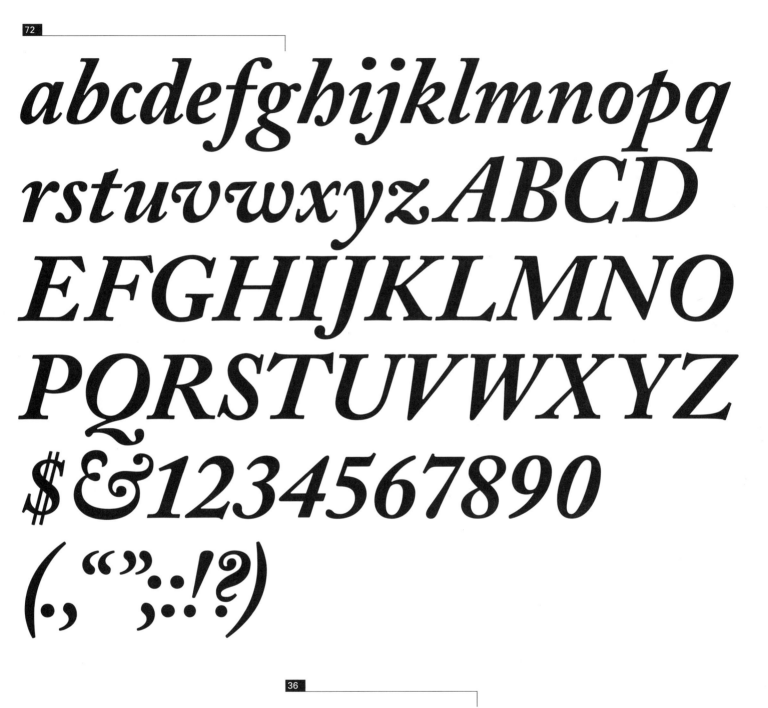

36

*abcdefghijklmnopqrstuvwxyz
ABCDEFGHIJKLMNOPQRSTU
VWXYZ$&1234567890(.,"";:!?)*

Caslon

abcdefghijklmnopqrstuvwxyz
ABCDEFGHIJKLMNOPQRSTUVWXYZ
$1234567890&(.,"";:!?)

abcdefghijklmnopqrstuvwxyz
ABCDEFGHIJKLMNOPQRSTUVWXYZ
$1234567890&(.,"";:!?)

8/8

Typography, the major communications advance between the invention of writing and the age of electronic mass communications in the twentieth cen tury, *played a pivotal role* in the social, economic, and religious upheavals that occurred during the fifteenth and sixteenth centuries. The modern nation deve loped as a result of the vigorous spirit of nationalism that swept over Europe and led to the American and French revolutions of the late eighteenth cent ury. In addition to being a powerful vehicle for spreading ideas about human rights and the sovereignty of the people, typographic printing stabilized and unified languages. Illiteracy, the inability to read and write, began a long, stea dy decline. Typography radically altered education. The medieval classroom had been a scriptorium of sorts, where each student penned his own book. Learn ing became an increasingly private, rather than communal, process. Human dialog, extended by type, began to take place on a global scale that bridged time and space. Gutenberg's invention was the first mechanization of a skilled

9/9

Typography, the major communications advance between the inven tion of writing and the age of electronic mass communications in the twentieth century, *played a pivotal role* in the social, economic, and rel igious upheavals that occurred during the fifteenth and sixteenth cen turies. The modern nation developed as a result of the vigorous spirit of nationalism that swept over Europe and led to the American and Fre nch revolutions of the late eighteenth century. In addition to being a powerful vehicle for spreading ideas about human rights and the sover eignty of the people, typographic printing stabilized and unified langu ages. Illiteracy, the inability to read and write, began a long, steady de cline. Typography radically altered education. The medieval classroom had been a scriptorium of sorts, where each student penned his own book. Learning became an increasingly private, rather than communal, pro

8/9

Typography, the major communications advance between the invention of writing and the age of electronic mass communications in the twentieth cen tury, *played a pivotal role* in the social, economic, and religious upheavals that occurred during the fifteenth and sixteenth centuries. The modern nation deve loped as a result of the vigorous spirit of nationalism that swept over Europe and led to the American and French revolutions of the late eighteenth cent ury. In addition to being a powerful vehicle for spreading ideas about human rights and the sovereignty of the people, typographic printing stabilized and unified languages. Illiteracy, the inability to read and write, began a long, stea dy decline. Typography radically altered education. The medieval classroom had been a scriptorium of sorts, where each student penned his own book. Learn ing became an increasingly private, rather than communal, process. Human dialog, extended by type, began to take place on a global scale that bridged time

9/10

Typography, the major communications advance between the inven tion of writing and the age of electronic mass communications in the twentieth century, *played a pivotal role* in the social, economic, and rel igious upheavals that occurred during the fifteenth and sixteenth cen turies. The modern nation developed as a result of the vigorous spirit of nationalism that swept over Europe and led to the American and Fre nch revolutions of the late eighteenth century. In addition to being a powerful vehicle for spreading ideas about human rights and the sover eignty of the people, typographic printing stabilized and unified langu ages. Illiteracy, the inability to read and write, began a long, steady de cline. Typography radically altered education. The medieval classroom had been a scriptorium of sorts, where each student penned his own book.

8/10

Typography, the major communications advance between the invention of writing and the age of electronic mass communications in the twentieth cen tury, *played a pivotal role* in the social, economic, and religious upheavals that occurred during the fifteenth and sixteenth centuries. The modern nation deve loped as a result of the vigorous spirit of nationalism that swept over Europe and led to the American and French revolutions of the late eighteenth cent ury. In addition to being a powerful vehicle for spreading ideas about human rights and the sovereignty of the people, typographic printing stabilized and unified languages. Illiteracy, the inability to read and write, began a long, stea dy decline. Typography radically altered education. The medieval classroom had been a scriptorium of sorts, where each student penned his own book. Learn ing became an increasingly private, rather than communal, process. Human

9/11

Typography, the major communications advance between the inven tion of writing and the age of electronic mass communications in the twentieth century, *played a pivotal role* in the social, economic, and rel igious upheavals that occurred during the fifteenth and sixteenth cen turies. The modern nation developed as a result of the vigorous spirit of nationalism that swept over Europe and led to the American and Fre nch revolutions of the late eighteenth century. In addition to being a powerful vehicle for spreading ideas about human rights and the sover eignty of the people, typographic printing stabilized and unified langu ages. Illiteracy, the inability to read and write, began a long, steady de cline. Typography radically altered education. The medieval classroom had

8/11

Typography, the major communications advance between the invention of writing and the age of electronic mass communications in the twentieth cen tury, *played a pivotal role* in the social, economic, and religious upheavals that occurred during the fifteenth and sixteenth centuries. The modern nation deve loped as a result of the vigorous spirit of nationalism that swept over Europe and led to the American and French revolutions of the late eighteenth cent ury. In addition to being a powerful vehicle for spreading ideas about human rights and the sovereignty of the people, typographic printing stabilized and unified languages. Illiteracy, the inability to read and write, began a long, stea dy decline. Typography radically altered education. The medieval classroom had been a scriptorium of sorts, where each student penned his own book. Learn

9/12

Typography, the major communications advance between the inven tion of writing and the age of electronic mass communications in the twentieth century, *played a pivotal role* in the social, economic, and rel igious upheavals that occurred during the fifteenth and sixteenth cen turies. The modern nation developed as a result of the vigorous spirit of nationalism that swept over Europe and led to the American and Fre nch revolutions of the late eighteenth century. In addition to being a powerful vehicle for spreading ideas about human rights and the sover eignty of the people, typographic printing stabilized and unified langu ages. Illiteracy, the inability to read and write, began a long, steady de

abcdefghijklmnopqrstuvwxyz
ABCDEFGHIJKLMNOPQRSTUVWXYZ
$1234567890&(.,"";:!?)

abcdefghijklmnopqrstuvwxyz
ABCDEFGHIJKLMNOPQRSTUVWXYZ
$1234567890&(.,"";:!?)

10/10

Typography, the major communications advance between the invention of writing and the age of electronic mass commu nications in the twentieth century, *played a pivotal role* in the social, economic, and religious upheavals that occurred during the fifteenth and sixteenth centuries. The modern nation devel oped as a result of the vigorous spirit of nationalism that swept over Europe and led to the American and French revolutions of the late eighteenth century. In addition to being a powerful ve hicle for spreading ideas about human rights and the sovereig nty of the people, typographic printing stabilized and unified languages. Illiteracy, the inability to read and write, began a lo

10/11

Typography, the major communications advance between the invention of writing and the age of electronic mass commu nications in the twentieth century, *played a pivotal role* in the social, economic, and religious upheavals that occurred during the fifteenth and sixteenth centuries. The modern nation devel oped as a result of the vigorous spirit of nationalism that swept over Europe and led to the American and French revolutions of the late eighteenth century. In addition to being a powerful ve hicle for spreading ideas about human rights and the sovereig nty of the people, typographic printing stabilized and unified

10/12

Typography, the major communications advance between the invention of writing and the age of electronic mass commu nications in the twentieth century, *played a pivotal role* in the social, economic, and religious upheavals that occurred during the fifteenth and sixteenth centuries. The modern nation devel oped as a result of the vigorous spirit of nationalism that swept over Europe and led to the American and French revolutions of the late eighteenth century. In addition to being a powerful ve hicle for spreading ideas about human rights and the sovereig

10/13

Typography, the major communications advance between the invention of writing and the age of electronic mass commu nications in the twentieth century, *played a pivotal role* in the social, economic, and religious upheavals that occurred during the fifteenth and sixteenth centuries. The modern nation devel oped as a result of the vigorous spirit of nationalism that swept over Europe and led to the American and French revolutions of the late eighteenth century. In addition to being a powerful ve hicle for spreading ideas about human rights and the sovereig

12/12

Typography, the major communications advance be tween the invention of writing and the age of electronic mass communications in the twentieth century, *played a pivotal role* in the social, economic, and religious uphea vals that occurred during the fifteenth and sixteenth cen turies. The modern nation developed as a result of the vig orous spirit of nationalism that swept over Europe and led to the American and French revolutions of the late eight eenth century. In addition to being a powerful vehicle for

12/13

Typography, the major communications advance be tween the invention of writing and the age of electronic mass communications in the twentieth century, *played a pivotal role* in the social, economic, and religious uphea vals that occurred during the fifteenth and sixteenth cen turies. The modern nation developed as a result of the vig orous spirit of nationalism that swept over Europe and led to the American and French revolutions of the late eight eenth century. In addition to being a powerful vehicle for

12/14

Typography, the major communications advance be tween the invention of writing and the age of electronic mass communications in the twentieth century, *played a pivotal role* in the social, economic, and religious uphea vals that occurred during the fifteenth and sixteenth cen turies. The modern nation developed as a result of the vig orous spirit of nationalism that swept over Europe and led to the American and French revolutions of the late eight

12/15

Typography, the major communications advance be tween the invention of writing and the age of electronic mass communications in the twentieth century, *played a pivotal role* in the social, economic, and religious uphea vals that occurred during the fifteenth and sixteenth cen turies. The modern nation developed as a result of the vig orous spirit of nationalism that swept over Europe and led to the American and French revolutions of the late eight

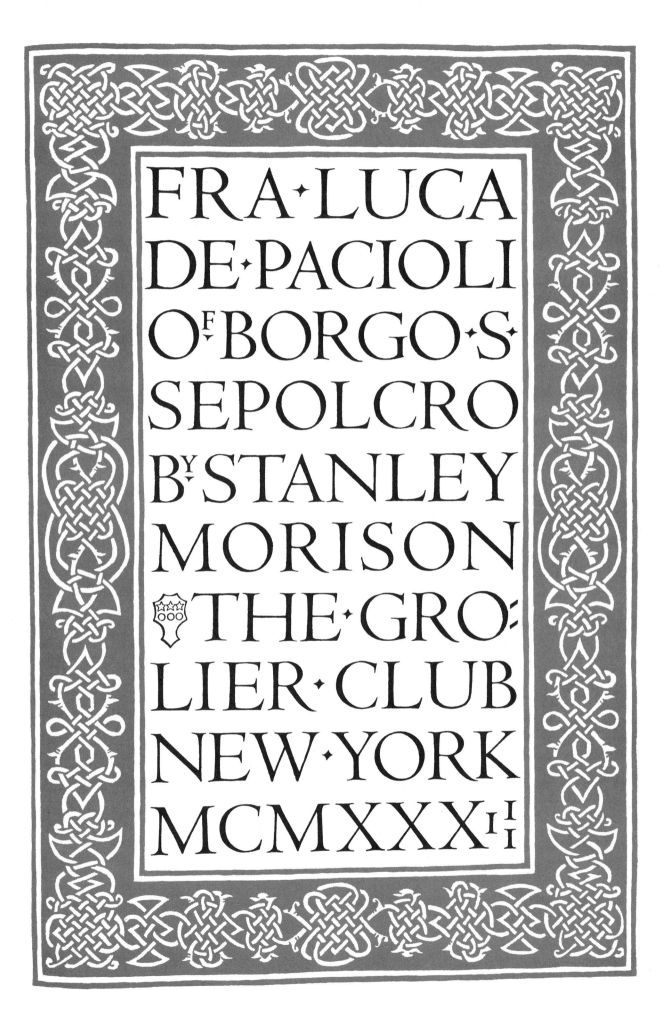

FRA·LUCA
DE·PACIOLI
O⸍·BORGO·S
SEPOLCRO
B⸍·STANLEY
MORISON
THE·GRO-
LIER·CLUB
NEW·YORK
MCMXXXII

Design: **Bruce Rogers**

Specimens are set in
Monotype Centaur

Centaur was designed by the American book designer Bruce Rogers, who based its design on Nicolas Jenson's 1470 Venetian roman type. Centaur was created for New York's Metropolitan Museum Press and first appeared in the Montague Press's 1916 edition of *The Centaur* by Maurice de Guerin. The initial handset type castings consisted of 14-point capital and lowercase letters. Additional fonts were cast in capitals only and named Museum Press Capitals. Rogers finally responded to numerous requests for Centaur to be available to others, and the English Monotype Company issued it for machineset composition in 1929.

An italic font was needed, but Rogers lacked confidence in his ability to design one; therefore, he asked Frederic Warde to permit Warde's excellent chancery italic typeface, Arrighi, to be used as the italic for Centaur. Warde agreed, and Arrighi is now also known as Centaur Italic. Arrighi had been designed as a private typeface; it was inspired by the work of the 16th century Italian calligrapher and type designer, Lodovico Arrighi.

Centaur is lighter in color and crisper in form than Nicolas Jenson's typefaces, and many other Jenson-inspired typefaces, including William Morris's Golden and Frederic Goudy's Kennerly and Goudy Old Styles. Rogers designed elegant and refined serifs, replaced the slab serifs on Jenson's **M** with smaller and more tapered serifs, and gave the Js a delicate tail.

Originally, Centaur did not have bold fonts; its primary use was for fine book typography and display designs such as invitations and title pages where an exquisite Venetian style was deemed appropriate.

abcdefghij
klmnopqrs
tuvwxyz
$1234567
890!?

abcdefghijklmnopqrstuvwxyz
ABCDEFGHIJKLMNOPQRSTUVWXYZ
$&1234567890(.,"";:!?)

72

abcdefghijklmnop
qrstuvwxyzABCDEF
GHIJKLMNOPQR
STUVWXYZ$&
1234567890(.,"";:!?)

36

abcdefghijklmnopqrstuvwxyz
ABCDEFGHIJKLMNOPQRSTUVW
XYZ$&1234567890(.,"";:!?)

abcdefghijklmnopqrstuvwxyz
ABCDEFGHIJKLMNOPQRSTUVWXYZ
$&1234567890(.,""';:!?)

18

72

abcdefghijklmnopqrstuvw
xyzABCDEFGHIJK
LMNOPQRSTUVW
XYZ$&1234567890
(.,"";:!?)

36

abcdefghijklmnopqrstuvwxyz
ABCDEFGHIJKLMNOPQRSTUVWXYZ
$&1234567890(.,"";:!?)

Centaur

abcdefghijklmnopqrstuvwxyz
ABCDEFGHIJKLMNOPQRSTUVWXYZ
$1234567890&(.,""";:!?)

abcdefghijklmnopqrstuvwxyz
ABCDEFGHIJKLMNOPQRSTUVWXYZ
$1234567890&(.,""";:!?)

8/8

Typography, the major communications advance between the invention of writing and the age of electronic mass communications in the twentieth century, *played a pivotal role* in the social, economic, and religious upheavals that occurred during the fifteenth and sixteenth centuries. The modern nation developed as a result of the vigorous spirit of nationalism that swept over Europe and led to the American and French revolutions of the late eighteenth century. In addition to being a powerful vehicle for spreading ideas about human rights and the sovereignty of the people, typographic printing stabilized and unified languages. Illiteracy, the inability to read and write, began a long, steady decline. Typography radically altered education. The medieval classroom had been a scriptorium of sorts, where each student penned his own book. Learning became an increasingly private, rather than communal, process. Human dialog, extended by type, began to take place on a global scale that bridged time and space. Gutenberg's invention was the first mechanization of a skilled handicraft. As such, it set into motion, over the next three hundred years, the machinations that would lead to the industrial revolution.

9/9

Typography, the major communications advance between the invention of writing and the age of electronic mass communications in the twentieth century, *played a pivotal role* in the social, economic, and religious upheavals that occurred during the fifteenth and sixteenth centuries. The modern nation developed as a result of the vigorous spirit of nationalism that swept over Europe and led to the American and French revolutions of the late eighteenth century. In addition to being a powerful vehicle for spreading ideas about human rights and the sovereignty of the people, typographic printing stabilized and unified languages. Illiteracy, the inability to read and write, began a long, steady decline. Typography radically altered education. The medieval classroom had been a scriptorium of sorts, where each student penned his own book. Learning became an increasingly private, rather than communal, process. Human dialog, extended by type, began to take place on

8/9

Typography, the major communications advance between the invention of writing and the age of electronic mass communications in the twentieth century, *played a pivotal role* in the social, economic, and religious upheavals that occurred during the fifteenth and sixteenth centuries. The modern nation developed as a result of the vigorous spirit of nationalism that swept over Europe and led to the American and French revolutions of the late eighteenth century. In addition to being a powerful vehicle for spreading ideas about human rights and the sovereignty of the people, typographic printing stabilized and unified languages. Illiteracy, the inability to read and write, began a long, steady decline. Typography radically altered education. The medieval classroom had been a scriptorium of sorts, where each student penned his own book. Learning became an increasingly private, rather than communal, process. Human dialog, extended by type, began to take place on a global scale that bridged time and space. Gutenberg's invention was the first mechanization of a skilled handicraft. As such, it set into

9/10

Typography, the major communications advance between the invention of writing and the age of electronic mass communications in the twentieth century, *played a pivotal role* in the social, economic, and religious upheavals that occurred during the fifteenth and sixteenth centuries. The modern nation developed as a result of the vigorous spirit of nationalism that swept over Europe and led to the American and French revolutions of the late eighteenth century. In addition to being a powerful vehicle for spreading ideas about human rights and the sovereignty of the people, typographic printing stabilized and unified languages. Illiteracy, the inability to read and write, began a long, steady decline. Typography radically altered education. The medieval classroom had been a scriptorium of sorts, where each student penned his own book. Learning became an increasingly private, rather than

8/10

Typography, the major communications advance between the invention of writing and the age of electronic mass communications in the twentieth century, *played a pivotal role* in the social, economic, and religious upheavals that occurred during the fifteenth and sixteenth centuries. The modern nation developed as a result of the vigorous spirit of nationalism that swept over Europe and led to the American and French revolutions of the late eighteenth century. In addition to being a powerful vehicle for spreading ideas about human rights and the sovereignty of the people, typographic printing stabilized and unified languages. Illiteracy, the inability to read and write, began a long, steady decline. Typography radically altered education. The medieval classroom had been a scriptorium of sorts, where each student penned his own book. Learning became an increasingly private, rather than communal, process. Human dialog, extended by type, began to take place on a global scale that bridged time and space. Gutenberg's

9/11

Typography, the major communications advance between the invention of writing and the age of electronic mass communications in the twentieth century, *played a pivotal role* in the social, economic, and religious upheavals that occurred during the fifteenth and sixteenth centuries. The modern nation developed as a result of the vigorous spirit of nationalism that swept over Europe and led to the American and French revolutions of the late eighteenth century. In addition to being a powerful vehicle for spreading ideas about human rights and the sovereignty of the people, typographic printing stabilized and unified languages. Illiteracy, the inability to read and write, began a long, steady decline. Typography radically altered education. The medieval classroom had been a scriptorium of sorts, where each student

8/11

Typography, the major communications advance between the invention of writing and the age of electronic mass communications in the twentieth century, *played a pivotal role* in the social, economic, and religious upheavals that occurred during the fifteenth and sixteenth centuries. The modern nation developed as a result of the vigorous spirit of nationalism that swept over Europe and led to the American and French revolutions of the late eighteenth century. In addition to being a powerful vehicle for spreading ideas about human rights and the sovereignty of the people, typographic printing stabilized and unified languages. Illiteracy, the inability to read and write, began a long, steady decline. Typography radically altered education. The medieval classroom had been a scriptorium of sorts, where each student penned his own book. Learning became an increasingly private, rather than communal, process. Human dialog, extended by type,

9/12

Typography, the major communications advance between the invention of writing and the age of electronic mass communications in the twentieth century, *played a pivotal role* in the social, economic, and religious upheavals that occurred during the fifteenth and sixteenth centuries. The modern nation developed as a result of the vigorous spirit of nationalism that swept over Europe and led to the American and French revolutions of the late eighteenth century. In addition to being a powerful vehicle for spreading ideas about human rights and the sovereignty of the people, typographic printing stabilized and unified languages. Illiteracy, the inability to read and write, began a long, steady decline. Typography radically altered education.

abcdefghijklmnopqrstuvwxyz
ABCDEFGHIJKLMNOPQRSTUVWXYZ
$1234567890&(.,""";:!?)

abcdefghijklmnopqrstuvwxyz
ABCDEFGHIJKLMNOPQRSTUVWXYZ
$1234567890&(.,""";:!?)

10/10

Typography, the major communications advance between the invention of writing and the age of electronic mass communications in the twentieth century, *played a pivotal role* in the social, economic, and religious upheavals that occurred during the fifteenth and sixteenth centuries. The modern nation developed as a result of the vigorous spirit of nationalism that swept over Europe and led to the American and French revolutions of the late eighteenth century. In addition to being a powerful vehicle for spreading ideas about human rights and the sovereignty of the people, typographic printing stabilized and unified languages. Illiteracy, the inability to read and write, began a long, steady decline. Typography radically altered education. The medieval classroom had been a scriptorium of sorts,

10/11

Typography, the major communications advance between the invention of writing and the age of electronic mass communications in the twentieth century, *played a pivotal role* in the social, economic, and religious upheavals that occurred during the fifteenth and sixteenth centuries. The modern nation developed as a result of the vigorous spirit of nationalism that swept over Europe and led to the American and French revolutions of the late eighteenth century. In addition to being a powerful vehicle for spreading ideas about human rights and the sovereignty of the people, typographic printing stabilized and unified languages. Illiteracy, the inability to read and write, began a long, steady decline. Typography radically altered

10/12

Typography, the major communications advance between the invention of writing and the age of electronic mass communications in the twentieth century, *played a pivotal role* in the social, economic, and religious upheavals that occurred during the fifteenth and sixteenth centuries. The modern nation developed as a result of the vigorous spirit of nationalism that swept over Europe and led to the American and French revolutions of the late eighteenth century. In addition to being a powerful vehicle for spreading ideas about human rights and the sovereignty of the people, typographic printing

10/13

Typography, the major communications advance between the invention of writing and the age of electronic mass communications in the twentieth century, *played a pivotal role* in the social, economic, and religious upheavals that occurred during the fifteenth and sixteenth centuries. The modern nation developed as a result of the vigorous spirit of nationalism that swept over Europe and led to the American and French revolutions of the late eighteenth century. In addition to being a powerful vehicle for spreading ideas about human rights and the sovereignty of the people, typographic printing

12/12

Typography, the major communications advance between the invention of writing and the age of electronic mass communications in the twentieth century, *played a pivotal role* in the social, economic, and religious upheavals that occurred during the fifteenth and sixteenth centuries. The modern nation developed as a result of the vigorous spirit of nationalism that swept over Europe and led to the American and French revolutions of the late eighteenth century. In addition to being a powerful vehicle for spreading ideas about human rights and the sovereignty

12/13

Typography, the major communications advance between the invention of writing and the age of electronic mass communications in the twentieth century, *played a pivotal role* in the social, economic, and religious upheavals that occurred during the fifteenth and sixteenth centuries. The modern nation developed as a result of the vigorous spirit of nationalism that swept over Europe and led to the American and French revolutions of the late eighteenth century. In addition to being a powerful vehicle for

12/14

Typography, the major communications advance between the invention of writing and the age of electronic mass communications in the twentieth century, *played a pivotal role* in the social, economic, and religious upheavals that occurred during the fifteenth and sixteenth centuries. The modern nation developed as a result of the vigorous spirit of nationalism that swept over Europe and led to the American and French revolutions of the late eighteenth

12/15

Typography, the major communications advance between the invention of writing and the age of electronic mass communications in the twentieth century, *played a pivotal role* in the social, economic, and religious upheavals that occurred during the fifteenth and sixteenth centuries. The modern nation developed as a result of the vigorous spirit of nationalism that swept over Europe and led to the American and French revolutions of the late eighteenth

Jack and Jill went up the hill
to fetch a pail of water.
Jack fell down and broke his
crown, and Jill c a m e
t u m b l i n g
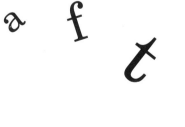
a f t

e r.

Century Schoolbook

Design: **Philip Meggs**

Specimens are set in
**Monotype Century
Schoolbook**

The original Century typeface was developed by Lynn Boyd Benton of the American Typefounders Company in conjunction with the renowned American printer Theodore De Vinne. It was specifically designed to print *Century* magazine beginning in 1896. Century maintained the narrow set width of modern style fonts used in periodicals, but the thin elements were thicker and serifs were strengthened. Century's strong acceptance led to the development of other variations. Benton's son, Morris F. Benton, became director of typeface development at ATF and designed over 225 typefaces, including a slightly wider version of Century called Century Expanded in 1900 and Century Schoolbook in 1915.

Century Schoolbook was specifically designed as an extremely readable typeface for school textbooks; legibility and perception research guided its development. Stroke weights, character heights, and spaces between and within letters were carefully determined, using vast amounts of research data to guide in a quest for a perfectly legible typeface for young readers. Century Schoolbook has prominent slab serifs with a gentle bracket. Thick and thin stroke weights are somewhat heavier than most serifed fonts, this hearty weight is offset by generous white spaces between and within the letters. The unique identifying visual characteristics of each letter are clear and even slightly exaggerated.

The clarity and legibility of Century Schoolbook make it a "user friendly" typeface. It has maintained great popularity, not only for educational materials, but for advertising, book design, and corporate work as well.

ABCDEF
GHIJKL
MNOPQ
RSTUVW
XYZ&(,""::)

abcdefghi
jklmnopq
rstuvwxy
z$123456
7890!?

abcdefghijklmnopqrstuvwxyz
ABCDEFGHIJKLMNOPQRSTU
VWXYZ$&1234567890(.,"";:!?)

72

abcdefghijklmno
pqrstuvwxyzA
BCDEFGHIJKL
MNOPQRSTU
VWXYZ$&1234
567890(.,"";:!?)

36

abcdefghijklmnopqrstuvwxyz
ABCDEFGHIJKLMNOPQRSTU
VWXYZ$&1234567890(.,"";:!?)

abcdefghijklmnopqrstuvwxyz
ABCDEFGHIJKLMNOPQRSTU
VWXYZ$&1234567890(.,"";:!?)

18

72

abcdefghijklmno
pqrstuvwxyzABC
DEFGHIJKLM
NOPQRSTUVW
XYZ$&12345678
90(.,"";:!?)

36

abcdefghijklmnopqrstuvwxyz
ABCDEFGHIJKLMNOPQRSTU
VWXYZ$&1234567890(.,"";:!?)

abcdefghijklmnopqrstuvwxyz
ABCDEFGHIJKLMNOPQRSTU
VWXYZ$&1234567890(.,"";:!?)

70

abcdefghijklm
nopqrstuvwxyz
ABCDEFGHIJ
KLMNOPQRS
TUVWXYZ$&12
34567890(.,"";:!?)

35

abcdefghijklmnopqrstuvwxyz
ABCDEFGHIJKLMNOPQRST
UVWXYZ$&1234567890(.,"";:!?)

abcdefghijklmnopqrstuvwxyz
ABCDEFGHIJKLMNOPQRSTU
VWXYZ$&1234567890(.,"";:!?)

18

70

abcdefghijklm
nopqrstuvwxyz
ABCDEFGHIJ
KLMNOPQRST
UVWXYZ$&123
4567890(.,"";:!?)

35

abcdefghijklmnopqrstuvwxyz
ABCDEFGHIJKLMNOPQRST
UVWXYZ$&1234567890(.,"";:!?)

Century Schoolbook

abcdefghijklmnopqrstuvwxyz
ABCDEFGHIJKLMNOPQRSTUVWXYZ
$1234567890&(.,"";:!?)

abcdefghijklmnopqrstuvwxyz
ABCDEFGHIJKLMNOPQRSTUVWXYZ
$1234567890&(.,"";:!?)

8/8

Typography, the major communications advance between the invention of writing and the age of electronic mass communications in the twentieth century, *played a pivotal role* in the social, economic, and religious upheavals that occurred during the fifteenth and sixteenth centuries. The modern nation developed as a result of the vigorous spirit of nationalism that swept over Europe and led to the American and French revolutions of the late eighteenth century. In addition to being a powerful vehicle for spreading ideas about human rights and the sovereignty of the people, typographic printing stabilized and unified languages. Illiteracy, the inability to read and write, began a long, steady decline. Typography radically altered education. The medieval classroom had been a scriptorium of sorts, where each student penned his own book. Learning became an increasingly private, rather than communal, process. Human dia

9/9

Typography, the major communications advance between the invention of writing and the age of electronic mass communications in the twentieth century, *played a pivotal role* in the social, economic, and religious upheavals that occurred during the fifteenth and sixteenth centuries. The modern nation developed as a result of the vigorous spirit of nationalism that swept over Europe and led to the American and French revolutions of the late eighteenth century. In addition to being a powerful vehicle for spreading ideas about human rights and the sovereignty of the people, typographic printing stabilized and unified languages. Illiteracy, the inability to read and write, began a long, steady decline. Typography radically altered education. The medieval class room had been a script

8/9

Typography, the major communications advance between the invention of writing and the age of electronic mass communications in the twentieth century, *played a pivotal role* in the social, economic, and religious upheavals that occurred during the fifteenth and sixteenth centuries. The modern nation developed as a result of the vigorous spirit of nationalism that swept over Europe and led to the American and French revolutions of the late eighteenth century. In addition to being a powerful vehicle for spreading ideas about human rights and the sovereignty of the people, typographic printing stabilized and unified languages. Illiteracy, the inability to read and write, began a long, steady decline. Typography radically altered education. The medieval classroom had been a scriptorium of sorts, where each student penned his own book. Learning became an

9/10

Typography, the major communications advance between the invention of writing and the age of electronic mass communications in the twentieth century, *played a pivotal role* in the social, economic, and religious upheavals that occurred during the fifteenth and sixteenth centuries. The modern nation developed as a result of the vigorous spirit of nationalism that swept over Europe and led to the American and French revolutions of the late eighteenth century. In addition to being a powerful vehicle for spreading ideas about human rights and the sovereignty of the people, typographic printing stabilized and unified languages. Illiteracy, the inability to read and write, began a long, steady decline. Typography radically alte

8/10

Typography, the major communications advance between the invention of writing and the age of electronic mass communications in the twentieth century, *played a pivotal role* in the social, economic, and religious upheavals that occurred during the fifteenth and sixteenth centuries. The modern nation developed as a result of the vigorous spirit of nationalism that swept over Europe and led to the American and French revolutions of the late eighteenth century. In addition to being a powerful vehicle for spreading ideas about human rights and the sovereignty of the people, typographic printing stabilized and unified languages. Illiteracy, the inability to read and write, began a long, steady decline. Typography radically altered education. The medieval classroom had been a scriptorium of sorts,

9/11

Typography, the major communications advance between the invention of writing and the age of electronic mass communications in the twentieth century, *played a pivotal role* in the social, economic, and religious upheavals that occurred during the fifteenth and sixteenth centuries. The modern nation developed as a result of the vigorous spirit of nationalism that swept over Europe and led to the American and French revolutions of the late eighteenth century. In addition to being a powerful vehicle for spreading ideas about human rights and the sovereignty of the people, typographic printing stabilized and unified languages. Illiteracy, the inability to read and

8/11

Typography, the major communications advance between the invention of writing and the age of electronic mass communications in the twentieth century, *played a pivotal role* in the social, economic, and religious upheavals that occurred during the fifteenth and sixteenth centuries. The modern nation developed as a result of the vigorous spirit of nationalism that swept over Europe and led to the American and French revolutions of the late eighteenth century. In addition to being a powerful vehicle for spreading ideas about human rights and the sovereignty of the people, typographic printing stabilized and unified languages. Illiteracy, the inability to read and write, began a long, steady decline. Typography radically altered ed

9/12

Typography, the major communications advance between the invention of writing and the age of electronic mass communications in the twentieth century, *played a pivotal role* in the social, economic, and religious upheavals that occurred during the fifteenth and sixteenth centuries. The modern nation developed as a result of the vigorous spirit of nationalism that swept over Europe and led to the American and French revolutions of the late eighteenth century. In addition to being a powerful vehicle for spreading ideas about human rights and the sovereignty of the people, typographic printing stabilized

abcdefghijklmnopqrstuvwxyz
ABCDEFGHIJKLMNOPQRSTUVWXYZ
$1234567890&(.,"";:!?)

abcdefghijklmnopqrstuvwxyz
ABCDEFGHIJKLMNOPQRSTUVWXYZ
$1234567890&(.,"";:!?)

10/10

Typography, the major communications advance bet ween the invention of writing and the age of electron ic mass communications during the twentieth cent ury, *played a pivotal role* in the social, economic, and religious upheavals that occurred during the fifteenth and sixteenth centuries. The modern nation developed as a result of the vigorous spirit of nationalism that swept over Europe and led to the American and Fre nch revolutions of the late eighteenth century. In addi tion to being a powerful vehicle for spreading ideas about human rights and the sovereignty of the people,

12/12

Typography, the major communications advan ce between the invention of writing and the age of electronic mass communications in the twenti eth century, *played a pivotal role* in the social, eco nomic, and religious upheavals that occurred dur ing the fifteenth and sixteenth centuries. The mod ern nation developed as a result of the vigorous spi rit of nationalism that swept over Europe and led to the American and French revolutions of the la

10/11

Typography, the major communications advance bet ween the invention of writing and the age of electron ic mass communications during the twentieth cent ury, *played a pivotal role* in the social, economic, and religious upheavals that occurred during the fifteenth and sixteenth centuries. The modern nation developed as a result of the vigorous spirit of nationalism that swept over Europe and led to the American and Fre nch revolutions of the late eighteenth century. In addi tion to being a powerful vehicle for spreading ideas about human rights and the sovereignty of the people,

12/13

Typography, the major communications advan ce between the invention of writing and the age of electronic mass communications in the twenti eth century, *played a pivotal role* in the social, eco nomic, and religious upheavals that occurred dur ing the fifteenth and sixteenth centuries. The mod ern nation developed as a result of the vigorous spi rit of nationalism that swept over Europe and led to the American and French revolutions of the la

10/12

Typography, the major communications advance bet ween the invention of writing and the age of electron ic mass communications during the twentieth cent ury, *played a pivotal role* in the social, economic, and religious upheavals that occurred during the fifteenth and sixteenth centuries. The modern nation developed as a result of the vigorous spirit of nationalism that swept over Europe and led to the American and Fre nch revolutions of the late eighteenth century. In addi

12/14

Typography, the major communications advan ce between the invention of writing and the age of electronic mass communications in the twenti eth century, *played a pivotal role* in the social, eco nomic, and religious upheavals that occurred dur ing the fifteenth and sixteenth centuries. The mod ern nation developed as a result of the vigorous spi rit of nationalism that swept over Europe and led

10/13

Typography, the major communications advance bet ween the invention of writing and the age of electron ic mass communications during the twentieth cent ury, *played a pivotal role* in the social, economic, and religious upheavals that occurred during the fifteenth and sixteenth centuries. The modern nation developed as a result of the vigorous spirit of nationalism that swept over Europe and led to the American and Fre nch revolutions of the late eighteenth century. In addi

12/15

Typography, the major communications advan ce between the invention of writing and the age of electronic mass communications in the twenti eth century, *played a pivotal role* in the social, eco nomic, and religious upheavals that occurred dur ing the fifteenth and sixteenth centuries. The mod ern nation developed as a result of the vigorous spi rit of nationalism that swept over Europe and led

Grunge • Yo! • Killer, dude • How's it hangin'? • Awesome • Bitchin' Slick • Groovy • Totally • Slam dunk Done Deal ...Not! Radical! • ...bba Dabba Doo! • Tech... • Chill out Hiphop • Illi... ...Mod • Yuppie Bummer • B... • Slimeball Homeboy • S... ...bag • Aggro Gag me • Do... ...e up, Scotty Trippin' • Sk... ...ion • Neato Gonzo • Jammin' • What's happenin'? Doohickey • Jive-ass • Interfacing Funky • Bone-head • Couch Potato Gnarly • DaKine • Cool • Main Squeeze

> The Americans are going to be the most fluent and melodious-voiced people in the world—and the most perfect users of words. The new world, the new times, the new people, the new vistas need a new tongue according—yes, what is more, they will have such a new tongue— will not be satisfied until it is evolved.
>
> WALT WHITMAN,
> *An American Primer*, 1904.

Design: **Kit Hinrichs / Pentagram**

Specimens are set in
ITC Cheltenham

Bertram Goodhue, the well-known American architect, designed Cheltenham (affectionately known as "Chelt") in 1896 to function as a legible text face. It was simultaneously released in 1902 by Mergenthaler Linotype and American Type Founders. From its inception, Cheltenham has been a design of considerable controversy. Loved or hated by typographic practitioners, the popularity of the face is largely due to the storm of debate surrounding its use.

To achieve the purpose of creating a legible text face, Goodhue designed Cheltenham with minimum contrast between strokes, short descenders and long ascenders, a narrow set width, and serifs reminiscent of 19th century Clarendon. The capital letters are quite wide, and the lowercase letters have a small x-height. Of interest is the lowercase **g** with its open loop, and the capital **G** with its protruding terminal. The **W** has crossing stems with serifs that touch; the **C** does not have a bottom serif.

By 1915, under the direction of Morris F. Benton, ATF had cut twenty-one variations of Cheltenham to establish a sizable family of faces. In years to follow, other firms, such as Linotype, Monotype, Ludlow, and Intertype also developed new variants. Ironically, because of the large number of selections available, Cheltenham has been perceived first as a display face and second as the text face intended by Goodhue. In 1975, it was released by the International Typeface Corporation and made widely available.

Currently, Cheltenham is used as display and text type in advertising and job printing. Typographic tastes among book publishers have shifted to typefaces other than Cheltenham, however. Despite the ups and downs of a typeface's acceptance, the popularity of this type family will most likely endure for years to come.

ABCDEF
GHIJKLM
NOPQRS
TUVWX
YZ&("",,;,)

abcdefgh
ijklmnop
qrstuvwx
yz$12345
67890!?

18

abcdefghijklmnopqrstuvwxyz
ABCDEFGHIJKLMNOPQRSTUVWXYZ
$&1234567890(.,"";:!?)

72

abcdefghijklmno
pqrstuvwxyzAB
CDEFGHIJKLMN
OPQRSTUVW
XYZ$&12345678
90(.,"";:!?)

36

abcdefghijklmnopqrstuvwxyz
ABCDEFGHIJKLMNOPQRSTUVW
XYZ$&1234567890(.,"";:!?)

abcdefghijklmnopqrstuvwxyz
ABCDEFGHIJKLMNOPQRSTUVWXYZ
$&1234567890(.,"";:!?)

18

72

abcdefghijklmn
opqrstuvwxyzAB
CDEFGHIJKLM
NOPQRSTUVWX
YZ$&1234567890
(.,"";:!?)

36

abcdefghijklmnopqrstuvwxyz
ABCDEFGHIJKLMNOPQRSTUVW
XYZ$&1234567890(.,"";:!?)

abcdefghijklmnopqrstuvwxyz
ABCDEFGHIJKLMNOPQRSTUVWXYZ
$&1234567890(.,""::!?)

72

abcdefghijklmn
opqrstuvwxyz
ABCDEFGHIJK
LMNOPQRSTU
VWXYZ$&1234
567890(.,"";:!?)

36

abcdefghijklmnopqrstuvwxyz
ABCDEFGHIJKLMNOPQRSTUV
WXYZ$&1234567890(.,"";:!?)

Cheltenham Bold Italic

abcdefghijklmnopqrstuvwxyz
ABCDEFGHIJKLMNOPQRSTUVWXYZ
$&1234567890(,""";:!?)

72

abcdefghijklm
nopqrstuvwxyz
ABCDEFGHIJK
LMNOPQRSTU
VWXYZ$&1234
567890(,"";:!?)

36

abcdefghijklmnopqrstuvwxyz
ABCDEFGHIJKLMNOPRSTUW
XYZ$&1234567890(,"";:!?)

Cheltenham Book

abcdefghijklmnopqrstuvwxyz
ABCDEFGHIJKLMNOPQRSTUVWXYZ
$1234567890&(.,"";:!?)

abcdefghijklmnopqrstuvwxyz
ABCDEFGHIJKLMNOPQRSTUVWXYZ
$1234567890&(.,"";:!?)

8/8

Typography, the major communications advance between the invent ion of writing and the age of electronic mass communications in the t wentieth century, *played a pivotal role* in the social, economic, and r eligious upheavals that occurred during the fifteenth and sixteenth c enturies. The modern nation developed as a result of the vigorous sp irit of nationalism that swept over Europe and led to the American a nd French revolutions of the late eighteenth century. In addition to b eing a powerful vehicle for spreading ideas about human rights and the sovereignty of the people, typographic printing stabilized and un ified languages. Illiteracy, the inability to read and write, began a lon g, steady decline. Typography radically altered education. The medi eval classroom had been a scriptorium of sorts, where each student penned his own book. Learning became an increasingly private, rath er than communal, process. Human dialog, extended by type, began to take place on a global scale that bridged time and space. Gutenbe

9/9

Typography, the major communications advance between th e invention of writing and the age of electronic mass commu nications in the twentieth century, *played a pivotal role* in the social, economic, and religious upheavals that occurred duri ng the fifteenth and sixteenth centuries. The modern nation d eveloped as a result of the vigorous spirit of nationalism that swept over Europe and led to the American and French revol utions of the late eighteenth century. In addition to being a p owerful vehicle for spreading ideas about human rights and the sovereignty of the people, typographic printing stabilized and unified languages. Illiteracy, the inability to read and writ e, began a long, steady decline. Typography radically altered education. The medieval classroom had been a scriptorium o

8/9

Typography, the major communications advance between the invent ion of writing and the age of electronic mass communications in the t wentieth century, *played a pivotal role* in the social, economic, and r eligious upheavals that occurred during the fifteenth and sixteenth c enturies. The modern nation developed as a result of the vigorous sp irit of nationalism that swept over Europe and led to the American a nd French revolutions of the late eighteenth century. In addition to b eing a powerful vehicle for spreading ideas about human rights and the sovereignty of the people, typographic printing stabilized and un ified languages. Illiteracy, the inability to read and write, began a lon g, steady decline. Typography radically altered education. The medi eval classroom had been a scriptorium of sorts, where each student penned his own book. Learning became an increasingly private, rath

9/10

Typography, the major communications advance between th e invention of writing and the age of electronic mass commu nications in the twentieth century, *played a pivotal role* in the social, economic, and religious upheavals that occurred duri ng the fifteenth and sixteenth centuries. The modern nation d eveloped as a result of the vigorous spirit of nationalism that swept over Europe and led to the American and French revol utions of the late eighteenth century. In addition to being a p owerful vehicle for spreading ideas about human rights and the sovereignty of the people, typographic printing stabilized and unified languages. Illiteracy, the inability to read and writ e, began a long, steady decline. Typography radically altered

8/10

Typography, the major communications advance between the invent ion of writing and the age of electronic mass communications in the t wentieth century, *played a pivotal role* in the social, economic, and r eligious upheavals that occurred during the fifteenth and sixteenth c enturies. The modern nation developed as a result of the vigorous sp irit of nationalism that swept over Europe and led to the American a nd French revolutions of the late eighteenth century. In addition to b eing a powerful vehicle for spreading ideas about human rights and the sovereignty of the people, typographic printing stabilized and un ified languages. Illiteracy, the inability to read and write, began a lon g, steady decline. Typography radically altered education. The medi eval classroom had been a scriptorium of sorts, where each student

9/11

Typography, the major communications advance between th e invention of writing and the age of electronic mass commu nications in the twentieth century, *played a pivotal role* in the social, economic, and religious upheavals that occurred duri ng the fifteenth and sixteenth centuries. The modern nation d eveloped as a result of the vigorous spirit of nationalism that swept over Europe and led to the American and French revol utions of the late eighteenth century. In addition to being a p owerful vehicle for spreading ideas about human rights and the sovereignty of the people, typographic printing stabilized and unified languages. Illiteracy, the inability to read and writ

8/11

Typography, the major communications advance between the invent ion of writing and the age of electronic mass communications in the t wentieth century, *played a pivotal role* in the social, economic, and r eligious upheavals that occurred during the fifteenth and sixteenth c enturies. The modern nation developed as a result of the vigorous sp irit of nationalism that swept over Europe and led to the American a nd French revolutions of the late eighteenth century. In addition to b eing a powerful vehicle for spreading ideas about human rights and the sovereignty of the people, typographic printing stabilized and un ified languages. Illiteracy, the inability to read and write, began a lon g, steady decline. Typography radically altered education. The medi

9/12

Typography, the major communications advance between th e invention of writing and the age of electronic mass commu nications in the twentieth century, *played a pivotal role* in the social, economic, and religious upheavals that occurred duri ng the fifteenth and sixteenth centuries. The modern nation d eveloped as a result of the vigorous spirit of nationalism that swept over Europe and led to the American and French revol utions of the late eighteenth century. In addition to being a p owerful vehicle for spreading ideas about human rights and the sovereignty of the people, typographic printing stabilized

abcdefghijklmnopqrstuvwxyz
ABCDEFGHIJKLMNOPQRSTUVWXYZ
$1234567890&(.,"";:!?)

abcdefghijklmnopqrstuvwxyz
ABCDEFGHIJKLMNOPQRSTUVWXYZ
&1234567890&(.,"";:!?)

10/10

Typography, the major communications advance betw een the invention of writing and the age of electronic m ass communications in the twentieth century, *played a pivotal role* in the social, economic, and religious uphe avals that occurred during the fifteenth and sixteenth c enturies. The modern nation developed as a result of t he vigorous spirit of nationalism that swept over Europ e and led to the American and French revolutions of th e late eighteenth century. In addition to being a powerf ul vehicle for spreading ideas about human rights and t he sovereignty of the people, typographic printing stab ilized and unified languages. Illiteracy, the inability to r

10/11

Typography, the major communications advance betw een the invention of writing and the age of electronic m ass communications in the twentieth century, *played a pivotal role* in the social, economic, and religious uphe avals that occurred during the fifteenth and sixteenth c enturies. The modern nation developed as a result of t he vigorous spirit of nationalism that swept over Europ e and led to the American and French revolutions of th e late eighteenth century. In addition to being a powerf ul vehicle for spreading ideas about human rights and t he sovereignty of the people, typographic printing stab

10/12

Typography, the major communications advance betw een the invention of writing and the age of electronic m ass communications in the twentieth century, *played a pivotal role* in the social, economic, and religious uphe avals that occurred during the fifteenth and sixteenth c enturies. The modern nation developed as a result of t he vigorous spirit of nationalism that swept over Europ e and led to the American and French revolutions of th e late eighteenth century. In addition to being a powerf ul vehicle for spreading ideas about human rights and t

10/13

Typography, the major communications advance betw een the invention of writing and the age of electronic m ass communications in the twentieth century, *played a pivotal role* in the social, economic, and religious uphe avals that occurred during the fifteenth and sixteenth c enturies. The modern nation developed as a result of t he vigorous spirit of nationalism that swept over Europ e and led to the American and French revolutions of th e late eighteenth century. In addition to being a powerf

12/12

Typography, the major communications adva nce between the invention of writing and the age of electronic mass communications in the twentieth century, *played a pivotal role* in the social, economic, and religious upheavals tha t occurred during the fifteenth and sixteenth centuries. The modern nation developed as a result of the vigorous spirit of nationalism tha t swept over Europe and led to the American and French revolutions of the late eighteenth

12/13

Typography, the major communications adva nce between the invention of writing and the age of electronic mass communications in the twentieth century, *played a pivotal role* in the social, economic, and religious upheavals tha t occurred during the fifteenth and sixteenth centuries. The modern nation developed as a result of the vigorous spirit of nationalism tha t swept over Europe and led to the American

12/14

Typography, the major communications adva nce between the invention of writing and the age of electronic mass communications in the twentieth century, *played a pivotal role* in the social, economic, and religious upheavals tha t occurred during the fifteenth and sixteenth centuries. The modern nation developed as a result of the vigorous spirit of nationalism tha t swept over Europe and led to the American

12/15

Typography, the major communications adva nce between the invention of writing and the age of electronic mass communications in the twentieth century, *played a pivotal role* in the social, economic, and religious upheavals tha t occurred during the fifteenth and sixteenth centuries. The modern nation developed as a result of the vigorous spirit of nationalism tha

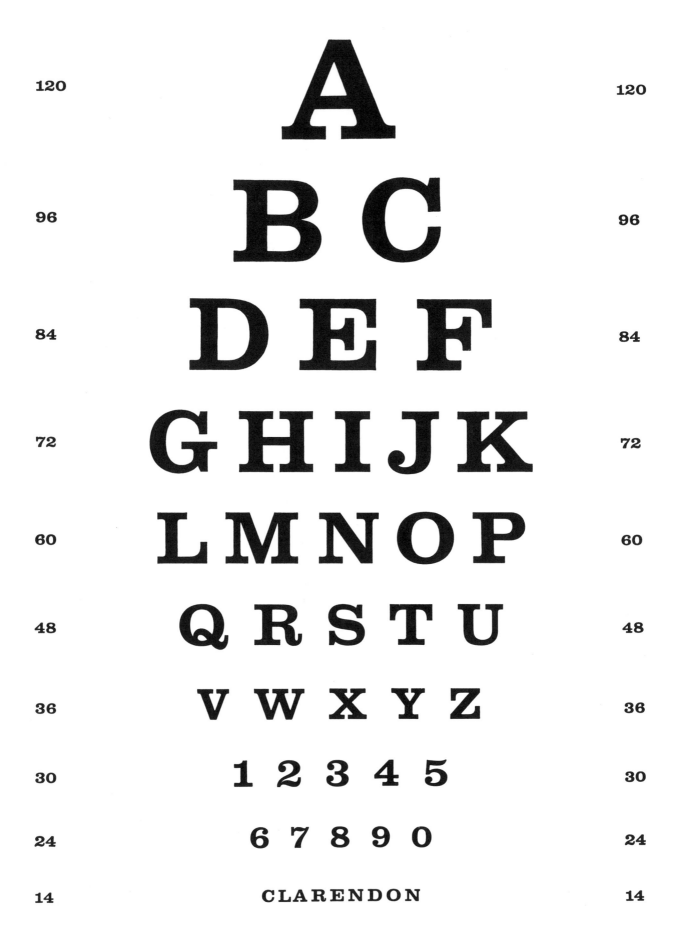

120	A	120
96	B C	96
84	D E F	84
72	G H I J K	72
60	L M N O P	60
48	Q R S T U	48
36	V W X Y Z	36
30	1 2 3 4 5	30
24	6 7 8 9 0	24
14	CLARENDON	14

Design: **Bradbury Thompson**

The term Clarendon represents not a single typeface, but a subcategory of square-serfed typefaces. Robert Beasley designed the first Clarendon for London's Fann Street Foundry in 1845; it was intended as a bold face for use with roman text type in dictionaries and reference books. Although the name may refer to the Clarendon Press at Oxford University, claims that the first Clarendon was cut for this press have been disputed. Beasley's Clarendon, the first typeface protected by England's three-year design-copyright law, was wildly popular and widely plagiarized. Clarendons enjoyed a revival during the 1950s. Important new versions released during that decade include Hermann Eidenbenz's 1951 Hass Clarendon for the Haas'sche foundry in Basel, Freeman Craw's 1956 Craw Clarendon for American Type Founders, and the 1955 Fortune – later renamed Fortuna – designed for Germany's Bauer foundry by K.F. Bauer and Walter Baum.

The strokes in Clarendon fonts are fairly heavy, with thick-and-thin weight contrast rather than the uniform stroke weight of many Egyptians. The square serifs are not as thick as most Egyptians and have subtle bracketing. In most Clarendons, a, c, g, and r have a round serif; the structure of the a, e, g, and t is based on the roman model rather than the Egyptian style, and the tail of the **R** ends in an upward curve rather than a squared serif.

Clarendons are often used as display rather than text types. Their boldly assertive designs find frequent application in broadcast graphics, advertising, and package design. Their beautiful abstract shapes have inspired use as initial letters, typographic trademarks, and numerals.

Specimens are set in
Linotype Clarendon

ABCDEF
GHIJKL
MNOPQR
STUVWX
YZ&(.,""'';:)

abcdefghi
jklmnopq
rstuvwxy
z$123456
7890!?

abcdefghijklmnopqrstuvwxyz
ABCDEFGHIJKLMNOPQRSTU
VWXYZ$&1234567890(.,"";:!?)

72

abcdefghijklmn
opqrstuvwxyzA
BCDEFGHIJKL
MNOPQRSTUV
WXYZ$&12345
67890(.,"";:!?)

36

abcdefghijklmnopqrstuvwxyz
ABCDEFGHIJKLMNOPQRST
UVWXYZ$&1234567890(.,"";:!?)

abcdefghijklmnopqrstuvwxyz
ABCDEFGHIJKLMNOPQRSTU
VWXYZ$&1234567890(.,"";:!?)

72

abcdefghijklmn
opqrstuvwxyz
ABCDEFGHIJK
LMNOPQRSTU
VWXYZ$&123
4567890(.,"";:!?)

36

abcdefghijklmnopqrstuvwxyz
ABCDEFGHIJKLMNOPQRST
UVWXYZ$&1234567890(.,"";:!?)

abcdefghijklmnopqrstuvwxyz
ABCDEFGHIJKLMNOPQRSTU
VWXYZ$&1234567890(.,"";:!?)

72

abcdefghijklmn
opqrstuvwxyz
ABCDEFGHIJ
KLMNOPQRST
UVWXYZ$&12
34567890(.,"";:!?)

36

abcdefghijklmnopqrstuvwxyz
ABCDEFGHIJKLMNOPQRST
UVWXYZ$&1234567890(.,"";:!?)

abcdefghijklmnopqrstuvwxyz
ABCDEFGHIJKLMNOPQRSTU
VWXYZ$&1234567890(.,"";:!?)

18

70

abcdefghijklmn
opqrstuvwxyz
ABCDEFGHIJK
LMNOPQRSTU
VWXYZ$&1234
567890(.,"";:!?)

34

abcdefghijklmnopqrstuvwxyz
ABCDEFGHIJKLMNOPQRSTU
VWXYZ$&1234567890(.,"";:!?)

Clarendon

abcdefghijklmnopqrstuvwxyz
ABCDEFGHIJKLMNOPQRSTUVWXYZ
$1234567890&(.,"";:!?)

abcdefghijklmnopqrstuvwxyz
ABCDEFGHIJKLMNOPQRSTUVWXYZ
$1234567890&(.,"";:!?)

Typography, the major communications advance between the invention of writing and the age of electronic mass communi cations in the twentieth century, *played a pivotal role* in the soc ial, economic, and religious upheavals that occurred during the fifteenth and sixteenth centuries. The modern nation developed as a result of the vigorous spirit of nationalism that swept over Europe and led to the American and French revolutions of the late eighteenth century. In addition to being a powerful vehicle for spreading ideas about human rights and the sovereignty of the peo ple, typographic printing stabilized and unified languages. Illit eracy, the inability to read and write, began a long, steady de cline. Typography radically altered education. The medieval cla ssroom had been a scriptorium of sorts, where each student pen ned his own book. Learning became an increasingly private, rat

Typography, the major communications advance between the invention of writing and the age of electronic mass communications in the twentieth century, *played a pivotal role* in the social, economic, and religious upheavals that oc curred during the fifteenth and sixteenth centuries. The modern nation developed as a result of the vigorous spirit of nationalism that swept over Europe and led to the Ame rican and French revolutions of the late eighteenth centu ry. In addition to being a powerful vehicle for spreading ide as about human rights and the sovereignty of the people, typ ographic printing stabilized and unified languages. Illite racy, the inability to read and write, began a long, steady decline. Typography radically altered education. The medi

Typography, the major communications advance between the invention of writing and the age of electronic mass communi cations in the twentieth century, *played a pivotal role* in the soc ial, economic, and religious upheavals that occurred during the fifteenth and sixteenth centuries. The modern nation developed as a result of the vigorous spirit of nationalism that swept over Europe and led to the American and French revolutions of the late eighteenth century. In addition to being a powerful vehicle for spreading ideas about human rights and the sovereignty of the peo ple, typographic printing stabilized and unified languages. Illit eracy, the inability to read and write, began a long, steady de cline. Typography radically altered education. The medieval cla ssroom had been a scriptorium of sorts, where each student pen

Typography, the major communications advance between the invention of writing and the age of electronic mass communications in the twentieth century, *played a pivotal role* in the social, economic, and religious upheavals that oc curred during the fifteenth and sixteenth centuries. The modern nation developed as a result of the vigorous spirit of nationalism that swept over Europe and led to the Ame rican and French revolutions of the late eighteenth centu ry. In addition to being a powerful vehicle for spreading ide as about human rights and the sovereignty of the people, typ ographic printing stabilized and unified languages. Illite racy, the inability to read and write, began a long, steady

Typography, the major communications advance between the invention of writing and the age of electronic mass communi cations in the twentieth century, *played a pivotal role* in the soc ial, economic, and religious upheavals that occurred during the fifteenth and sixteenth centuries. The modern nation developed as a result of the vigorous spirit of nationalism that swept over Europe and led to the American and French revolutions of the late eighteenth century. In addition to being a powerful vehicle for spreading ideas about human rights and the sovereignty of the peo ple, typographic printing stabilized and unified languages. Illit eracy, the inability to read and write, began a long, steady de cline. Typography radically altered education. The medieval cla

Typography, the major communications advance between the invention of writing and the age of electronic mass communications in the twentieth century, *played a pivotal role* in the social, economic, and religious upheavals that oc curred during the fifteenth and sixteenth centuries. The modern nation developed as a result of the vigorous spirit of nationalism that swept over Europe and led to the Ame rican and French revolutions of the late eighteenth centu ry. In addition to being a powerful vehicle for spreading ide as about human rights and the sovereignty of the people, typ ographic printing stabilized and unified languages. Illite

Typography, the major communications advance between the invention of writing and the age of electronic mass communi cations in the twentieth century, *played a pivotal role* in the soc ial, economic, and religious upheavals that occurred during the fifteenth and sixteenth centuries. The modern nation developed as a result of the vigorous spirit of nationalism that swept over Europe and led to the American and French revolutions of the late eighteenth century. In addition to being a powerful vehicle for spreading ideas about human rights and the sovereignty of the peo ple, typographic printing stabilized and unified languages. Illit eracy, the inability to read and write, began a long, steady de

Typography, the major communications advance between the invention of writing and the age of electronic mass communications in the twentieth century, *played a pivotal role* in the social, economic, and religious upheavals that oc curred during the fifteenth and sixteenth centuries. The modern nation developed as a result of the vigorous spirit of nationalism that swept over Europe and led to the Ame rican and French revolutions of the late eighteenth centu ry. In addition to being a powerful vehicle for spreading ide as about human rights and the sovereignty of the people, typ

abcdefghijklmnopqrstuvwxyz
ABCDEFGHIJKLMNOPQRSTUVWXYZ
$1234567890&(.,"";:!?)

abcdefghijklmnopqrstuvwxyz
ABCDEFGHIJKLMNOPQRSTUVWXYZ
$1234567890&(.,"";:!?)

10/10

Typography, the major communications advance be tween the invention of writing and the age of elec tronic mass communications in the twentieth century, *played a pivotal role* in the social, economic, and religi ous upheavals that occurred during the fifteenth and sixteenth centuries. The modern nation developed as a result of the vigorous spirit of nationalism that swept over Europe and led to the American and French revol utions of the late eighteenth century. In addition to be ing a powerful vehicle for spreading ideas about human rights and the sovereignty of the people, typographic pr

12/12

Typography, the major communications advan ce between the invention of writing and the age of electronic mass communications in the twe ntieth century, *played a pivotal role* in the so cial, economic, and religious upheavals that oc curred during the fifteenth and sixteenth cent uries. The modern nation developed as a resu lt of the vigorous spirit of nationalism that swe pt over Europe and led to the American and Fre

10/11

Typography, the major communications advance be tween the invention of writing and the age of elec tronic mass communications in the twentieth century, *played a pivotal role* in the social, economic, and religi ous upheavals that occurred during the fifteenth and sixteenth centuries. The modern nation developed as a result of the vigorous spirit of nationalism that swept over Europe and led to the American and French revol utions of the late eighteenth century. In addition to be ing a powerful vehicle for spreading ideas about human rights and the sovereignty of the people, typographic pr

12/13

Typography, the major communications advan ce between the invention of writing and the age of electronic mass communications in the twe ntieth century, *played a pivotal role* in the social, economic, and religious upheavals that oc curred during the fifteenth and sixteenth cent uries. The modern nation developed as a resu lt of the vigorous spirit of nationalism that swe pt over Europe and led to the American and Fre

10/12

Typography, the major communications advance be tween the invention of writing and the age of elec tronic mass communications in the twentieth century, *played a pivotal role* in the social, economic, and religi ous upheavals that occurred during the fifteenth and sixteenth centuries. The modern nation developed as a result of the vigorous spirit of nationalism that swept over Europe and led to the American and French revol utions of the late eighteenth century. In addition to be

12/14

Typography, the major communications advan ce between the invention of writing and the age of electronic mass communications in the twe ntieth century, *played a pivotal role* in the social, economic, and religious upheavals that oc curred during the fifteenth and sixteenth cent uries. The modern nation developed as a resu lt of the vigorous spirit of nationalism that swe

10/13

Typography, the major communications advance be tween the invention of writing and the age of elec tronic mass communications in the twentieth century, *played a pivotal role* in the social, economic, and religi ous upheavals that occurred during the fifteenth and sixteenth centuries. The modern nation developed as a result of the vigorous spirit of nationalism that swept over Europe and led to the American and French revol utions of the late eighteenth century. In addition to be

12/15

Typography, the major communications advan ce between the invention of writing and the age of electronic mass communications in the twe ntieth century, *played a pivotal role* in the social, economic, and religious upheavals that oc curred during the fifteenth and sixteenth cent uries. The modern nation developed as a resu lt of the vigorous spirit of nationalism that swe

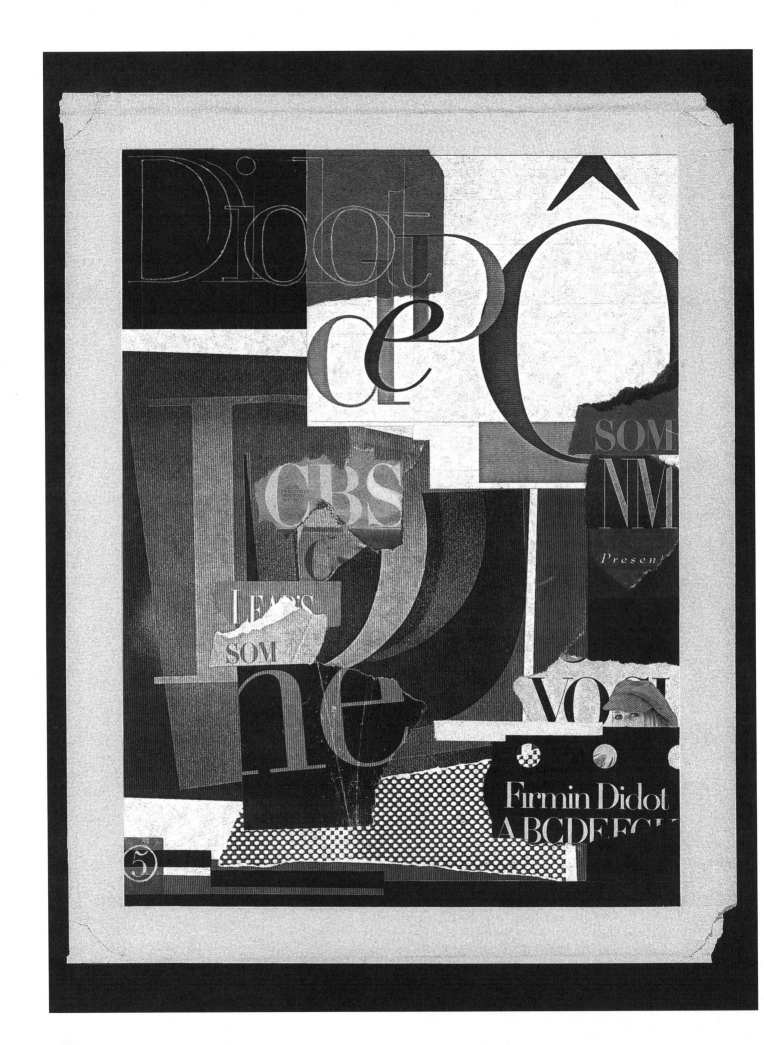

Design: **Ned Drew**

Specimens are set in
Linotype Didot

The Didot family from Paris was a highly innovative team of printers, publishers, typefounders, and papermakers; their accomplishments strongly influenced the development and evolution of type design. In 1784, Firmin Didot designed the first truly Modern typeface. This design predated the Modern faces of their Italian competitor and rival, Giambattista Bodoni; however, Bodoni and the Didots reciprocated influences, and both made permanent contributions.

By comparison, the original Didot typefaces were more mechanical and severe than those of Bodoni. For example, Bodoni's serifs are joined to the main strokes with a slight bracket, and the serifs of the lowercase letters are slightly concave. The straight-edged serifs in Didot's letters, on the other hand, possess no bracket. Other Modern features of Didot include a vertical stress, and a high contrast between the thick and thin strokes of letters. The **Q** has a curved tail, and the **R** a curved leg; the **E** carries the weight of heavy serifs, and the **W** has a stepped joint.

Several versions of Didot closely resemble the original, including Deberny & Peignot's Firmin Didot, and versions by Ludwig & Mayer, Linotype, and Monotype. In 1904, Monotype also issued Neo Didot, a revival that is a reasonable facsimile, but also an improvement upon earlier versions.

Though in recent years Didot has not received the same notoriety as Bodoni, it remains an exceptionally fine text face for book designers and a distinctive display face for advertising and newspapers.

Didot Roman

abcdefghij
klmnopq
rstuvwxyz
$1234567
890!?

abcdefghijklmnopqrstuvwxyz
ABCDEFGHIJKLMNOPQRSTUVWXYZ
$&1234567890(.,""";:!?)

72

abcdefghijklmn
opqrstuvwxyzA
BCDEFGHIJKL
MNOPQRSTU
VWXYZ$&1234
567890(,"";:!?)

36

abcdefghijklmnopqrstuvwxyz
ABCDEFGHIJKLMNOPQRSTU
VWXYZ$&1234567890(.,""";:!?)

abcdefghijklmnopqrstuvwxyz
ABCDEFGHIJKLMNOPQRSTUVWXYZ
$&1234567890(.,""":!?)

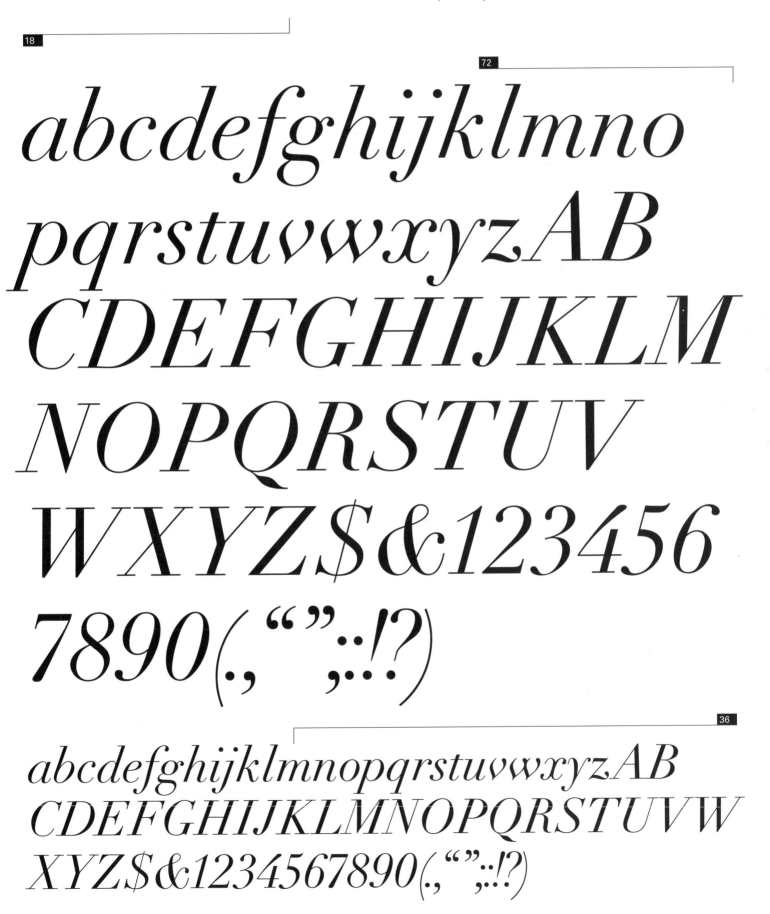

18

72

abcdefghijklmno

pqrstuvwxyzAB

CDEFGHIJKLM

NOPQRSTUV

WXYZ$&123456

7890(.,"":;:!?)

36

abcdefghijklmnopqrstuvwxyzAB
CDEFGHIJKLMNOPQRSTUVW
XYZ$&1234567890(.,"":;:!?)

abcdefghijklmnopqrstuvwxyz
ABCDEFGHIJKLMNOPQRSTUVWXYZ
$&1234567890(.,""::!?)

72

abcdefghijklmn
opqrstuvwxyzA
BCDEFGHIKL
MNOPQRSTU
VWXYZ$&1234
567890(,"""::!?)

36

abcdefghijklmnopqrstuvwxyz
ABCDEFGHIJKLMNOPQRST
UVWXYZ$&1234567890(,"""::!?)

abcdefghijklmnopqrstuvwxyz
ABCDEFGHIJKLMNOPQRSTUVWXYZ
$&1234567890(,""::!?)

18

72

abcdefghijklmno
pqrstuvwxyzABC
DEFGHIJKLM
NOPQRSTUV
WXYZ$&123456
7890(,"";:!?)

36

abcdefghijklmnopqrstuvwxyzAB
CDEFGHIJKLMNOPQRSTUVW
XYZ$&1234567890(,"";:!?)

Didot Roman

abcdefghijklmnopqrstuvwxyz
ABCDEFGHIJKLMNOPQRSTUVWXYZ
$1234567890&(.,"";:!?)

abcdefghijklmnopqrstuvwxyz
ABCDEFGHIJKLMNOPQRSTUVWXYZ
$1234567890&(.,"";:!?)

8/8

Typography, the major communications advance between the inventi on of writing and the age of electronic mass communications in the t wentieth century, *played a pivotal role* in the social, economic, and reli gious upheavals that occurred during the fifteenth and sixteenth cent uries. The modern nation developed as a result of the vigorous spirit of nationalism that swept over Europe and led to the American and F rench revolutions of the late eighteenth century. In addition to being a powerful vehicle for spreading ideas about human rights and the so vereignty of the people, typographic printing stabilized and unified la nguages. Illiteracy, the inability to read and write, began a long, stead y decline. Typography radically altered education. The medieval class room had been a scriptorium of sorts, where each student penned his own book. Learning became an increasingly private, rather than com munal, process. Human dialog, extended by type, began to take place on a global scale that bridged time and space. Gutenberg's invention

9/9

Typography, the major communications advance between the invention of writing and the age of electronic mass communic ations in the twentieth century, *played a pivotal role* in the soci al, economic, and religious upheavals that occurred during th e fifteenth and sixteenth centuries. The modern nation develo ped as a result of the vigorous spirit of nationalism that swept over Europe and led to the American and French revolutions of the late eighteenth century. In addition to being a powerful vehicle for spreading ideas about human rights and the sovere ignty of the people, typographic printing stabilized and unifie d languages. Illiteracy, the inability to read and write, began a long, steady decline. Typography radically altered education. The medieval class room had been a scriptorium of sorts, whe

8/9

Typography, the major communications advance between the inventi on of writing and the age of electronic mass communications in the t wentieth century, *played a pivotal role* in the social, economic, and reli gious upheavals that occurred during the fifteenth and sixteenth cent uries. The modern nation developed as a result of the vigorous spirit of nationalism that swept over Europe and led to the American and F rench revolutions of the late eighteenth century. In addition to being a powerful vehicle for spreading ideas about human rights and the so vereignty of the people, typographic printing stabilized and unified la nguages. Illiteracy, the inability to read and write, began a long, stead y decline. Typography radically altered education. The medieval class room had been a scriptorium of sorts, where each student penned his own book. Learning became an increasingly private, rather than com

9/10

Typography, the major communications advance between the invention of writing and the age of electronic mass communic ations in the twentieth century, *played a pivotal role* in the soci al, economic, and religious upheavals that occurred during th e fifteenth and sixteenth centuries. The modern nation develo ped as a result of the vigorous spirit of nationalism that swept over Europe and led to the American and French revolutions of the late eighteenth century. In addition to being a powerful vehicle for spreading ideas about human rights and the sovere ignty of the people, typographic printing stabilized and unifie d languages. Illiteracy, the inability to read and write, began a long, steady decline. Typography radically altered education.

8/10

Typography, the major communications advance between the inventi on of writing and the age of electronic mass communications in the t wentieth century, *played a pivotal role* in the social, economic, and reli gious upheavals that occurred during the fifteenth and sixteenth cent uries. The modern nation developed as a result of the vigorous spirit of nationalism that swept over Europe and led to the American and F rench revolutions of the late eighteenth century. In addition to being a powerful vehicle for spreading ideas about human rights and the so vereignty of the people, typographic printing stabilized and unified la nguages. Illiteracy, the inability to read and write, began a long, stead y decline. Typography radically altered education. The medieval class room had been a scriptorium of sorts, where each student penned his

9/11

Typography, the major communications advance between the invention of writing and the age of electronic mass communic ations in the twentieth century, *played a pivotal role* in the soci al, economic, and religious upheavals that occurred during th e fifteenth and sixteenth centuries. The modern nation develo ped as a result of the vigorous spirit of nationalism that swept over Europe and led to the American and French revolutions of the late eighteenth century. In addition to being a powerful vehicle for spreading ideas about human rights and the sovere ignty of the people, typographic printing stabilized and unifie d languages. Illiteracy, the inability to read and write, began a

8/11

Typography, the major communications advance between the inventi on of writing and the age of electronic mass communications in the t wentieth century, *played a pivotal role* in the social, economic, and reli gious upheavals that occurred during the fifteenth and sixteenth cent uries. The modern nation developed as a result of the vigorous spirit of nationalism that swept over Europe and led to the American and F rench revolutions of the late eighteenth century. In addition to being a powerful vehicle for spreading ideas about human rights and the so vereignty of the people, typographic printing stabilized and unified la nguages. Illiteracy, the inability to read and write, began a long, stead y decline. Typography radically altered education. The medieval class

9/12

Typography, the major communications advance between the invention of writing and the age of electronic mass communic ations in the twentieth century, *played a pivotal role* in the soci al, economic, and religious upheavals that occurred during th e fifteenth and sixteenth centuries. The modern nation develo ped as a result of the vigorous spirit of nationalism that swept over Europe and led to the American and French revolutions of the late eighteenth century. In addition to being a powerful vehicle for spreading ideas about human rights and the sovere ignty of the people, typographic printing stabilized and unifie

abcdefghijklmnopqrstuvwxyz
ABCDEFGHIJKLMNOPQRSTUVWXYZ
$1234567890&(.,"";:!?)

abcdefghijklmnopqrstuvwxyz
ABCDEFGHIJKLMNOPQRSTUVWXYZ
$1234567890&(.,"";:!?)

10/10

Typography, the major communications advance betwe en the invention of writing and the age of electronic ma ss communications in the twentieth century, *played a pi votal role* in the social, economic, and religious upheaval s that occurred during the fifteenth and sixteenth centu ries. The modern nation developed as a result of the vig orous spirit of nationalism that swept over Europe and l ed to the American and French revolutions of the late e ighteenth century. In addition to being a powerful vehi cle for spreading ideas about human rights and the sove reignty of the people, typographic printing stabilized an d unified languages. Illiteracy, the inability to read and

---

10/11

Typography, the major communications advance betwe en the invention of writing and the age of electronic ma ss communications in the twentieth century, *played a pi votal role* in the social, economic, and religious upheaval s that occurred during the fifteenth and sixteenth centu ries. The modern nation developed as a result of the vig orous spirit of nationalism that swept over Europe and l ed to the American and French revolutions of the late e ighteenth century. In addition to being a powerful vehi cle for spreading ideas about human rights and the sove reignty of the people, typographic printing stabilized an

---

10/12

Typography, the major communications advance betwe en the invention of writing and the age of electronic ma ss communications in the twentieth century, *played a pi votal role* in the social, economic, and religious upheaval s that occurred during the fifteenth and sixteenth centu ries. The modern nation developed as a result of the vig orous spirit of nationalism that swept over Europe and l ed to the American and French revolutions of the late e ighteenth century. In addition to being a powerful vehi cle for spreading ideas about human rights and the sove

---

10/13

Typography, the major communications advance betwe en the invention of writing and the age of electronic ma ss communications in the twentieth century, *played a pi votal role* in the social, economic, and religious upheaval s that occurred during the fifteenth and sixteenth centu ries. The modern nation developed as a result of the vig orous spirit of nationalism that swept over Europe and l ed to the American and French revolutions of the late e ighteenth century. In addition to being a powerful vehi

---

12/12

Typography, the major communications advan ce between the invention of writing and the ag e of electronic mass communications in the tw entieth century, *played a pivotal role* in the soci al, economic, and religious upheavals that occ urred during the fifteenth and sixteenth centu ries. The modern nation developed as a result of the vigorous spirit of nationalism that swept over Europe and led to the American and Fren ch revolutions of the late eighteenth century. I

12/13

Typography, the major communications advan ce between the invention of writing and the ag e of electronic mass communications in the tw entieth century, *played a pivotal role* in the soci al, economic, and religious upheavals that occ urred during the fifteenth and sixteenth centu ries. The modern nation developed as a result of the vigorous spirit of nationalism that swept over Europe and led to the American and Fren

---

12/14

Typography, the major communications advan ce between the invention of writing and the ag e of electronic mass communications in the tw entieth century, *played a pivotal role* in the soci al, economic, and religious upheavals that occ urred during the fifteenth and sixteenth centu ries. The modern nation developed as a result of the vigorous spirit of nationalism that swept over Europe and led to the American and Fren

---

12/15

Typography, the major communications advan ce between the invention of writing and the ag e of electronic mass communications in the tw entieth century, *played a pivotal role* in the soci al, economic, and religious upheavals that occ urred during the fifteenth and sixteenth centu ries. The modern nation developed as a result of the vigorous spirit of nationalism that swept

Design: **Philip Meggs**

Specimens are set in
Bauer Folio

Folio was designed by Konrad Bauer and Walter Baum at the Bauer foundry in Germany. Released in 1957, it was one of numerous new sans-serif typefaces to become available during the 1950s, reflecting a shift in the design sensibilities of the era. Geometric sans-serif faces such as Futura had been dominant from the late 1920s until the middle 1950s, when a reaction against them occurred. Art directors and designers turned toward less geometric sans-serif fonts based on 19th century fonts, such as Akzidenz-Grotesk and Venus. This inspired a spate of other new sans-serif typefaces as foundries competed for a share of the shifting market.

The design of Folio is modelled more closely upon Akzidenz-Grotesk than either Helvetica or Univers, both of which have larger x-heights. In addition to Folio, Univers, and Helvetica, other new offerings designed in 1957 included Mercator, designed by Dick Dooijes for Amsterdam Typefoundry; and Recta, designed by Aldo Novarese for the Nebiolo foundry in Turin, Italy. Unlike Mercator and Recta, Folio was widely used in the United States because Bauer had an effective sales and distribution center for its handset metal type in the United States, and Folio was licensed for machine setting on the Intertype linecasting machine.

The tail of the **Q** is centered below the oval; and the **R** had two versions, one with a straight tail and one with a curved tail. The capital **J** and lowercase **j** had a very slight hook; these details were changed in some phototype versions developed in the 1960s. Folio offers an alternative to the more widely used typefaces in its category of sans-serif types.

Folio Medium

ABCDEF
GHIJKLM
NOPQRS
TUVWXY
Z&(.,"" ";:)

abcdefgh
ijklmnopq
rstuvwxy
z$123456
7890!?

abcdefghijklmnopqrstuvwxyz
ABCDEFGHIJKLMNOPQRSTUVWXYZ
$&1234567890(.," ";:!?)

72

abcdefghijklmnop
qrstuvwxyzABC
DEFGHIJKLMNO
PQRSTUVWXYZ
$&1234567890
(.,"";:!?)

36

abcdefghijklmnopqrstuvwxyz
ABCDEFGHIJKLMNOPQRSTUW
XYZ$&1234567890(.,"";:!?)

abcdefghijklmnopqrstuvwxyz
ABCDEFGHIJKLMNOPQRSTUVWXYZ
$&1234567890(.," ";:!?)

18

72

abcdefghijklmnop
qrstuvwxyzABC
DEFGHIJKLMNO
PQRSTUVWXYZ
$&1234567890
(.," ";:!?)

36

abcdefghijklmnopqrstuvwxyz
ABCDEFGHIJKLMNOPQRSTUV
WXYZ$&1234567890(.," ";:!?)

abcdefghijklmnopqrstuvwxyz
ABCDEFGHIJKLMNOPQRSTUVWXYZ
$&1234567890(.,"";:!?)

72

abcdefghijklmno
pqrstuvwxyz
ABCDEFGHIJKL
MNOPQRSTUV
WXYZ$&1234567
890(.,"";:!?)

36

abcdefghijklmnopqrstuvwxyz
ABCDEFGHIJKLMNOPQRSTUV
WXYZ$&1234567890(.,"";:!?)

abcdefghijklmnopqrstuvwxyz
ABCDEFGHIJKLMNOPQRSTUV
WXYZ$&1234567890(.,"";:!?)

18

68

abcdefghijklm
nopqrstuvwxyz
ABCDEFGHIJK
LMNOPQRSTU
VWXYZ$&1234
567890(.,"";:!?)

33

abcdefghijklmnopqrstuvwxyz
ABCDEFGHIJKLMNOPQRSTU
VWXYZ$&1234567890(.,"";:!?)

abcdefghijklmnopqrstuvwxyz
ABCDEFGHIJKLMNOPQRSTUVWXYZ
$&1234567890(.,""";:!?)

72

abcdefghijklm
nopqrstuvwxyz
ABCDEFGHIJKL
MNOPQRSTUVW
XYZ$&1234567
890(.,""";:!?)

36

abcdefghijklmnopqrstuvwxyz
ABCDEFGHIJKLMNOPQRSTUVWXYZ
$&1234567890(.,""";:!?)

abcdefghijklmnopqrstuvw
xyzABCDEFGHIJKLMNOPQRSTUV
WXYZ$&1234567890[.,""";:!?]

18

67

abcdefghijklm
nopqrstuvwxy
zABCDEFGHIJK
LMNOPQRSTUV
WXYZ$&12345
67890[.,"",;:!?]

33

abcdefghijklmnopqrstuvwxy
zABCDEFGHIJKLMNOPQRSTUV
WXYZ$&1234567890[.,"",;:!?]

Folio Light

abcdefghijklmnopqrstuvwxyz
ABCDEFGHIJKLMNOPQRSTUVWXYZ
$1234567890&(.," ";:!?)

abcdefghijklmnopqrstuvwxyz
ABCDEFGHIJKLMNOPQRSTUVWXYZ
$1234567890&(.," ";:!?)

8/8

Typography, the major communications advance between the invention of writing and the age of electronic mass communications in the twentieth century, *played a pivotal role* in the social, economic, and religious upheavals that occurred during the fifteenth and sixteenth centuries. The modern nation developed as a result of the vigorous spirit of nationalism that swept over Europe and led to the American and French revolutions of the late eighteenth century. In addition to being a powerful vehicle for spreading ideas about human rights and the sovereignty of the people, typographic printing stabilized and unified languages. Illiteracy, the inability to read and write, began a long, steady decline. Typography radically altered education. The medieval classroom had been a scriptorium of sorts, where each student penned his own book. Learning became an increasingly private, rather than communal, process. Human dialog, extended by type, began to take place on a global scale that bridged time and space. Gutenberg's invention was the

9/9

Typography, the major communications advance between the invention of writing and the age of electronic mass communications in the twentieth century, *played a pivotal role* in the social, economic, and religious upheavals that occurred during the fifteenth and sixteenth centuries. The modern nation developed as a result of the vigorous spirit of nationalism that swept over Europe and led to the American and French revolutions of the late eighteenth century. In addition to being a powerful vehicle for spreading ideas about human rights and the sovereignty of the people, typographic printing stabilized and unified languages. Illiteracy, the inability to read and write, began a long, steady decline. Typography radically altered education. The medieval classroom had been a scriptorium of sorts, where each student penned his own book. Learning became

8/9

Typography, the major communications advance between the invention of writing and the age of electronic mass communications in the twentieth century, *played a pivotal role* in the social, economic, and religious upheavals that occurred during the fifteenth and sixteenth centuries. The modern nation developed as a result of the vigorous spirit of nationalism that swept over Europe and led to the American and French revolutions of the late eighteenth century. In addition to being a powerful vehicle for spreading ideas about human rights and the sovereignty of the people, typographic printing stabilized and unified languages. Illiteracy, the inability to read and write, began a long, steady decline. Typography radically altered education. The medieval classroom had been a scriptorium of sorts, where each student penned his own book. Learning became an increasingly private, rather than communal,

9/10

Typography, the major communications advance between the invention of writing and the age of electronic mass communications in the twentieth century, *played a pivotal role* in the social, economic, and religious upheavals that occurred during the fifteenth and sixteenth centuries. The modern nation developed as a result of the vigorous spirit of nationalism that swept over Europe and led to the American and French revolutions of the late eighteenth century. In addition to being a powerful vehicle for spreading ideas about human rights and the sovereignty of the people, typographic printing stabilized and unified languages. Illiteracy, the inability to read and write, began a long, steady decline. Typography radically altered education. The medieval classroom had been a scriptorium of

8/10

Typography, the major communications advance between the invention of writing and the age of electronic mass communications in the twentieth century, *played a pivotal role* in the social, economic, and religious upheavals that occurred during the fifteenth and sixteenth centuries. The modern nation developed as a result of the vigorous spirit of nationalism that swept over Europe and led to the American and French revolutions of the late eighteenth century. In addition to being a powerful vehicle for spreading ideas about human rights and the sovereignty of the people, typographic printing stabilized and unified languages. Illiteracy, the inability to read and write, began a long, steady decline. Typography radically altered education. The medieval classroom had been a scriptorium of sorts, where each student penned his own

9/11

Typography, the major communications advance between the invention of writing and the age of electronic mass communications in the twentieth century, *played a pivotal role* in the social, economic, and religious upheavals that occurred during the fifteenth and sixteenth centuries. The modern nation developed as a result of the vigorous spirit of nationalism that swept over Europe and led to the American and French revolutions of the late eighteenth century. In addition to being a powerful vehicle for spreading ideas about human rights and the sovereignty of the people, typographic printing stabilized and unified languages. Illiteracy, the inability to read and write, began a long, steady decline. Typography radically alter

8/11

Typography, the major communications advance between the invention of writing and the age of electronic mass communications in the twentieth century, *played a pivotal role* in the social, economic, and religious upheavals that occurred during the fifteenth and sixteenth centuries. The modern nation developed as a result of the vigorous spirit of nationalism that swept over Europe and led to the American and French revolutions of the late eighteenth century. In addition to being a powerful vehicle for spreading ideas about human rights and the sovereignty of the people, typographic printing stabilized and unified languages. Illiteracy, the inability to read and write, began a long, steady decline. Typography radically altered education. The medieval classroom

9/12

Typography, the major communications advance between the invention of writing and the age of electronic mass communications in the twentieth century, *played a pivotal role* in the social, economic, and religious upheavals that occurred during the fifteenth and sixteenth centuries. The modern nation developed as a result of the vigorous spirit of nationalism that swept over Europe and led to the American and French revolutions of the late eighteenth century. In addition to being a powerful vehicle for spreading ideas about human rights and the sovereignty of the people, typographic printing stabilized and unified languages. Illiteracy, the inability to read

abcdefghijklmnopqrstuvwxyz
ABCDEFGHIJKLMNOPQRSTUVWXYZ
$1234567890&(.,"";:!?)

abcdefghijklmnopqrstuvwxyz
ABCDEFGHIJKLMNOPQRSTUVWXYZ
$1234567890&(.,"";:!?)

10/10

Typography, the major communications advance between the invention of writing and the age of electronic mass com munications in the twentieth century, *played a pivotal role* in the social, economic, and religious upheavals that occurred during the fifteenth and sixteenth centuries. The modern na tion developed as a result of the vigorous spirit of nation alism that swept over Europe and led to the American and French revolutions of the late eighteenth century. In addition to being a powerful vehicle for spreading ideas about hum an rights and the sovereignty of the people, typographic pri nting stabilized and unified languages. Illiteracy, the inability to read and write, began a long, steady decline. Typography

10/11

Typography, the major communications advance between the invention of writing and the age of electronic mass com munications in the twentieth century, *played a pivotal role* in the social, economic, and religious upheavals that occurred during the fifteenth and sixteenth centuries. The modern na tion developed as a result of the vigorous spirit of nation alism that swept over Europe and led to the American and French revolutions of the late eighteenth century. In addition to being a powerful vehicle for spreading ideas about hum an rights and the sovereignty of the people, typographic pri nting stabilized and unified languages. Illiteracy, the inability

10/12

Typography, the major communications advance between the invention of writing and the age of electronic mass com munications in the twentieth century, *played a pivotal role* in the social, economic, and religious upheavals that occurred during the fifteenth and sixteenth centuries. The modern na tion developed as a result of the vigorous spirit of nation alism that swept over Europe and led to the American and French revolutions of the late eighteenth century. In addition to being a powerful vehicle for spreading ideas about hum

10/13

Typography, the major communications advance between the invention of writing and the age of electronic mass com munications in the twentieth century, *played a pivotal role* in the social, economic, and religious upheavals that occurred during the fifteenth and sixteenth centuries. The modern na tion developed as a result of the vigorous spirit of nation alism that swept over Europe and led to the American and French revolutions of the late eighteenth century. In addition to being a powerful vehicle for spreading ideas about hum

12/12

Typography, the major communications advan ce between the invention of writing and the age of electronic mass communications in the twentieth century, *played a pivotal role* in the social, econo mic, and religious upheavals that occurred during the fifteenth and sixteenth centuries. The modern nation developed as a result of the vigorous spirit of nationalism that swept over Europe and led to the American and French revolutions of the late ei ghteenth century. In addition to being a powerful

12/13

Typography, the major communications advan ce between the invention of writing and the age of electronic mass communications in the twentieth century, *played a pivotal role* in the social, econo mic, and religious upheavals that occurred during the fifteenth and sixteenth centuries. The modern nation developed as a result of the vigorous spirit of nationalism that swept over Europe and led to the American and French revolutions of the late ei

12/14

Typography, the major communications advan ce between the invention of writing and the age of electronic mass communications in the twentieth century, *played a pivotal role* in the social, econo mic, and religious upheavals that occurred during the fifteenth and sixteenth centuries. The modern nation developed as a result of the vigorous spirit of nationalism that swept over Europe and led to

12/15

Typography, the major communications advan ce between the invention of writing and the age of electronic mass communications in the twentieth century, *played a pivotal role* in the social, econo mic, and religious upheavals that occurred during the fifteenth and sixteenth centuries. The modern nation developed as a result of the vigorous spirit of nationalism that swept over Europe and led to

A   B   C

D   E   **Franklin Gothic**

H   I   J   K

L   M   N   O

designed 1904

P   Q   R   S

T   U   V   W

X   Y   Z

digitized 1980

HELLO

YOUR ATTENTION IS CALLED TO
THIS NEW AND HANDSOME FACE
FRANKLIN GOTHIC CONDENSED

**Get on
the Line**

The careless printer who doesn't keep up
with modern demands will be all alone, he
will be left in the rear. The buying public
is beginning to appreciate good work and
demand the latest and best in type design

1910 advertisement

Malcolm Grear

Design: **Malcolm Grear, Malcolm Grear Designers**

Franklin Gothic was designed in 1904 by Morris Benton, type designer at American Type Founders, and it was released by the company in 1905. That same year the company offered a condensed version of the face, and the following year an extra condensed was issued.

The term "gothic" was erroneously given to sans-serif typefaces originating in the United States at the beginning of the 20th century. With the exception of letterform weight, there is no relationship between the modern gothics and the true black letter gothics of the medieval period. It is thought, however, that this is the reason for the label. In Europe, the term "grotesque" is synonymous with "gothic."

Benton's design of Franklin Gothic was influenced by Akzidenz-Grotesk. It is a sans-serif typeface with a large x-height that retains anatomical characteristics common to roman forms. Evidence of this is found in the double-storied **a** and the closed-loop **g**, both of which are typical roman characters. Franklin Gothic is a bold face with no stroke contrast, except for a slight thinning where curved strokes meet stems. Further, the **A** is topped by a flat apex, the **C** and **e** terminate with angled strokes, and the **Q** has a curved tail.

During this century, Franklin Gothic has survived the onslaught of the geometric sans serifs inspired by the Bauhaus and the development of more recent competitors to become one of the most favored sans-serif typefaces. It is used widely as both a text and display face. Currently, Franklin Gothic is available from several type manufacturers, including Monotype, Adobe, Bitstream (Gothic 744), and Linotype.

Specimens are set in
Monotype Franklin Gothic

ABCDEF
GHIJKLM
NOPQRS
TUVWXY
Z&(.,""",;:)

abcdefgh
ijklmnop
qrstuvwx
yz$1234
567890!

abcdefghijklmnopqrstuvwxyz
ABCDEFGHIJKLMNOPQRSTUVWXYZ
$&1234567890(.," ";:!?)

72

abcdefghijklmno
pqrstuvwxyzAB
CDEFGHIJKLMN
OPQRSTUVWXYZ
$&1234567890
(.," ";:!?)

36

abcdefghijklmnopqrstuvwxyz
ABCDEFGHIJKLMNOPQRSTUVWX
YZ$&1234567890(.," ";:!?)

Franklin Gothic Book Oblique

abcdefghijklmnopqrstuvwxyz
ABCDEFGHIJKLMNOPQRSTUVWXYZ
$&1234567890(.,"";:!?)

18

72

abcdefghijklmno
pqrstuvwxyzAB
CDEFGHIJKLMN
OPQRSTUVWXYZ
$&1234567890
(.,"";:!?)

36

abcdefghijklmnopqrstuvwxyz
ABCDEFGHIJKLMNOPQRSTUVWX
YZ$&1234567890(.,"";:!?)

Franklin Gothic Demi

abcdefghijklmnopqrstuvwxyz
ABCDEFGHIJKLMNOPQRSTUVWXYZ
$&1234567890(.,""::!?)

72

abcdefghijklmn
opqrstuvwxyz
ABCDEFGHIJKL
MNOPQRSTUV
WXYZ$&12345
67890(.," ";:!?)

36

abcdefghijklmnopqrstuvwxyz
ABCDEFGHIJKLMNOPQRSTUVW
XYZ$&1234567890(.," ";:!?)

abcdefghijklmnopqrstuvwxyz
ABCDEFGHIJKLMNOPQRSTUVWXYZ
$&1234567890(.,""";:!?)

18

72

abcdefghijklmn
opqrstuvwxyz
ABCDEFGHIJKL
MNOPQRSTUV
WXYZ$&12345
67890(.,"";:!?)

36

abcdefghijklmnopqrstuvwxyz
ABCDEFGHIJKLMNOPQRSTUVW
XYZ$&1234567890(.,"";:!?)

abcdefghijklmnopqrstuvwxyz
ABCDEFGHIJKLMNOPQRSTUVWX
YZ$&1234567890(.,"";:!?)

abcdefghijklmn
opqrstuvwxyzA
BCDEFGHIJKL
MNOPQRSTUV
WXYZ$&1234
567890(.,"";:!?)

abcdefghijklmnopqrstuvwxyz
ABCDEFGHIJKLMNOPQRSTUV
WXYZ$&1234567890(.,"";:!?)

abcdefghijklmnopqrstuvwxyz
ABCDEFGHIJKLMNOPQRSTUVWXYZ
$&1234567890(.,""";:!?)

18

72

abcdefghijklmnop
qrstuvwxyzABCDE
FGHIJKLMNOPQR
STUVWXYZ$&123
4567890(.,""";:!?)

36

abcdefghijklmnopqrstuvwxyz
ABCDEFGHIJKLMNOPQRSTUVWXYZ
$&1234567890(.,""";:!?)

Franklin Gothic Book

abcdefghijklmnopqrstuvwxyz
ABCDEFGHIJKLMNOPQRSTUVWXYZ
$1234567890&(.,""::!?)

abcdefghijklmnopqrstuvwxyz
ABCDEFGHIJKLMNOPQRSTUVWXYZ
$1234567890&(.,""::!?)

Typography, the major communications advance between the invention of writing and the age of electronic mass communications in the twenti eth century, *played a pivotal role* in the social, economic, and religious upheavals that occurred during the fifteenth and sixteenth centuries. Th e modern nation developed as a result of the vigorous spirit of nationali sm that swept over Europe and led to the American and French revoluti ons of the late eighteenth century. In addition to being a powerful vehicl e for spreading ideas about human rights and the sovereignty of the pe ople, typographic printing stabilized and unified languages. Illiteracy, th e inability to read and write, began a long, steady decline. Typography r adically altered education. The medieval classroom had been a scriptori um of sorts, where each student penned his own book. Learning becam e an increasingly private, rather than communal, process. Human dialo g, extended by type, began to take place on a global scale that bridged time and space. Gutenberg's invention was the first mechanization of a

Typography, the major communications advance between the invention of writing and the age of electronic mass communicati ons in the twentieth century, *played a pivotal role* in the social, economic, and religious upheavals that occurred during the fifte enth and sixteenth centuries. The modern nation developed as a result of the vigorous spirit of nationalism that swept over Eur ope and led to the American and French revolutions of the late eighteenth century. In addition to being a powerful vehicle for s preading ideas about human rights and the sovereignty of the p eople, typographic printing stabilized and unified languages. Illit eracy, the inability to read and write, began a long, steady decli ne. Typography radically altered education. The medieval classr oom had been a scriptorium of sorts, where each student penn

Typography, the major communications advance between the invention of writing and the age of electronic mass communications in the twenti eth century, *played a pivotal role* in the social, economic, and religious upheavals that occurred during the fifteenth and sixteenth centuries. Th e modern nation developed as a result of the vigorous spirit of nationali sm that swept over Europe and led to the American and French revoluti ons of the late eighteenth century. In addition to being a powerful vehicl e for spreading ideas about human rights and the sovereignty of the pe ople, typographic printing stabilized and unified languages. Illiteracy, th e inability to read and write, began a long, steady decline. Typography r adically altered education. The medieval classroom had been a scriptori um of sorts, where each student penned his own book. Learning becam e an increasingly private, rather than communal, process. Human dialo

Typography, the major communications advance between the invention of writing and the age of electronic mass communicati ons in the twentieth century, *played a pivotal role* in the social, economic, and religious upheavals that occurred during the fifte enth and sixteenth centuries. The modern nation developed as a result of the vigorous spirit of nationalism that swept over Eur ope and led to the American and French revolutions of the late eighteenth century. In addition to being a powerful vehicle for s preading ideas about human rights and the sovereignty of the p eople, typographic printing stabilized and unified languages. Illit eracy, the inability to read and write, began a long, steady decli ne. Typography radically altered education. The medieval classr

Typography, the major communications advance between the invention of writing and the age of electronic mass communications in the twenti eth century, *played a pivotal role* in the social, economic, and religious upheavals that occurred during the fifteenth and sixteenth centuries. Th e modern nation developed as a result of the vigorous spirit of nationali sm that swept over Europe and led to the American and French revoluti ons of the late eighteenth century. In addition to being a powerful vehicl e for spreading ideas about human rights and the sovereignty of the pe ople, typographic printing stabilized and unified languages. Illiteracy, th e inability to read and write, began a long, steady decline. Typography r adically altered education. The medieval classroom had been a scriptori um of sorts, where each student penned his own book. Learning becam

Typography, the major communications advance between the invention of writing and the age of electronic mass communicati ons in the twentieth century, *played a pivotal role* in the social, economic, and religious upheavals that occurred during the fifte enth and sixteenth centuries. The modern nation developed as a result of the vigorous spirit of nationalism that swept over Eur ope and led to the American and French revolutions of the late eighteenth century. In addition to being a powerful vehicle for s preading ideas about human rights and the sovereignty of the p eople, typographic printing stabilized and unified languages. Illit eracy, the inability to read and write, began a long, steady decli

Typography, the major communications advance between the invention of writing and the age of electronic mass communications in the twenti eth century, *played a pivotal role* in the social, economic, and religious upheavals that occurred during the fifteenth and sixteenth centuries. Th e modern nation developed as a result of the vigorous spirit of nationali sm that swept over Europe and led to the American and French revoluti ons of the late eighteenth century. In addition to being a powerful vehicl e for spreading ideas about human rights and the sovereignty of the pe ople, typographic printing stabilized and unified languages. Illiteracy, th e inability to read and write, began a long, steady decline. Typography r adically altered education. The medieval classroom had been a scriptori

Typography, the major communications advance between the invention of writing and the age of electronic mass communicati ons in the twentieth century, *played a pivotal role* in the social, economic, and religious upheavals that occurred during the fifte enth and sixteenth centuries. The modern nation developed as a result of the vigorous spirit of nationalism that swept over Eur ope and led to the American and French revolutions of the late eighteenth century. In addition to being a powerful vehicle for s preading ideas about human rights and the sovereignty of the p eople, typographic printing stabilized and unified languages. Illit

Franklin Gothic Book

abcdefghijklmnopqrstuvwxyz
ABCDEFGHIJKLMNOPQRSTUVWXYZ
$1234567890&(.,""";:!?)

abcdefghijklmnopqrstuvwxyz
ABCDEFGHIJKLMNOPQRSTUVWXYZ
$1234567890&(.,""";:!?)

10/10

Typography, the major communications advance betwee n the invention of writing and the age of electronic mass communications in the twentieth century, *played a pivotal role* in the social, economic, and religious upheavals that occurred during the fifteenth and sixteenth centuries. The modern nation developed as a result of the vigorous spiri t of nationalism that swept over Europe and led to the A merican and French revolutions of the late eighteenth ce ntury. In addition to being a powerful vehicle for spreadin g ideas about human rights and the sovereignty of the p eople, typographic printing stabilized and unified languag es. Illiteracy, the inability to read and write, began a long,

12/12

Typography, the major communications advanc e between the invention of writing and the age of electronic mass communications in the twen tieth century, played *a pivotal role* in the social, economic, and religious upheavals that occurred during the fifteenth and sixteenth centuries. The modern nation developed as a result of the vig orous spirit of nationalism that swept over Eur ope and led to the American and French revolut ions of the late eighteenth century. In addition to

10/11

Typography, the major communications advance betwee n the invention of writing and the age of electronic mass communications in the twentieth century, *played a pivotal role* in the social, economic, and religious upheavals that occurred during the fifteenth and sixteenth centuries. The modern nation developed as a result of the vigorous spiri t of nationalism that swept over Europe and led to the A merican and French revolutions of the late eighteenth ce ntury. In addition to being a powerful vehicle for spreadin g ideas about human rights and the sovereignty of the p eople, typographic printing stabilized and unified languag

12/13

Typography, the major communications advanc e between the invention of writing and the age of electronic mass communications in the twen tieth century, played *a pivotal role* in the social, economic, and religious upheavals that occurred during the fifteenth and sixteenth centuries. The modern nation developed as a result of the vig orous spirit of nationalism that swept over Eur ope and led to the American and French revolut

10/12

Typography, the major communications advance betwee n the invention of writing and the age of electronic mass communications in the twentieth century, *played a pivotal role* in the social, economic, and religious upheavals that occurred during the fifteenth and sixteenth centuries. The modern nation developed as a result of the vigorous spiri t of nationalism that swept over Europe and led to the A merican and French revolutions of the late eighteenth ce ntury. In addition to being a powerful vehicle for spreadin g ideas about human rights and the sovereignty of the p

12/14

Typography, the major communications advanc e between the invention of writing and the age of electronic mass communications in the twen tieth century, played *a pivotal role* in the social, economic, and religious upheavals that occurred during the fifteenth and sixteenth centuries. The modern nation developed as a result of the vig orous spirit of nationalism that swept over Eur ope and led to the American and French revolut

10/13

Typography, the major communications advance betwee n the invention of writing and the age of electronic mass communications in the twentieth century, *played a pivotal role* in the social, economic, and religious upheavals that occurred during the fifteenth and sixteenth centuries. The modern nation developed as a result of the vigorous spiri t of nationalism that swept over Europe and led to the A merican and French revolutions of the late eighteenth ce ntury. In addition to being a powerful vehicle for spreadin

12/15

Typography, the major communications advanc e between the invention of writing and the age of electronic mass communications in the twen tieth century, played *a pivotal role* in the social, economic, and religious upheavals that occurred during the fifteenth and sixteenth centuries. The modern nation developed as a result of the vig orous spirit of nationalism that swept over Eur

While it resembles Univers in weight and form, it is more humanistic in feel.

Design: **Julie Sebastianelli**
Photograph: **Oi, R. David Chambers**

Specimens are set in
Linotype Frutiger

Frutiger was originally designed by Adrian Frutiger as lettering for the signage at Charles de Gaulle Airport in Rossey, France, which opened during 1975. The Stempel foundry and Linotype released Frutiger as a new typeface in 1976. Frutiger is available in five stroke weights, four italics, and five condensed versions.

During the mid-1970s, Adrian Frutiger believed the most widely used sans-serif typefaces such as Helvetica and Univers were becoming dated. He sought a renewed sans-serif approach by blending properties of Univers with organic and proportional aspects found in less geometric sans-serif typefaces such as Gill Sans. The result of this synthesis is a typeface of great legibility and distinctiveness. Because Frutiger was originally conceived for signage requiring distant viewing, ascenders and descenders are prominent and the individual characteristics of each letterform are stressed; for example, the **c** and **e** have large apertures to better separate them from the **o**; the **G** has a wide aperture as well. **B**, **E**, **F**, and **H** are fairly narrow, reflecting the classical proportions of traditional roman inscriptional lettering.

Designers find Frutiger to be very useful when they want the texture and color of a sans-serif typeface, with enhanced readability and strong character differentiation. Although the fourteen members of the Frutiger family lack the full diversity of the 21-member Univers family, they provide the same level of compatibility. Frutiger expanded the range of sans-serif expression, adding a valuable interval to the typographic palette.

ABCDEF
GHIJKLM
NOPQRS
TUVWX
YZ&(.,""'':)

abcdefgh
ijklmnop
qrstuvwx
yz$12345
67890!?

abcdefghijklmnopqrstuvwxyz
ABCDEFGHIJKLMNOPQRSTUVWXYZ
$&1234567890(.,""";:!?)

72

abcdefghijklmn
opqrstuvwxyz
ABCDEFGHIJKL
MNOPQRSTUV
WXYZ$&123456
7890(.,"";:!?)

36

abcdefghijklmnopqrstuvwxyz
ABCDEFGHIJKLMNOPQRSTUVW
XYZ$&1234567890(.,"";:!?)

Frutiger Roman Italic

abcdefghijklmnopqrstuvwxyz
ABCDEFGHIJKLMNOPQRSTUVWXYZ
$&1234567890(.,""";:!?)

18

72

abcdefghijklmn
opqrstuvwxyz
ABCDEFGHIJKL
MNOPQRSTUV
WXYZ$&123456
7890(.,"";:!?)

36

abcdefghijklmnopqrstuvwxyz
ABCDEFGHIJKLMNOPQRSTUV
WXYZ$&1234567890(.,"";:!?)

abcdefghijklmnopqrstuvwxyz
ABCDEFGHIJKLMNOPQRSTUVWXYZ
$&1234567890(.,"";:!?)

72

abcdefghijklmn
opqrstuvwxyz
ABCDEFGHIJKL
MNOPQRSTUV
WXYZ$&123456
7890(.,"";:!?)

36

abcdefghijklmnopqrstuvwxyz
ABCDEFGHIJKLMNOPQRSTUVW
XYZ$&1234567890(.,"";:!?)

72

abcdefghijklmn
opqrstuvwxyz
ABCDEFGHIJKL
MNOPQRSTUV
WXYZ$&123456
7890(.,"";:!?)

36

abcdefghijklmnopqrstuvwxyz
ABCDEFGHIJKLMNOPQRSTUVW
XYZ$&1234567890(.,"";:!?)

Frutiger Roman

abcdefghijklmnopqrstuvwxyz
ABCDEFGHIJKLMNOPQRSTUVWXYZ
1234567890&(.,""";:!?)

abcdefghijklmnopqrstuvwxyz
ABCDEFGHIJKLMNOPQRSTUVWXYZ
1234567890&(.,""";:!?)

8/8

Typography, the major communications advance between the invention of writing and the age of electronic mass communications in the twentieth century, *played a pivotal role* in the social, economic, and religious upheavals that occurred during the fifteenth and sixteenth centuries. The modern nation developed as a result of the vigorous spirit of nationalism that swept over Europe and led to the American and French revolutions of the late eighteenth century. In addition to being a powerful vehicle for spreading ideas about human rights and the sovereignty of the people, typographic printing stabilized and unified languages. Illiteracy, the inability to read and write, began a long, steady decline. Typography radically altered education. The medieval classroom had been a scriptorium of sorts, where each student penned his own book. Learning became an increasingly private, rather than communal, process. Human dialog, extended by type, began to take place on a global scale that bridged time and space.

9/9

Typography, the major communications advance between the invention of writing and the age of electronic mass communications in the twentieth century, *played a pivotal role* in the social, economic, and religious upheavals that occurred during the fifteenth and sixteenth centuries. The modern nation developed as a result of the vigorous spirit of nationalism that swept over Europe and led to the American and French revolutions of the late eighteenth century. In addition to being a powerful vehicle for spreading ideas about human rights and the sovereignty of the people, typographic printing stabilized and unified languages. Illiteracy, the inability to read and write, began a long, steady decline. Typography radically altered education. The medieval classroom had been a scriptorium of sorts, where

8/9

Typography, the major communications advance between the invention of writing and the age of electronic mass communications in the twentieth century, *played a pivotal role* in the social, economic, and religious upheavals that occurred during the fifteenth and sixteenth centuries. The modern nation developed as a result of the vigorous spirit of nationalism that swept over Europe and led to the American and French revolutions of the late eighteenth century. In addition to being a powerful vehicle for spreading ideas about human rights and the sovereignty of the people, typographic printing stabilized and unified languages. Illiteracy, the inability to read and write, began a long, steady decline. Typography radically altered education. The medieval classroom had been a scriptorium of sorts, where each student penned his own book. Learning became an increasingly priva

9/10

Typography, the major communications advance between the invention of writing and the age of electronic mass communications in the twentieth century, *played a pivotal role* in the social, economic, and religious upheavals that occurred during the fifteenth and sixteenth centuries. The modern nation developed as a result of the vigorous spirit of nationalism that swept over Europe and led to the American and French revolutions of the late eighteenth century. In addition to being a powerful vehicle for spreading ideas about human rights and the sovereignty of the people, typographic printing stabilized and unified languages. Illiteracy, the inability to read and write, began a long, steady decline. Typography radically altered education. The

8/10

Typography, the major communications advance between the invention of writing and the age of electronic mass communications in the twentieth century, *played a pivotal role* in the social, economic, and religious upheavals that occurred during the fifteenth and sixteenth centuries. The modern nation developed as a result of the vigorous spirit of nationalism that swept over Europe and led to the American and French revolutions of the late eighteenth century. In addition to being a powerful vehicle for spreading ideas about human rights and the sovereignty of the people, typographic printing stabilized and unified languages. Illiteracy, the inability to read and write, began a long, steady decline. Typography radically altered education. The medieval classroom had been a scriptorium of sorts, where each

9/11

Typography, the major communications advance between the invention of writing and the age of electronic mass communications in the twentieth century, *played a pivotal role* in the social, economic, and religious upheavals that occurred during the fifteenth and sixteenth centuries. The modern nation developed as a result of the vigorous spirit of nationalism that swept over Europe and led to the American and French revolutions of the late eighteenth century. In addition to being a powerful vehicle for spreading ideas about human rights and the sovereignty of the people, typographic printing stabilized and unified languages. Illiteracy, the inability to read and write, began a

8/11

Typography, the major communications advance between the invention of writing and the age of electronic mass communications in the twentieth century, *played a pivotal role* in the social, economic, and religious upheavals that occurred during the fifteenth and sixteenth centuries. The modern nation developed as a result of the vigorous spirit of nationalism that swept over Europe and led to the American and French revolutions of the late eighteenth century. In addition to being a powerful vehicle for spreading ideas about human rights and the sovereignty of the people, typographic printing stabilized and unified languages. Illiteracy, the inability to read and write, began a long, steady decline. Typography radically altered education. The

9/12

Typography, the major communications advance between the invention of writing and the age of electronic mass communications in the twentieth century, *played a pivotal role* in the social, economic, and religious upheavals that occurred during the fifteenth and sixteenth centuries. The modern nation developed as a result of the vigorous spirit of nationalism that swept over Europe and led to the American and French revolutions of the late eighteenth century. In addition to being a powerful vehicle for spreading ideas about human rights and the sovereignty of the people, typographic printing stabilized and unified

abcdefghijklmnopqrstuvwxyz
ABCDEFGHIJKLMNOPQRSTUVWXYZ
1234567890&(.,"";:!?)

abcdefghijklmnopqrstuvwxyz
ABCDEFGHIJKLMNOPQRSTUVWXYZ
1234567890&(.,"";:!?)

10/10

Typography, the major communications advance bet
ween the invention of writing and the age of electronic
mass communications in the twentieth century, *played a
pivotal role* in the social, economic, and religious up
heavals that occurred during the fifteenth and sixteenth
centuries. The modern nation developed as a result of the
vigorous spirit of nationalism that swept over Europe and
led to the American and French revolutions of the late ei
ghteenth century. In addition to being a powerful vehicle
for spreading ideas about human rights and the sovereig
nty of the people, typographic printing stabilized and uni
fied languages. Illiteracy, the inability to read and write,

12/12

Typography, the major communications advance
between the invention of writing and the age of
electronic mass communications in the twentieth
century, *played a pivotal role* in the social, econo
mic, and religious upheavals that occurred during
the fifteenth and sixteenth centuries. The mod
ern nation developed as a result of the vigorous
spirit of nationalism that swept over Europe and
led to the American and French revolutions of the
late eighteenth century. In addition to being a po

10/11

Typography, the major communications advance bet
ween the invention of writing and the age of electronic
mass communications in the twentieth century, *played a
pivotal role* in the social, economic, and religious up
heavals that occurred during the fifteenth and sixteenth
centuries. The modern nation developed as a result of the
vigorous spirit of nationalism that swept over Europe and
led to the American and French revolutions of the late ei
ghteenth century. In addition to being a powerful vehicle
for spreading ideas about human rights and the sovereig
nty of the people, typographic printing stabilized and uni

12/13

Typography, the major communications advance
between the invention of writing and the age of
electronic mass communications in the twentieth
century, *played a pivotal role* in the social, econo
mic, and religious upheavals that occurred during
the fifteenth and sixteenth centuries. The mod
ern nation developed as a result of the vigorous
spirit of nationalism that swept over Europe and
led to the American and French revolutions of the

10/12

Typography, the major communications advance bet
ween the invention of writing and the age of electronic
mass communications in the twentieth century, *played a
pivotal role* in the social, economic, and religious up
heavals that occurred during the fifteenth and sixteenth
centuries. The modern nation developed as a result of the
vigorous spirit of nationalism that swept over Europe and
led to the American and French revolutions of the late ei
ghteenth century. In addition to being a powerful vehicle

12/14

Typography, the major communications advance
between the invention of writing and the age of
electronic mass communications in the twentieth
century, *played a pivotal role* in the social, econo
mic, and religious upheavals that occurred during
the fifteenth and sixteenth centuries. The mod
ern nation developed as a result of the vigorous
spirit of nationalism that swept over Europe and

10/13

Typography, the major communications advance bet
ween the invention of writing and the age of electronic
mass communications in the twentieth century, *played a
pivotal role* in the social, economic, and religious up
heavals that occurred during the fifteenth and sixteenth
centuries. The modern nation developed as a result of the
vigorous spirit of nationalism that swept over Europe and
led to the American and French revolutions of the late ei
ghteenth century. In addition to being a powerful vehicle

12/15

Typography, the major communications advance
between the invention of writing and the age of
electronic mass communications in the twentieth
century, *played a pivotal role* in the social, econo
mic, and religious upheavals that occurred during
the fifteenth and sixteenth centuries. The mod
ern nation developed as a result of the vigorous
spirit of nationalism that swept over Europe and

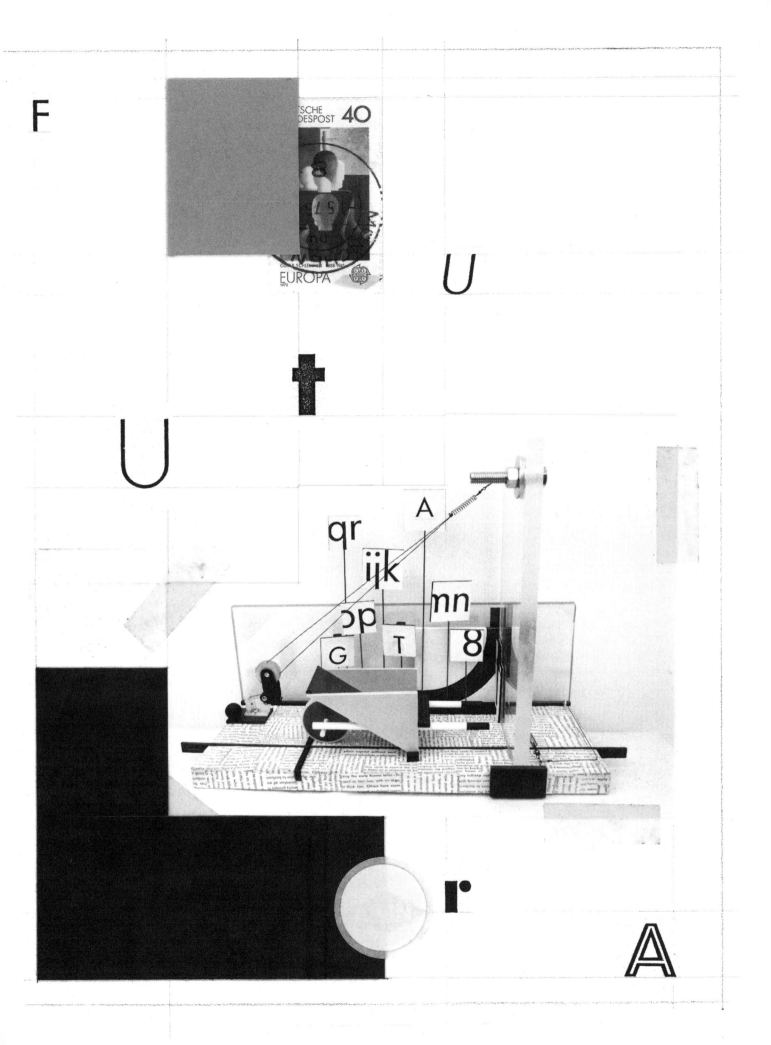

Design: **John Malinoski**

Specimens are set in
Bauer Futura

Inspired by the Dutch De Stijl and Russian Constructivist movements – along with the Bauhaus school and its dictum that "form follows function"– European designers explored elemental geometry during the 1920s. Futura reflects this passion. It was designed by the German book designer and educator Paul Renner, who applied elementary geometric form to typeface design by constructing Futura with a T-square, triangle, and compass. Renner's original concept was quite abstract; numerous changes occurred before the Bauer foundry released it from 1927-30. The original family had six weights, plus three condensed weights, and an inline design.

All strokes in each font are made of a single line weight, and the number of strokes to create each letter are minimized. The **o** is a perfect circle, and **a**, **b**, **d**, **p**, and **q** were designed by adding a single straight line to it. The **t** is composed of two straight lines, and the tail of the **j** does not curve. The **G** has no foot serif, and the **Q** is a perfect circle broken by a diagonal slash.

Futura and the host of other geometric sans-serif fonts were embraced during the late 1920s and 1930s as an expression of modernism and industrial culture. Type companies rushed to bring out competing fonts; similar faces include Jakob Erbar's 1922-30 Erbar, Rudolf Koch's 1927-29 Kabel, William A. Dwiggins's 1929-30 Metro, R. Hunter Middleton's 1930-54 Tempo, and Sol Hess's 1951-54 Spartan. Geometric sans serifs were extremely popular until the 1960s, when sans serifs such as Helvetica and Univers became dominant. Futura is widely used by contemporary designers for its crisp geometry and formal simplicity.

ABCDEF
GHIJKLM
NOPQRS
TUVWXY
Z&(.,""''":;)

abcdefgh
ijklmnopq
rstuvwxyz
$123456
7890!?

abcdefghijklmnopqrstuvwxyz
ABCDEFGHIJKLMNOPQRSTUVWXYZ
$&1234567890(.,"";:!?)

72

abcdefghijklmno
pqrstuvwxyzABC
DEFGHIJKLMNO
PQRSTUVWXYZ
$&1234567890
(.,"";:!?)

36

abcdefghijklmnopqrstuvwxyz
ABCDEFGHIJKLMNOPQRSTUV
WXYZ$&1234567890(.,"";:!?)

abcdefghijklmnopqrstuvwxyz
ABCDEFGHIJKLMNOPQRSTUVWXYZ
$&1234567890(.,"";:!?)

18

72

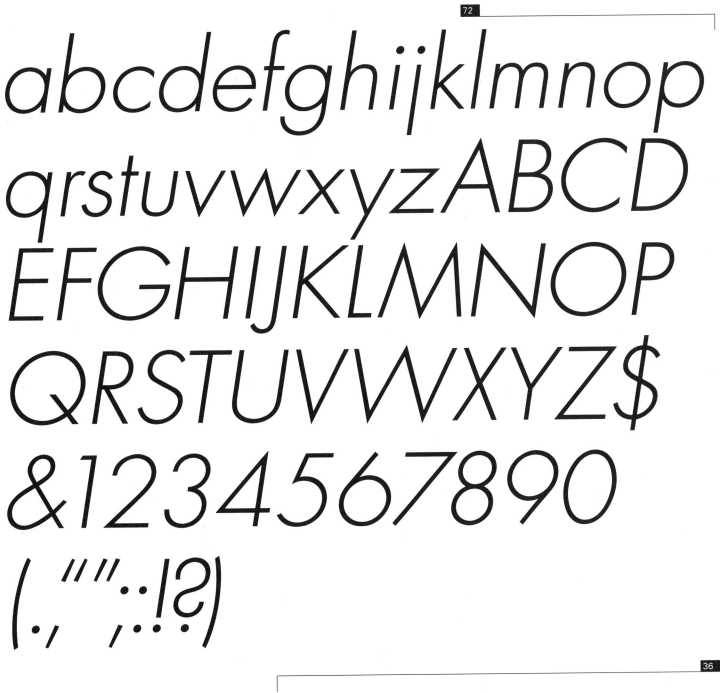

abcdefghijklmnop
qrstuvwxyzABCD
EFGHIJKLMNOP
QRSTUVWXYZ$
&1234567890
(.,"";:!?)

36

abcdefghijklmnopqrstuvwxyz
ABCDEFGHIJKLMNOPQRSTUV
WXYZ$&1234567890(.,"";:!?)

abcdefghijklmnopqrstuvwxyz
ABCDEFGHIJKLMNOPQRSTUVWXYZ
$&1234567890(.,"";:!?)

72

abcdefghijklmno
pqrstuvwxyzABC
DEFGHIJKLMNO
PQRSTUVWXYZ
$&1234567890
(.,"";:!?)

36

abcdefghijklmnopqrstuvwxyz
ABCDEFGHIJKLMNOPQRSTUV
WXYZ$&1234567890(.,"";:!?)

abcdefghijklmnopqrstuvwxyz
ABCDEFGHIJKLMNOPQRSTUVWXYZ
$&1234567890(.,"";:!?)

abcdefghijklmno
pqrstuvwxyzABC
DEFGHIJKLMNO
PQRSTUVWXYZ
$&1234567890
(.,"";:!?)

abcdefghijklmnopqrstuvwxyz
ABCDEFGHIJKLMNOPQRSTUV
WXYZ$&1234567890(.,"";:!?)

abcdefghijklmnopqrstuvwxyz
ABCDEFGHIJKLMNOPQRSTUVWXYZ
$&1234567890(.,"";:!?)

72

abcdefghijklmno
pqrstuvwxyzABC
DEFGHIJKLMNO
PQRSTUVWXYZ
$&1234567890
(.,"";:!?)

36

abcdefghijklmnopqrstuvwxyz
ABCDEFGHIJKLMNOPQRSTUVW
XYZ$&1234567890(.,"";:!?)

abcdefghijklmnopqrstuvwxyz
ABCDEFGHIJKLMNOPQRSTUVWXYZ
$&1234567890(.,"";:!?)

abcdefghijklmno
pqrstuvwxyzABC
DEFGHIJKLMNO
PQRSTUVWXYZ
$&1234567890
(.,"";:!?)

abcdefghijklmnopqrstuvwxyz
ABCDEFGHIJKLMNOPQRSTUVW
XYZ$&1234567890(.,"";:!?)

abcdefghijklmnopqrstuvwxyz
ABCDEFGHIJKLMNOPQRSTUVWXYZ
$&1234567890(.,""";:!?)

72

abcdefghijklm
nopqrstuvwxy
zABCDEFGHIJK
LMNOPQRSTU
VWXYZ$&1234
567890(.,""";:!?)

36

abcdefghijklmnopqrstuvwxyz
ABCDEFGHIJKLMNOPQRSTUV
WXYZ$&1234567890(.,""";:!?)

Futura Extrabold

abcdefghijklmnopqrstuvwx
yzABCDEFGHIJKLMNOPQRSTUV
WXYZ$&1234567890(.,""¡:!?)

abcdefghijklmn
opqrstuvwxyzA
BCDEFGHIJKLM
NOPQRSTUVW
XYZ$&123456
7890(.,"";:!?)

abcdefghijklmnopqrstuvwxyz
ABCDEFGHIJKLMNOPQRSTUVW
XYZ$&1234567890(.,"";:!?)

abcdefghijklmnopqrstuvwxyz
ABCDEFGHIJKLMNOPQRSTUVWXYZ
$&1234567890(.,"";:!?)

72

abcdefghijklmnopqrs
tuvwxyzABCDEFGHI
JKLMNOPQRSTUVW
XYZ$&1234567890
(.,"";:!?)

36

abcdefghijklmnopqrstuvwxyz
ABCDEFGHIJKLMNOPQRSTUVWXYZ
$&1234567890(.,"";:!?)

abcdefghijklmnopqrstuvwxyz
ABCDEFGHIJKLMNOPQRSTUVWXYZ
$&1234567890(.,"";:!?)

18

72

abcdefghijklmno
pqrstuvwxyzAB
CDEFGHIJKLMNO
PQRSTUVWXYZ$
&1234567890
(.,"";:!?)

36

abcdefghijklmnopqrstuvwxyz
ABCDEFGHIJKLMNOPQRSTUVWX
YZ$&1234567890(.,"";:!?)

Futura Book

abcdefghijklmnopqrstuvwxyz
ABCDEFGHIJKLMNOPQRSTUVWXYZ
$1234567890&(.,"";:!?)

abcdefghijklmnopqrstuvwxyz
ABCDEFGHIJKLMNOPQRSTUVWXYZ
$1234567890&(.,"";:!?)

8/8

Typography, the major communications advance between the invention of writing and the age of electronic mass communications in the twentieth century, *played a pivotal role* in the social, economic, and religious upheavals that occurred during the fifteenth and sixteenth centuries. The modern nation developed as a result of the vigorous spirit of nationalism that swept over Europe and led to the American and French revolutions of the late eighteenth century. In addition to being a powerful vehicle for spreading ideas about human rights and the sovereignty of the people, typographic printing stabilized and unified languages. Illiteracy, the inability to read and write, began a long, steady decline. Typography radically altered education. The medieval classroom had been a scriptorium of sorts, where each student penned his own book. Learning became an increasingly private, rather than communal, process. Human dialog, extended by type, began to take place on a global scale that bri

---

9/9

Typography, the major communications advance between the invention of writing and the age of electronic mass communications in the twentieth century, *played a pivotal role* in the social, economic, and religious upheavals that occurred during the fifteenth and sixteenth centuries. The modern nation developed as a result of the vigorous spirit of nationalism that swept over Europe and led to the American and French revolutions of the late eighteenth century. In addition to being a powerful vehicle for spreading ideas about human rights and the sovereignty of the people, typographic printing stabilized and unified languages. Illiteracy, the inability to read and write, began a long, steady decline. Typography radically altered education. The medieval classroom had been a scriptorium of sorts, where each student penned

---

8/9

Typography, the major communications advance between the invention of writing and the age of electronic mass communications in the twentieth century, *played a pivotal role* in the social, economic, and religious upheavals that occurred during the fifteenth and sixteenth centuries. The modern nation developed as a result of the vigorous spirit of nationalism that swept over Europe and led to the American and French revolutions of the late eighteenth century. In addition to being a powerful vehicle for spreading ideas about human rights and the sovereignty of the people, typographic printing stabilized and unified languages. Illiteracy, the inability to read and write, began a long, steady decline. Typography radically altered education. The medieval classroom had been a scriptorium of sorts, where each student penned his own book. Learning became an increasingly private, rather than communal, process. Human

---

9/10

Typography, the major communications advance between the invention of writing and the age of electronic mass communications in the twentieth century, *played a pivotal role* in the social, economic, and religious upheavals that occurred during the fifteenth and sixteenth centuries. The modern nation developed as a result of the vigorous spirit of nationalism that swept over Europe and led to the American and French revolutions of the late eighteenth century. In addition to being a powerful vehicle for spreading ideas about human rights and the sovereignty of the people, typographic printing stabilized and unified languages. Illiteracy, the inability to read and write, began a long, steady decline. Typography radically altered education. The medieval class

---

8/10

Typography, the major communications advance between the invention of writing and the age of electronic mass communications in the twentieth century, *played a pivotal role* in the social, economic, and religious upheavals that occurred during the fifteenth and sixteenth centuries. The modern nation developed as a result of the vigorous spirit of nationalism that swept over Europe and led to the American and French revolutions of the late eighteenth century. In addition to being a powerful vehicle for spreading ideas about human rights and the sovereignty of the people, typographic printing stabilized and unified languages. Illiteracy, the inability to read and write, began a long, steady decline. Typography radically altered education. The medieval classroom had been a scriptorium of sorts, where each student penned his own book. Learning

---

9/11

Typography, the major communications advance between the invention of writing and the age of electronic mass communications in the twentieth century, *played a pivotal role* in the social, economic, and religious upheavals that occurred during the fifteenth and sixteenth centuries. The modern nation developed as a result of the vigorous spirit of nationalism that swept over Europe and led to the American and French revolutions of the late eighteenth century. In addition to being a powerful vehicle for spreading ideas about human rights and the sovereignty of the people, typographic printing stabilized and unified languages. Illiteracy, the inability to read and write, began a long, steady dec

---

8/11

Typography, the major communications advance between the invention of writing and the age of electronic mass communications in the twentieth century, *played a pivotal role* in the social, economic, and religious upheavals that occurred during the fifteenth and sixteenth centuries. The modern nation developed as a result of the vigorous spirit of nationalism that swept over Europe and led to the American and French revolutions of the late eighteenth century. In addition to being a powerful vehicle for spreading ideas about human rights and the sovereignty of the people, typographic printing stabilized and unified languages. Illiteracy, the inability to read and write, began a long, steady decline. Typography radically altered education. The medieval classroom had been a

---

9/12

Typography, the major communications advance between the invention of writing and the age of electronic mass communications in the twentieth century, *played a pivotal role* in the social, economic, and religious upheavals that occurred during the fifteenth and sixteenth centuries. The modern nation developed as a result of the vigorous spirit of nationalism that swept over Europe and led to the American and French revolutions of the late eighteenth century. In addition to being a powerful vehicle for spreading ideas about human rights and the sovereignty of the people, typographic printing stabilized and unified languages. Illite

abcdefghijklmnopqrstuvwxyz
ABCDEFGHIJKLMNOPQRSTUVWXYZ
$1234567890&(.,"";:!?)

abcdefghijklmnopqrstuvwxyz
ABCDEFGHIJKLMNOPQRSTUVWXYZ
$1234567890&(.,"";:!?)

10/10

Typography, the major communications advance betwe
en the invention of writing and the age of electronic mass
communications in the twentieth century, *played a pivotal
role* in the social, economic, and religious upheavals that
occurred during the fifteenth and sixteenth centuries. The
modern nation developed as a result of the vigorous spirit
of nationalism that swept over Europe and led to the Ame
rican and French revolutions of the late eighteenth century.
In addition to being a powerful vehicle for spreading ideas
about human rights and the sovereignty of the people, typo
graphic printing stabilized and unified languages. Illitera

12/12

Typography, the major communications advan
ce between the invention of writing and the age of
electronic mass communications in the twentieth
century, *played a pivotal role* in the social, econo
mic, and religious upheavals that occurred during
the fifteenth and sixteenth centuries. The modern
nation developed as a result of the vigorous spirit
of nationalism that swept over Europe and led to
the American and French revolutions of the late ei
ghteenth century. In addition to being a powerful

10/11

Typography, the major communications advance betwe
en the invention of writing and the age of electronic mass
communications in the twentieth century, *played a pivotal
role* in the social, economic, and religious upheavals that
occurred during the fifteenth and sixteenth centuries. The
modern nation developed as a result of the vigorous spirit
of nationalism that swept over Europe and led to the Ame
rican and French revolutions of the late eighteenth century.
In addition to being a powerful vehicle for spreading ideas
about human rights and the sovereignty of the people, typo

12/13

Typography, the major communications advan
ce between the invention of writing and the age of
electronic mass communications in the twentieth
century, *played a pivotal role* in the social, econo
mic, and religious upheavals that occurred during
the fifteenth and sixteenth centuries. The modern
nation developed as a result of the vigorous spirit
of nationalism that swept over Europe and led to
the American and French revolutions of the late ei

10/12

Typography, the major communications advance betwe
en the invention of writing and the age of electronic mass
communications in the twentieth century, *played a pivotal
role* in the social, economic, and religious upheavals that
occurred during the fifteenth and sixteenth centuries. The
modern nation developed as a result of the vigorous spirit
of nationalism that swept over Europe and led to the Ame
rican and French revolutions of the late eighteenth century.
In addition to being a powerful vehicle for spreading ideas

12/14

Typography, the major communications advan
ce between the invention of writing and the age of
electronic mass communications in the twentieth
century, *played a pivotal role* in the social, econo
mic, and religious upheavals that occurred during
the fifteenth and sixteenth centuries. The modern
nation developed as a result of the vigorous spirit
of nationalism that swept over Europe and led to

10/13

Typography, the major communications advance betwe
en the invention of writing and the age of electronic mass
communications in the twentieth century, *played a pivotal
role* in the social, economic, and religious upheavals that
occurred during the fifteenth and sixteenth centuries. The
modern nation developed as a result of the vigorous spirit
of nationalism that swept over Europe and led to the Ame
rican and French revolutions of the late eighteenth century.
In addition to being a powerful vehicle for spreading ideas

12/15

Typography, the major communications advan
ce between the invention of writing and the age of
electronic mass communications in the twentieth
century, *played a pivotal role* in the social, econo
mic, and religious upheavals that occurred during
the fifteenth and sixteenth centuries. The modern
nation developed as a result of the vigorous spirit
of nationalism that swept over Europe and led to

Matthew Carter's

Galliard

ITC Galliard Roman & *Italic* digitized
by their designer. Complete with

Roman Small Capitals
ABCDEFGHIJKLMNOPQRSTUVWXYZ&ÆŒ

Old Style figures 1234567890 *1234567890*

Superiors & inferiors 12345/67890 *12345/67890*

Nut fractions 1 1 3 1 3 5 7 1 2 *1 1 3 1 3 5 7 1 2*
4 2 4 8 8 8 8 3 3 *4 2 4 8 8 8 8 3 3*

Ligatures fffiflffiffiflfjctstß *fffiflffiffiflffrctspstß*

&Call the trimmings Q t ȧ ḋ ė ṅ ṙ ṫ
z ct st & *Q as is us ȧ ė ė g m t v nt*

¶ In Type 1 & TrueType for the MAC & PC

Carter & Cone Type Inc.
2155 Massachusetts Avenue
Cambridge MA 02140

To order call 617 576–0398

Design: **Matthew Carter**

Galliard, designed by Matthew Carter for Linotype and first released in 1978, is a distinctive old style font specifically developed for phototypesetting. Carter based Galliard on 16th century fonts by Robert Granjon which are spirited, tense, and individualistic compared to their contemporaries. Granjon may have been the first punchcutter to give his fonts names other than size references. Granjon named an 8-point font from about 1570 *La Gaillarde,* after a lively dance of the time. The name Galliard is derived from it. Galliard italic is based on the most atypical and calligraphic of Granjon's four discernable approaches to italic font design. Carter chose it as his model because it achieved "the now accepted relationship between roman and italic of matching size and color but contrasting texture."

Although Granjon's specimens inspired Galliard, the forms are not copies; rather, the feeling and energy of Granjon's fonts were used as inspiration. Comparison of Galliard to earlier old style fonts reveals subtle but pronounced differences: the x-height is larger, but not overly exaggerated as in many typefaces designed for photocomposition; and the forms are crisp and angular. Thick-and-thin contrast is more pronounced, and serifs are slightly larger and sharper. The **a** has a straight diagonal stroke at the top of the bowl. The hook of the **f** has a larger overhang, made possible by the kerning capabilities of photocomposition. The **G** has a unique foot serif; the italic *g* is distinctive.

Galliard is available in four weights with matching italics and has found growing acceptance as a book face and in advertising. Its vibrant design re-energizes the traditional values of old style type.

Specimens are set in
ITC Galliard CC

ABCDEF
GHIJKL
MNOPQ
RSTUVW
XYZ&(,""",;:)

abcdefghij
klmnopqrs
tuvwxyz
$1234567
890!?

abcdefghijklmnopqrstuvwxyz
ABCDEFGHIJKLMNOPQRSTU
VWXYZ$&1234567890(.,""‚:!?)

72

abcdefghijklmnop
qrstuvwxyzABC
DEFGHIJKLM
NOPQRSTUVW
XYZ$&12345678
90(.,""‚:!?)

36

abcdefghijklmnopqrstuvwxyz
ABCDEFGHIJKLMNOPQRSTU
VWXYZ$&1234567890(.,""‚:!?)

abcdefghijklmnopqrstuvwxyz
ABCDEFGHIJKLMNOPQRSTU
VWXYZ$&1234567890(.,"";:!?)

18

72

abcdefghijklmnopq
rstuvwxyzABCDE
FGHIJKLMNOP
QRSTUVWXYZ
$&1234567890
(.,"";:!?)

36

abcdefghijklmnopqrstuvwxyz
ABCDEFGHIJKLMNOPQRSTU
VWXYZ$&1234567890(.,"";:!?)

abcdefghijklmnopqrstuvwxyz
ABCDEFGHIJKLMNOPQRSTU
VWXYZ$&1234567890(.,""";:!?)

abcdefghijklmn
opqrstuvwxyzA
BCDEFGHIJK
LMNOPQRST
UVWXYZ$&12
34567890(.,"";:!?)

abcdefghijklmnopqrstuvwxyzA
BCDEFGHIJKLMNOPQRSTU
VWXYZ$&1234567890(.,"";:!?)

abcdefghijklmnopqrstuvwxyz
ABCDEFGHIJKLMNOPQRSTU
VWXYZ$&1234567890(.,"";:!?)

18

70

abcdefghijklmnop
qrstuvwxyzABC
DEFGHIJKLM
NOPQRSTUVW
XYZ$&12345678
90(.,"";:!?)

32

abcdefghijklmnopqrstuvwxyz
ABCDEFGHIJKLMNOPQRST
UVWXYZ$&1234567890(.,"";:!?)

Galliard

abcdefghijklmnopqrstuvwxyz
ABCDEFGHIJKLMNOPQRSTUVWXYZ
$1234567890&(.,"";:!?)

abcdefghijklmnopqrstuvwxyz
ABCDEFGHIJKLMNOPQRSTUVWXYZ
$1234567890&(.,"";:!?)

8/8

Typography, the major communications advance between the invention of writing and the age of electronic mass communications in the twentieth century, *played a pivotal role* in the social, economic, and religious upheavals that occurred during the fifteenth and sixteenth centuries. The modern nation developed as a result of the vigorous spirit of nationalism that swept over Europe and led to the American and French revolutions of the late eighteenth century. In addition to being a powerful vehicle for spreading ideas about human rights and the sovereignty of the people, typographic printing stabilized and unified languages. Illiteracy, the inability to read and write, began a long, steady decline. Typography radically altered education. The medieval classroom had been a scriptorium of sorts, where each student penned his own book. Learning became an increasingly private, rather than communal, process. Human dialog, extended by type, began to take place on a global scale that bridged time and space. Gutenberg's invention was the first mechanization of a

9/9

Typography, the major communications advance between the invention of writing and the age of electronic mass communications in the twentieth century, *played a pivotal role* in the social, economic, and religious upheavals that occurred during the fifteenth and sixteenth centuries. The modern nation developed as a result of the vigorous spirit of nationalism that swept over Europe and led to the American and French revolutions of the late eighteenth century. In addition to being a powerful vehicle for spreading ideas about human rights and the sovereignty of the people, typographic printing stabilized and unified languages. Illiteracy, the inability to read and write, began a long, steady decline. Typography radically altered education. The medieval classroom had been a scriptorium of sorts, where each student penned his own book. Le

8/9

Typography, the major communications advance between the invention of writing and the age of electronic mass communications in the twentieth century, *played a pivotal role* in the social, economic, and religious upheavals that occurred during the fifteenth and sixteenth centuries. The modern nation developed as a result of the vigorous spirit of nationalism that swept over Europe and led to the American and French revolutions of the late eighteenth century. In addition to being a powerful vehicle for spreading ideas about human rights and the sovereignty of the people, typographic printing stabilized and unified languages. Illiteracy, the inability to read and write, began a long, steady decline. Typography radically altered education. The medieval classroom had been a scriptorium of sorts, where each student penned his own book. Learning became an increasingly private, rather than communal, process. Human

9/10

Typography, the major communications advance between the invention of writing and the age of electronic mass communications in the twentieth century, *played a pivotal role* in the social, economic, and religious upheavals that occurred during the fifteenth and sixteenth centuries. The modern nation developed as a result of the vigorous spirit of nationalism that swept over Europe and led to the American and French revolutions of the late eighteenth century. In addition to being a powerful vehicle for spreading ideas about human rights and the sovereignty of the people, typographic printing stabilized and unified languages. Illiteracy, the inability to read and write, began a long, steady decline. Typography radically altered education. The medieval classroom had been a

8/10

Typography, the major communications advance between the invention of writing and the age of electronic mass communications in the twentieth century, *played a pivotal role* in the social, economic, and religious upheavals that occurred during the fifteenth and sixteenth centuries. The modern nation developed as a result of the vigorous spirit of nationalism that swept over Europe and led to the American and French revolutions of the late eighteenth century. In addition to being a powerful vehicle for spreading ideas about human rights and the sovereignty of the people, typographic printing stabilized and unified languages. Illiteracy, the inability to read and write, began a long, steady decline. Typography radically altered education. The medieval classroom had been a scriptorium of sorts, where each student penned his own book. Learning

9/11

Typography, the major communications advance between the invention of writing and the age of electronic mass communications in the twentieth century, *played a pivotal role* in the social, economic, and religious upheavals that occurred during the fifteenth and sixteenth centuries. The modern nation developed as a result of the vigorous spirit of nationalism that swept over Europe and led to the American and French revolutions of the late eighteenth century. In addition to being a powerful vehicle for spreading ideas about human rights and the sovereignty of the people, typographic printing stabilized and unified languages. Illiteracy, the inability to read and write, began a long, steady decline. Typography

8/11

Typography, the major communications advance between the invention of writing and the age of electronic mass communications in the twentieth century, *played a pivotal role* in the social, economic, and religious upheavals that occurred during the fifteenth and sixteenth centuries. The modern nation developed as a result of the vigorous spirit of nationalism that swept over Europe and led to the American and French revolutions of the late eighteenth century. In addition to being a powerful vehicle for spreading ideas about human rights and the sovereignty of the people, typographic printing stabilized and unified languages. Illiteracy, the inability to read and write, began a long, steady decline. Typography radically altered education. The medieval classroom had been a

9/12

Typography, the major communications advance between the invention of writing and the age of electronic mass communications in the twentieth century, *played a pivotal role* in the social, economic, and religious upheavals that occurred during the fifteenth and sixteenth centuries. The modern nation developed as a result of the vigorous spirit of nationalism that swept over Europe and led to the American and French revolutions of the late eighteenth century. In addition to being a powerful vehicle for spreading ideas about human rights and the sovereignty of the people, typographic printing stabilized and unified languages. Illiteracy, the in

abcdefghijklmnopqrstuvwxyz
ABCDEFGHIJKLMNOPQRSTUVWXYZ
$1234567890&(.,"";:!?)

abcdefghijklmnopqrstuvwxyz
ABCDEFGHIJKLMNOPQRSTUVWXYZ
$1234567890&(.,"";:!?)

10/10

Typography, the major communications advance between the invention of writing and the age of electronic mass communications in the twentieth century, *played a pivotal role* in the social, economic, and religious upheavals that occurred during the fifteenth and sixteenth centuries. The modern nation developed as a result of the vigorous spirit of nationalism that swept over Europe and led to the American and French revolutions of the late eighteenth century. In addition to being a powerful vehicle for spreading ideas about human rights and the sovereignty of the people, typographic printing stabilized and unified languages. Illiteracy, the inability to read and write, began a

12/12

Typography, the major communications advance between the invention of writing and the age of electronic mass communications in the twentieth century, *played a pivotal role* in the social, economic, and religious upheavals that occurred during the fifteenth and sixteenth centuries. The modern nation developed as a result of the vigorous spirit of nationalism that swept over Europe and led to the American and French revolutions of the late eighteenth century. In

10/11

Typography, the major communications advance between the invention of writing and the age of electronic mass communications in the twentieth century, *played a pivotal role* in the social, economic, and religious upheavals that occurred during the fifteenth and sixteenth centuries. The modern nation developed as a result of the vigorous spirit of nationalism that swept over Europe and led to the American and French revolutions of the late eighteenth century. In addition to being a powerful vehicle for spreading ideas about human rights and the sovereignty of the people, typographic printing stabilized and unified

12/13

Typography, the major communications advance between the invention of writing and the age of electronic mass communications in the twentieth century, *played a pivotal role* in the social, economic, and religious upheavals that occurred during the fifteenth and sixteenth centuries. The modern nation developed as a result of the vigorous spirit of nationalism that swept over Europe and led to the American and French

10/12

Typography, the major communications advance between the invention of writing and the age of electronic mass communications in the twentieth century, *played a pivotal role* in the social, economic, and religious upheavals that occurred during the fifteenth and sixteenth centuries. The modern nation developed as a result of the vigorous spirit of nationalism that swept over Europe and led to the American and French revolutions of the late eighteenth century. In addition to being a powerful vehicle for

12/14

Typography, the major communications advance between the invention of writing and the age of electronic mass communications in the twentieth century, *played a pivotal role* in the social, economic, and religious upheavals that occurred during the fifteenth and sixteenth centuries. The modern nation developed as a result of the vigorous spirit of nationalism that swept over

10/13

Typography, the major communications advance between the invention of writing and the age of electronic mass communications in the twentieth century, *played a pivotal role* in the social, economic, and religious upheavals that occurred during the fifteenth and sixteenth centuries. The modern nation developed as a result of the vigorous spirit of nationalism that swept over Europe and led to the American and French revolutions of the late eighteenth century. In addition to being a powerful vehicle for

12/15

Typography, the major communications advance between the invention of writing and the age of electronic mass communications in the twentieth century, *played a pivotal role* in the social, economic, and religious upheavals that occurred during the fifteenth and sixteenth centuries. The modern nation developed as a result of the vigorous spirit of nationalism that swept over

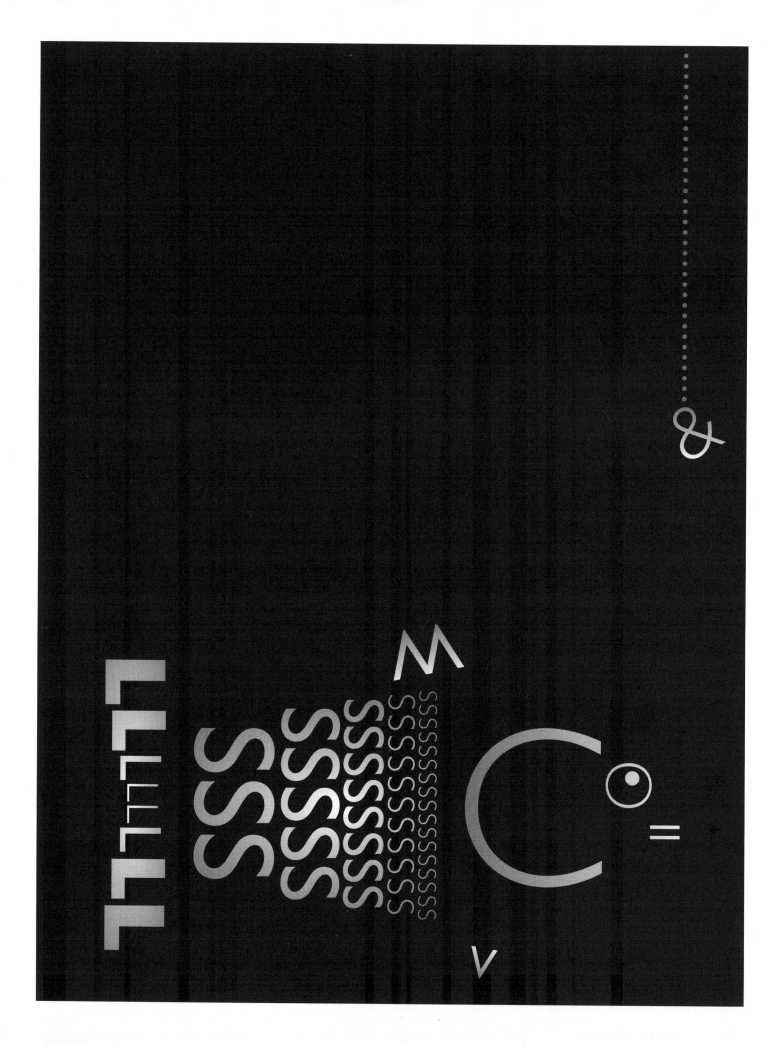

Design: **Larry Clarkson**

Specimens are set in
Monotype Gill Sans

Gill Sans, a typeface inspired by Edward Johnston's type for the London Underground Railroad of 1916, was designed by Eric Gill in 1928. Stanley Morison, who had seen Gill's letters on a store front sign, urged the designer to develop the letters into a typeface. Morison's foresight resulted in the design and release of Gill Sans by Monotype in 1929. It quickly became the most popular sans-serif typeface in Great Britain. This typeface is thought to be Gill's most significant design accomplishment.

Gill Sans is a humanist face meticulously patterned after classic roman character proportions; this gained it a reputation as the most legible sans-serif design of the time. It is interesting to note that Gill Sans is very similar in structure to Perpetua, another of Gill's most popular type designs. As a text face, however, Gill Sans is not without flaws. It has been criticized for having a book weight that is too heavy and a light weight that is too light for running text. When set as text, Gill Sans is informal and friendly in appearance. It was designed in four weights, italics (slanted roman letters), a condensed face, and Gill Shadow, a three-dimensional version.

Some of the more distinctive earmarks that characterize this face are an **M** with a high, pointed central junction; an **R** with a curved leg; a **j** with a short tail; and a **W** and **V** with pointed bases. In the italic, the stem and bowl of the *p* overlap and the *a* is a single-storied letter.

While Gill Sans is not as popular among typographic designers as it once was, it is still adventurously used by designers for a wide variety of applications. The legibility and visual resonance of the face provide Gill Sans with a permanent home in type specimen books.

ABCDEF
GHIJKLM
NOPQRS
TUVWX
YZ&("",:,;:)

abcdefghij
klmnopqr
stuvwxyz
$1234567
890!?

abcdefghijklmnopqrstuvwxyz
ABCDEFGHIJKLMNOPQRSTUVWXYZ
$&1234567890(.,"''";:!?)

72

abcdefghijklmnopq
rstuvwxyzABCDE
FGHIJKLMNOPQ
RSTUVWXYZ$&1
234567890(.,"''";:!?)

36

abcdefghijklmnopqrstuvwxyz
ABCDEFGHIJKLMNOPQRSTUVW
XYZ$&1234567890(.,"''";:!?)

abcdefghijklmnopqrstuvwxyz
ABCDEFGHIJKLMNOPQRSTUVWXYZ
$&1234567890(.,"";:!?)

18

72

abcdefghijklmnopq
rstuvwxyzABCDEFG
HIJKLMNOPQRST
UVWXYZ$&12345
67890(.,"";:·!?)

36

abcdefghijklmnopqrstuvwxyz
ABCDEFGHIJKLMNOPQRSTUVWX
YZ$&1234567890(.,"";:!?)

abcdefghijklmnopqrstuvwxyz
ABCDEFGHIJKLMNOPQRSTUVWXYZ
$&1234567890(.,“”;:!?)

72

abcdefghijklmn
opqrstuvwxyzA
BCDEFGHIJKL
MNOPQRSTU
VWXYZ$&1234
567890(.,“”;:!?)

36

abcdefghijklmnopqrstuvwxyz
ABCDEFGHIJKLMNOPQRSTU
VWXYZ$&1234567890(.,“”;:!?)

abcdefghijklmnopqrstuvwxyz
ABCDEFGHIJKLMNOPQRSTUVWXYZ
$&1234567890(.,""";:!?)

18

72

abcdefghijklmno
pqrstuvwxyzAB
CDEFGHIJKLM
NOPQRSTUVW
XYZ$&12345678
90(.,"""';:.!?)

36

abcdefghijklmnopqrstuvwxyz
ABCDEFGHIJKLMNOPQRSTUW
XYZ$&1234567890(.,""";:!?)

Gill Sans Regular

abcdefghijklmnopqrstuvwxyz
ABCDEFGHIJKLMNOPQRSTUVWXYZ
$1234567890&(.,"";:!?)

abcdefghijklmnopqrstuvwxyz
ABCDEFGHIJKLMNOPQRSTUVWXYZ
$1234567890&(.,"";:!?)

8/8

Typography, the major communications advance between the invention of writing and the age of electronic mass communications in the twentieth century, *played a pivotal role* in the social, economic, and religious upheavals that occurred during the fifteenth and sixteenth centuries. The modern nation developed as a result of the vigorous spirit of nationalism that swept over Europe and led to the American and French revolutions of the late eighteenth century. In addition to being a powerful vehicle for spreading ideas about human rights and the sovereignty of the people, typographic printing stabilized and unified languages. Illiteracy, the inability to read and write, began a long, steady decline. Typography radically altered education. The medieval classroom had been a scriptorium of sorts, where each student penned his own book. Learning became an increasingly private, rather than communal, process. Human dialog, extended by type, began to take place on a global scale that bridged time and space. Gutenberg's invention was the first mechanization of a skilled handicraft. As such, it set into motion, over the next three hundred years, th

9/9

Typography, the major communications advance between the invention of writing and the age of electronic mass communications in the twentieth century, *played a pivotal role* in the social, economic, and religious upheavals that occurred during the fifteenth and sixteenth centuries. The modern nation developed as a result of the vigorous spirit of nationalism that swept over Europe and led to the American and French revolutions of the late eighteenth century. In addition to being a powerful vehicle for spreading ideas about human rights and the sovereignty of the people, typographic printing stabilized and unified languages. Illiteracy, the inability to read and write, began a long, steady decline. Typography radically altered education. The medieval classroom had been a scriptorium of sorts, where each student penned his own book. Learning became an increasingly private, rather than communal, process. Human dialog, extended by type, began to

8/9

Typography, the major communications advance between the invention of writing and the age of electronic mass communications in the twentieth century, *played a pivotal role* in the social, economic, and religious upheavals that occurred during the fifteenth and sixteenth centuries. The modern nation developed as a result of the vigorous spirit of nationalism that swept over Europe and led to the American and French revolutions of the late eighteenth century. In addition to being a powerful vehicle for spreading ideas about human rights and the sovereignty of the people, typographic printing stabilized and unified languages. Illiteracy, the inability to read and write, began a long, steady decline. Typography radically altered education. The medieval classroom had been a scriptorium of sorts, where each student penned his own book. Learning became an increasingly private, rather than communal, process. Human dialog, extended by type, began to take place on a global scale that bridged

9/10

Typography, the major communications advance between the invention of writing and the age of electronic mass communications in the twentieth century, *played a pivotal role* in the social, economic, and religious upheavals that occurred during the fifteenth and sixteenth centuries. The modern nation developed as a result of the vigorous spirit of nationalism that swept over Europe and led to the American and French revolutions of the late eighteenth century. In addition to being a powerful vehicle for spreading ideas about human rights and the sovereignty of the people, typographic printing stabilized and unified languages. Illiteracy, the inability to read and write, began a long, steady decline. Typography radically altered education. The medieval classroom had been a scriptorium of sorts, where each student penn

8/10

Typography, the major communications advance between the invention of writing and the age of electronic mass communications in the twentieth century, *played a pivotal role* in the social, economic, and religious upheavals that occurred during the fifteenth and sixteenth centuries. The modern nation developed as a result of the vigorous spirit of nationalism that swept over Europe and led to the American and French revolutions of the late eighteenth century. In addition to being a powerful vehicle for spreading ideas about human rights and the sovereignty of the people, typographic printing stabilized and unified languages. Illiteracy, the inability to read and write, began a long, steady decline. Typography radically altered education. The medieval classroom had been a scriptorium of sorts, where each student penned his own book. Learning became an increasingly private, rather than communal, process. Hum

9/11

Typography, the major communications advance between the invention of writing and the age of electronic mass communications in the twentieth century, *played a pivotal role* in the social, economic, and religious upheavals that occurred during the fifteenth and sixteenth centuries. The modern nation developed as a result of the vigorous spirit of nationalism that swept over Europe and led to the American and French revolutions of the late eighteenth century. In addition to being a powerful vehicle for spreading ideas about human rights and the sovereignty of the people, typographic printing stabilized and unified languages. Illiteracy, the inability to read and write, began a long, steady decline. Typography radically altered education. The medieval

8/11

Typography, the major communications advance between the invention of writing and the age of electronic mass communications in the twentieth century, *played a pivotal role* in the social, economic, and religious upheavals that occurred during the fifteenth and sixteenth centuries. The modern nation developed as a result of the vigorous spirit of nationalism that swept over Europe and led to the American and French revolutions of the late eighteenth century. In addition to being a powerful vehicle for spreading ideas about human rights and the sovereignty of the people, typographic printing stabilized and unified languages. Illiteracy, the inability to read and write, began a long, steady decline. Typography radically altered education. The medieval classroom had been a scriptorium of sorts, where each student penned his own book. L

9/12

Typography, the major communications advance between the invention of writing and the age of electronic mass communications in the twentieth century, *played a pivotal role* in the social, economic, and religious upheavals that occurred during the fifteenth and sixteenth centuries. The modern nation developed as a result of the vigorous spirit of nationalism that swept over Europe and led to the American and French revolutions of the late eighteenth century. In addition to being a powerful vehicle for spreading ideas about human rights and the sovereignty of the people, typographic printing stabilized and unified languages. Illiteracy, the inability to read and write, began a long,

abcdefghijklmnopqrstuvwxyz
ABCDEFGHIJKLMNOPQRSTUVWXYZ
$1234567890&(.,"";:!?)

abcdefghijklmnopqrstuvwxyz
ABCDEFGHIJKLMNOPQRSTUVWXYZ
$1234567890&(.,"";:!?)

10/10

Typography, the major communications advance between t
he invention of writing and the age of electronic mass commu
nications in the twentieth century, *played a pivotal role* in the s
ocial, economic, and religious upheavals that occurred during
the fifteenth and sixteenth centuries. The modern nation dev
eloped as a result of the vigorous spirit of nationalism that sw
ept over Europe and led to the American and French revoluti
ons of the late eighteenth century. In addition to being a pow
erful vehicle for spreading ideas about human rights and the s
overeignty of the people, typographic printing stabilized and u
nified languages. Illiteracy, the inability to read and write, bega
n a long, steady decline. Typography radically altered educatio

10/11

Typography, the major communications advance between t
he invention of writing and the age of electronic mass commu
nications in the twentieth century, *played a pivotal role* in the s
ocial, economic, and religious upheavals that occurred during
the fifteenth and sixteenth centuries. The modern nation dev
eloped as a result of the vigorous spirit of nationalism that sw
ept over Europe and led to the American and French revoluti
ons of the late eighteenth century. In addition to being a pow
erful vehicle for spreading ideas about human rights and the s
overeignty of the people, typographic printing stabilized and u
nified languages. Illiteracy, the inability to read and write, bega

10/12

Typography, the major communications advance between t
he invention of writing and the age of electronic mass commu
nications in the twentieth century, *played a pivotal role* in the s
ocial, economic, and religious upheavals that occurred during
the fifteenth and sixteenth centuries. The modern nation dev
eloped as a result of the vigorous spirit of nationalism that sw
ept over Europe and led to the American and French revoluti
ons of the late eighteenth century. In addition to being a pow
erful vehicle for spreading ideas about human rights and the s
overeignty of the people, typographic printing stabilized and u

10/13

Typography, the major communications advance between t
he invention of writing and the age of electronic mass commu
nications in the twentieth century, *played a pivotal role* in the s
ocial, economic, and religious upheavals that occurred during
the fifteenth and sixteenth centuries. The modern nation dev
eloped as a result of the vigorous spirit of nationalism that sw
ept over Europe and led to the American and French revoluti
ons of the late eighteenth century. In addition to being a pow
erful vehicle for spreading ideas about human rights and the s

12/12

Typography, the major communications advance b
etween the invention of writing and the age of elect
ronic mass communications in the twentieth centur
y, *played a pivotal role* in the social, economic, and r
eligious upheavals that occurred during the fifteenth
and sixteenth centuries. The modern nation develo
ped as a result of the vigorous spirit of nationalism
that swept over Europe and led to the American an
d French revolutions of the late eighteenth century.
In addition to being a powerful vehicle for spreadin

12/13

Typography, the major communications advance b
etween the invention of writing and the age of elect
ronic mass communications in the twentieth centur
y, *played a pivotal role* in the social, economic, and r
eligious upheavals that occurred during the fifteenth
and sixteenth centuries. The modern nation develo
ped as a result of the vigorous spirit of nationalism
that swept over Europe and led to the American an
d French revolutions of the late eighteenth century.

12/14

Typography, the major communications advance b
etween the invention of writing and the age of elect
ronic mass communications in the twentieth centur
y, *played a pivotal role* in the social, economic, and r
eligious upheavals that occurred during the fifteenth
and sixteenth centuries. The modern nation develo
ped as a result of the vigorous spirit of nationalism
that swept over Europe and led to the American an
d French revolutions of the late eighteenth century.

12/15

Typography, the major communications advance b
etween the invention of writing and the age of elect
ronic mass communications in the twentieth centur
y, *played a pivotal role* in the social, economic, and r
eligious upheavals that occurred during the fifteenth
and sixteenth centuries. The modern nation develo
ped as a result of the vigorous spirit of nationalism
that swept over Europe and led to the American an

Design: **Paula Scher and Ron Louie / Pentagram**

Specimens are set in
Adobe Garamond

The 16th century has been called "the golden age of French typography;" French publisher/printers produced exquisitely designed books using Old Style types inspired by types cut for Aldus Manutius by Francesco Griffo in Venice. Claude Garamond was an independent punchcutter whose fonts appearing in books from Paris in the 1530s achieved a high standard of design excellence. Many revivals of French Renaissance typefaces bear his name, even though some early 20th century versions were actually based on types cut by Jean Jannon, who modelled his types after Garamond's fonts, but with design changes in several characters. The American Type Founders's 1917 Garamond – designed by Morris F. Benton and T.M. Cleland, and also issued as Garamond No. 3 by Linotype – was based on Jannon's work. This inspired an international revival of Garamond with many versions produced around the world.

Garamonds are characterized by large counters in the **a** and **e**, which has a horizontal crossbar. Ascenders and descenders are long, and the **f** has a strong hook. Most top serifs slope downward toward the left; the influence of calligraphy is evident.

The Garamond shown here was designed by Robert Slimbach for Adobe Systems; it was selected from the many variations because of its wide availability and close modelling upon original Garamond roman types shown on a 1592 specimen sheet from the Egenolff-Berner foundry. Adobe Garamond italic is based on italics designed by Robert Granjon and appearing on the same specimen sheet. Garamond, one of the most popular typefaces in this century, is used across the spectrum of graphic design applications.

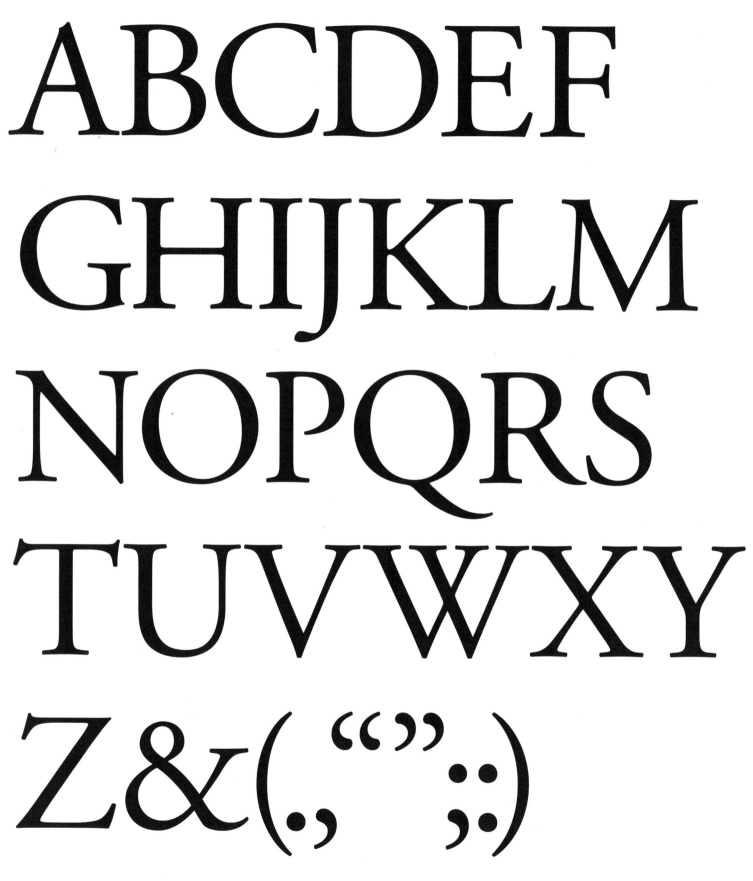

ABCDEF
GHIJKLM
NOPQRS
TUVWXY
Z&ʒ(,""";:)

abcdefghijk

lmnopqrst

uvwxyz$12

34567890!?

abcdefghijklmnopqrstuvwxyz
ABCDEFGHIJKLMNOPQRSTU
VWXYZ$&1234567890(.,"";:!?)

abcdefghijklmnopq
rstuvwxyzABCDE
FGHIJKLMNOP
QRSTUVWXYZ
$&1234567890
(.,"";:!?)

abcdefghijklmnopqrstuvwxyz
ABCDEFGHIJKLMNOPQRSTUV
WXYZ$&1234567890(.,"";:!?)

abcdefghijklmnopqrstuvwxyz
ABCDEFGHIJKLMNOPQRSTU
VWXYZ$&1234567890(.,"";:!?)

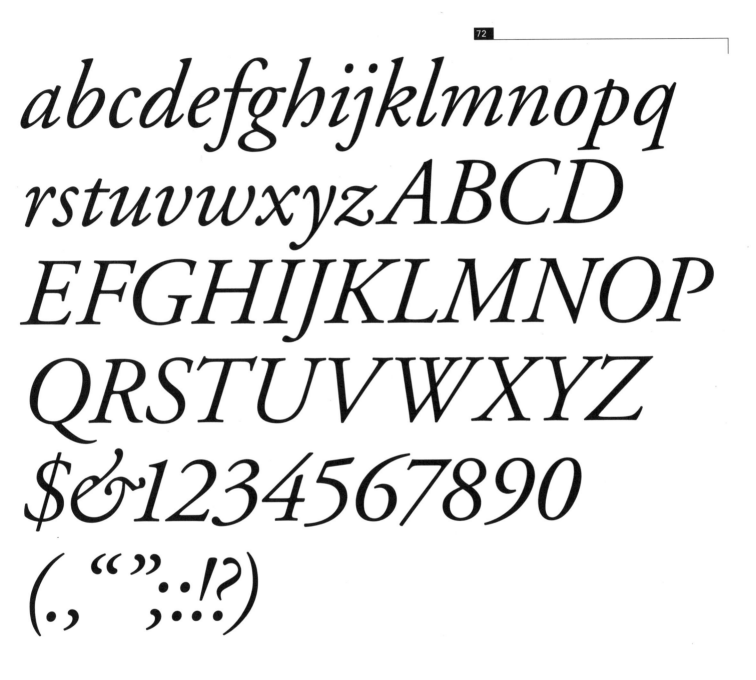

abcdefghijklmnopq
rstuvwxyzABCD
EFGHIJKLMNOP
QRSTUVWXYZ
$&1234567890
(.,"";:!?)

abcdefghijklmnopqrstuvwxyz
ABCDEFGHIJKLMNOPQRSTU
VWXYZ$&1234567890(.,"";:!?)

abcdefghijklmnopqrstuvwxyz
ABCDEFGHIJKLMNOPQRSTU
VWXYZ$&1234567890(.,"";:!?)

72

abcdefghijklmnop
qrstuvwxyzABCD
EFGHIJKLMNO
PQRSTUVWXY
Z$&1234567890
(.,"";:!?)

36

abcdefghijklmnopqrstuvwxyz
ABCDEFGHIJKLMNOPQRSTU
VWXYZ$&1234567890(.,"";:!?)

Garamond Semibold Italic

abcdefghijklmnopqrstuvwxyz
ABCDEFGHIJKLMNOPQRSTU
VWXYZ$&1234567890(.,""::!?)

18

70

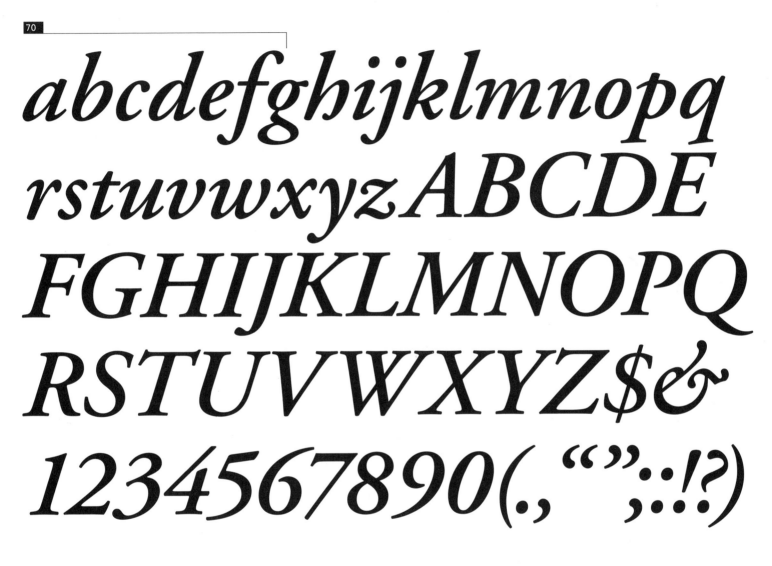

32

abcdefghijklmnopqrstuvwxyz
ABCDEFGHIJKLMNOPQRSTU
VWXYZ$&1234567890(.,""::!?)

Garamond

abcdefghijklmnopqrstuvwxyz
ABCDEFGHIJKLMNOPQRSTUVWXYZ
$1234567890&(.,"";:!?)

abcdefghijklmnopqrstuvwxyz
ABCDEFGHIJKLMNOPQRSTUVWXYZ
$1234567890&(.,"";:!?)

8/8

Typography, the major communications advance between the invention of writing and the age of electronic mass communications in the twentieth century, *played a pivotal role* in the social, economic, and religious upheavals that occurred during the fifteenth and sixteenth centuries. The modern nation developed as a result of the vigorous spirit of nationalism that swept over Europe and led to the American and French revolutions of the late eighteenth century. In addition to being a powerful vehicle for spreading ideas about human rights and the sovereignty of the people, typographic printing stabilized and unified languages. Illiteracy, the inability to read and write, began a long, steady decline. Typography radically altered education. The medieval classroom had been a scriptorium of sorts, where each student penned his own book. Learning became an increasingly private, rather than communal, process. Human dialog, extended by type, began to take place on a global scale that bridged time and space. Gutenberg's invention was the first mechanization of a skilled handicraft. As such, it set into motion, over the next three hundred years, the machinations that would lead to the

9/9

Typography, the major communications advance between the invention of writing and the age of electronic mass communications in the twentieth century, *played a pivotal role* in the social, economic, and religious upheavals that occurred during the fifteenth and sixteenth centuries. The modern nation developed as a result of the vigorous spirit of nationalism that swept over Europe and led to the American and French revolutions of the late eighteenth century. In addition to being a powerful vehicle for spreading ideas about human rights and the sovereignty of the people, typographic printing stabilized and unified languages. Illiteracy, the inability to read and write, began a long, steady decline. Typography radically altered education. The medieval classroom had been a scriptorium of sorts, where each student penned his own book. Learning became an increasingly private, rather than com

8/9

Typography, the major communications advance between the invention of writing and the age of electronic mass communications in the twentieth century, *played a pivotal role* in the social, economic, and religious upheavals that occurred during the fifteenth and sixteenth centuries. The modern nation developed as a result of the vigorous spirit of nationalism that swept over Europe and led to the American and French revolutions of the late eighteenth century. In addition to being a powerful vehicle for spreading ideas about human rights and the sovereignty of the people, typographic printing stabilized and unified languages. Illiteracy, the inability to read and write, began a long, steady decline. Typography radically altered education. The medieval classroom had been a scriptorium of sorts, where each student penned his own book. Learning became an increasingly private, rather than communal, process. Human dialog, extended by type, began to take place on a global scale that bridged time and space. Gutenberg's invention

9/10

Typography, the major communications advance between the invention of writing and the age of electronic mass communications in the twentieth century, *played a pivotal role* in the social, economic, and religious upheavals that occurred during the fifteenth and sixteenth centuries. The modern nation developed as a result of the vigorous spirit of nationalism that swept over Europe and led to the American and French revolutions of the late eighteenth century. In addition to being a powerful vehicle for spreading ideas about human rights and the sovereignty of the people, typographic printing stabilized and unified languages. Illiteracy, the inability to read and write, began a long, steady decline. Typography radically altered education. The medieval classroom had been a scriptorium of sorts, where each student penned his

8/10

Typography, the major communications advance between the invention of writing and the age of electronic mass communications in the twentieth century, *played a pivotal role* in the social, economic, and religious upheavals that occurred during the fifteenth and sixteenth centuries. The modern nation developed as a result of the vigorous spirit of nationalism that swept over Europe and led to the American and French revolutions of the late eighteenth century. In addition to being a powerful vehicle for spreading ideas about human rights and the sovereignty of the people, typographic printing stabilized and unified languages. Illiteracy, the inability to read and write, began a long, steady decline. Typography radically altered education. The medieval classroom had been a scriptorium of sorts, where each student penned his own book. Learning became an increasingly private, rather than communal, process. Human dialog, extended by type, began

9/11

Typography, the major communications advance between the invention of writing and the age of electronic mass communications in the twentieth century, *played a pivotal role* in the social, economic, and religious upheavals that occurred during the fifteenth and sixteenth centuries. The modern nation developed as a result of the vigorous spirit of nationalism that swept over Europe and led to the American and French revolutions of the late eighteenth century. In addition to being a powerful vehicle for spreading ideas about human rights and the sovereignty of the people, typographic printing stabilized and unified languages. Illiteracy, the inability to read and write, began a long, steady decline. Typography radically altered education. The medieval class

8/11

Typography, the major communications advance between the invention of writing and the age of electronic mass communications in the twentieth century, *played a pivotal role* in the social, economic, and religious upheavals that occurred during the fifteenth and sixteenth centuries. The modern nation developed as a result of the vigorous spirit of nationalism that swept over Europe and led to the American and French revolutions of the late eighteenth century. In addition to being a powerful vehicle for spreading ideas about human rights and the sovereignty of the people, typographic printing stabilized and unified languages. Illiteracy, the inability to read and write, began a long, steady decline. Typography radically altered education. The medieval classroom had been a scriptorium of sorts, where each student penned his own book. Learning became an increasingly

9/12

Typography, the major communications advance between the invention of writing and the age of electronic mass communications in the twentieth century, *played a pivotal role* in the social, economic, and religious upheavals that occurred during the fifteenth and sixteenth centuries. The modern nation developed as a result of the vigorous spirit of nationalism that swept over Europe and led to the American and French revolutions of the late eighteenth century. In addition to being a powerful vehicle for spreading ideas about human rights and the sovereignty of the people, typographic printing stabilized and unified languages. Illiteracy, the inability to read and write, began a long, steady

abcdefghijklmnopqrstuvwxyz
ABCDEFGHIJKLMNOPQRSTUVWXYZ
$1234567890&(.,"";:!?)

abcdefghijklmnopqrstuvwxyz
ABCDEFGHIJKLMNOPQRSTUVWXYZ
$1234567890&(.,"";:!?)

10/10

Typography, the major communications advance between the invention of writing and the age of electronic mass commu nications in the twentieth century, *played a pivotal role* in the soc ial, economic, and religious upheavals that occurred during the fi fteenth and sixteenth centuries. The modern nation developed as a result of the vigorous spirit of nationalism that swept over Eu rope and led to the American and French revolutions of the late eighteenth century. In addition to being a powerful vehicle for spreading ideas about human rights and the sovereignty of the people, typographic printing stabilized and unified languages. Illiteracy, the inability to read and write, began a long, steady decline. Typography radically altered education. The medieval

12/12

Typography, the major communications advance be tween the invention of writing and the age of elec tronic mass communications in the twentieth century, *played a pivotal role* in the social, economic, and rel igious upheavals that occurred during the fifteenth and sixteenth centuries. The modern nation devel oped as a result of the vigorous spirit of nationalism that swept over Europe and led to the American and French revolutions of the late eighteenth century. In addition to being a powerful vehicle for spreading

10/11

Typography, the major communications advance between the invention of writing and the age of electronic mass commu nications in the twentieth century, *played a pivotal role* in the soc ial, economic, and religious upheavals that occurred during the fi fteenth and sixteenth centuries. The modern nation developed as a result of the vigorous spirit of nationalism that swept over Eu rope and led to the American and French revolutions of the late eighteenth century. In addition to being a powerful vehicle for spreading ideas about human rights and the sovereignty of the people, typographic printing stabilized and unified languages. Illiteracy, the inability to read and write, began a long, steady

12/13

Typography, the major communications advance be tween the invention of writing and the age of elec tronic mass communications in the twentieth century, *played a pivotal role* in the social, economic, and rel igious upheavals that occurred during the fifteenth and sixteenth centuries. The modern nation devel oped as a result of the vigorous spirit of nationalism that swept over Europe and led to the American and French revolutions of the late eighteenth century. In

10/12

Typography, the major communications advance between the invention of writing and the age of electronic mass commu nications in the twentieth century, *played a pivotal role* in the soc ial, economic, and religious upheavals that occurred during the fi fteenth and sixteenth centuries. The modern nation developed as a result of the vigorous spirit of nationalism that swept over Eu rope and led to the American and French revolutions of the late eighteenth century. In addition to being a powerful vehicle for spreading ideas about human rights and the sovereignty of the

12/14

Typography, the major communications advance be tween the invention of writing and the age of elec tronic mass communications in the twentieth century, *played a pivotal role* in the social, economic, and rel igious upheavals that occurred during the fifteenth and sixteenth centuries. The modern nation devel oped as a result of the vigorous spirit of nationalism that swept over Europe and led to the American and

10/13

Typography, the major communications advance between the invention of writing and the age of electronic mass commu nications in the twentieth century, *played a pivotal role* in the soc ial, economic, and religious upheavals that occurred during the fi fteenth and sixteenth centuries. The modern nation developed as a result of the vigorous spirit of nationalism that swept over Eu rope and led to the American and French revolutions of the late eighteenth century. In addition to being a powerful vehicle for spreading ideas about human rights and the sovereignty of the

12/15

Typography, the major communications advance be tween the invention of writing and the age of elec tronic mass communications in the twentieth century, *played a pivotal role* in the social, economic, and rel igious upheavals that occurred during the fifteenth and sixteenth centuries. The modern nation devel oped as a result of the vigorous spirit of nationalism that swept over Europe and led to the American and

GOUDY OLD STYLE

produced by the American Type Founders Co. from drawings made by the writer,

is an individual design, neither the prototype nor an adaptation of any other type hitherto offered.

It is the result of an attempt to realize in one type a versatile face

adapted either to classic or commercial requirements.

F W G

The capitals were based on, or rather were suggested by some capitals introduced into a portrait painted by Hans Holbein,

but soon drew away from the pattern in the process of making, finally exhibited a character more nearly that of the monumental square

capitals derived by the early scribes from the best lapidary inscriptions of the first century.

lowercase forms

The next problem was to devise a lower case alphabet that would harmonize with

them; difficult because lower case forms came into existence centuries after the capitals

whose forms had been accepted by the first printer without alteration.

PACK
BOX W
FIVE DOZEN
LIQUOR
1234567
& The quic
brownfxjumps
over th lazy dog

With the exception of a few minor details the Foundry

rendered fairly the writer's design; but he feels, however

that the slight changes that were made

do not   in any degree add to the

beauty of the face. A type designer who knows his

business is certainly a better judge of what he wishes to

express than the mechanical executor of the design.

Sample page of Goudy Old Style taken from the *Elements of Lettering* by
Frederic W. Goudy, 1922. Page composition and design by Bertha M. Goudy.

Goudy
Old Style

Design: **Roger E. Baer**

Specimens are set in
Monotype
Goudy Old Style

Goudy Old Style was designed in 1915 by one of America's most renowned and prolific type designers, Frederic Goudy. As is true of all his types, Goudy produced the original drawings for this typeface freehand. The face was commissioned by American Type Founders with the agreement that the foundry not interfere with his designs; Goudy was above all a perfectionist, seeking always to find the ideal roman typeface.

A most distinctive quality of Goudy Old Style is the beautifully drawn classic capitals, which are often used by book designers for title pages and headings. The full-bodied letters are characterized by a low contrast between the thick-and-thin strokes, serifs that are slightly concave, and an oblique stress. A most notable trait is the abbreviated descenders of the lowercase letters, which provide an economical use of the vertical space. Looking closer, the **g** has a very peculiar upturned ear; the counter of the **P** is open; the **Q** has a tail with two ends, and the **i** has a diamond-shaped dot. The *Goudy Old Style Italic* is only slightly slanted.

In 1917, two years after the release of Goudy Old Style, a new member of the Goudy family was introduced – Goudy Title. And continuously thereafter, other variants were designed, including Goudy Bold in 1920.

Goudy Old Style is heralded as one of the most successful typefaces ever produced by ATF. In 1927 the company published a 124-page specimen book containing only the Goudy family. It has been particularly popular in advertising where an elegant, legible, and space-saving roman is needed.

ABCDEF
GHIJKL
MNOPQR
STUVWX
YZ&(.,''"";:)

abcdefghij
klmnopqrs
tuvwxyz
$12345678
90!?

abcdefghijklmnopqrstuvwxyz
ABCDEFGHIJKLMNOPQRSTUVWXYZ
$&1234567890(.,"";:!?)

abcdefghijklmno
pqrstuvwxyzAB
CDEFGHIJKLM
NOPQRSTUV
WXYZ$&12345
67890(.,"";:!?)

abcdefghijklmnopqrstuvwxyz
ABCDEFGHIJKLMNOPQRSTU
VWXYZ$&1234567890(.,"";:!?)

Goudy Old Style Regular Italic

abcdefghijklmnopqrstuvwxyz
ABCDEFGHIJKLMNOPQRSTUVWXYZ
$&1234567890(.,""";:!?)

18

72

abcdefghijklmnop

qrstuvwxyzABCD

EFGHIJKLMN

OPQRSTUVWX

YZ$&123456789

0(.,""";:!?)

36

abcdefghijklmnopqrstuvwxyz
ABCDEFGHIJKLMNOPQRSTU
VWXYZ$&1234567890(.,""";:!?)

abcdefghijklmnopqrstuvwxyz
ABCDEFGHIJKLMNOPQRSTUVWXY
Z$&1234567890(.,""'';:!?)

72

abcdefghijklmno
pqrstuvwxyzAB
CDEFGHIJKL
MNOPQRSTU
VWXYZ$&1234
567890(.,""'';:!?)

36

abcdefghijklmnopqrstuvwxyz
ABCDEFGHIJKLMNOPQRST
UVWXYZ$&1234567890(.,""'';:!?)

abcdefghijklmnopqrstuvwxyz
ABCDEFGHIJKLMNOPQRSTUVWXYZ
$&1234567890(„""";:!?)

18

72

abcdefghijklmn
opqrstuvwxyzAB
CDEFGHIJKL
MNOPQRSTU
VWXYZ$&1234
567890(„"";:!?)

36

abcdefghijklmnopqrstuvwxyz
ABCDEFGHIJKLMNOPQRST
UVWXYZ$&1234567890(„"";:!?)

Goudy Old Style Regular

abcdefghijklmnopqrstuvwxyz
ABCDEFGHIJKLMNOPQRSTUVWXYZ
$1234567890&(.,"";:!?)

abcdefghijklmnopqrstuvwxyz
ABCDEFGHIJKLMNOPQRSTUVWXYZ
$1234567890&(.,"";:!?)

Typography, the major communications advance between the invention of writing and the age of electronic mass communications in the twentieth century, *played a pivotal role* in the social, economic, and religious upheavals that occurred during the fifteenth and sixteenth centuries. The modern nation developed as a result of the vigorous spirit of nationalism that swept over Europe and led to the American and French revolutions of the late eighteenth century. In addition to being a powerful vehicle for spreading ideas about a human rights and the sovereignty of the people, typogr aphic printing stabilized and unified languages. Illiteracy, the inability to r ead and write, began a long, steady decline. Typography radically altered education. The medieval classroom had been a scriptorium of sorts, wher e each student penned his own book. Learning became an increasingly pri vate, rather than communal, process. Human dialog, extended by type, b egan to take place on a global scale that bridged time and space. Gutenber g's invention was the first

Typography, the major communications advance between the invention of writing and the age of electronic mass communicatio ns in the twentieth century, *played a pivotal role* in the social, eco nomic, and religious upheavals that occurred during the fifteenth and sixteenth centuries. The modern nation developed as a result of the vigorous spirit of nationalism that swept over Europe and l ed to the American and French revolutions of the late eighteenth century. In addition to being a powerful vehicle for spreading ide as about human rights and the sovereignty of the people, typogra phic printing stabilized and unified languages. Illiteracy, the inabi lity to read and write, began a long, steady decline. Typography r adically altered education. The medieval classroom had been a sc riptorium of sorts, where each student penned his own book. Le

Typography, the major communications advance between the invention of writing and the age of electronic mass communications in the twentiet h century, *played a pivotal role* in the social, economic, and religious uphe avals that occurred during the fifteenth and sixteenth centuries. The mod ern nation developed as a result of the vigorous spirit of nationalism that swept over Europe and led to the American and French revolutions of th e late eighteenth century. In addition to being a powerful vehicle for spre ading ideas about a human rights and the sovereignty of the people, typogr aphic printing stabilized and unified languages. Illiteracy, the inability to r ead and write, began a long, steady decline. Typography radically altered education. The medieval classroom had been a scriptorium of sorts, wher e each student penned his own book. Learning became an increasingly pri vate, rather than communal, process. Human

Typography, the major communications advance between the invention of writing and the age of electronic mass communicatio ns in the twentieth century, *played a pivotal role* in the social, eco nomic, and religious upheavals that occurred during the fifteenth and sixteenth centuries. The modern nation developed as a result of the vigorous spirit of nationalism that swept over Europe and l ed to the American and French revolutions of the late eighteenth century. In addition to being a powerful vehicle for spreading ide as about human rights and the sovereignty of the people, typogra phic printing stabilized and unified languages. Illiteracy, the inabi lity to read and write, began a long, steady decline. Typography r adically altered education. The medieval classroom had been a sc

Typography, the major communications advance between the invention of writing and the age of electronic mass communications in the twentiet h century, *played a pivotal role* in the social, economic, and religious uphe avals that occurred during the fifteenth and sixteenth centuries. The mod ern nation developed as a result of the vigorous spirit of nationalism that swept over Europe and led to the American and French revolutions of th e late eighteenth century. In addition to being a powerful vehicle for spre ading ideas about a human rights and the sovereignty of the people, typogr aphic printing stabilized and unified languages. Illiteracy, the inability to r ead and write, began a long, steady decline. Typography radically altered education. The medieval classroom had been a scriptorium of sorts, wher e each student penned his own book. Learning

Typography, the major communications advance between the invention of writing and the age of electronic mass communicatio ns in the twentieth century, *played a pivotal role* in the social, eco nomic, and religious upheavals that occurred during the fifteenth and sixteenth centuries. The modern nation developed as a result of the vigorous spirit of nationalism that swept over Europe and l ed to the American and French revolutions of the late eighteenth century. In addition to being a powerful vehicle for spreading ide as about human rights and the sovereignty of the people, typogra phic printing stabilized and unified languages. Illiteracy, the inabi lity to read and write, began a long, steady decline. Typography r

Typography, the major communications advance between the invention of writing and the age of electronic mass communications in the twentiet h century, *played a pivotal role* in the social, economic, and religious uphe avals that occurred during the fifteenth and sixteenth centuries. The mod ern nation developed as a result of the vigorous spirit of nationalism that swept over Europe and led to the American and French revolutions of th e late eighteenth century. In addition to being a powerful vehicle for spre ading ideas about a human rights and the sovereignty of the people, typogr aphic printing stabilized and unified languages. Illiteracy, the inability to r ead and write, began a long, steady decline. Typography radically altered education. The medieval classroom had been a

Typography, the major communications advance between the invention of writing and the age of electronic mass communicatio ns in the twentieth century, *played a pivotal role* in the social, eco nomic, and religious upheavals that occurred during the fifteenth and sixteenth centuries. The modern nation developed as a result of the vigorous spirit of nationalism that swept over Europe and l ed to the American and French revolutions of the late eighteenth century. In addition to being a powerful vehicle for spreading ide as about human rights and the sovereignty of the people, typogra phic printing stabilized and unified languages. Illiteracy, the inabi

abcdefghijklmnopqrstuvwxyz
ABCDEFGHIJKLMNOPQRSTUVWXYZ
$1234567890&(.,"";:!?)

abcdefghijklmnopqrstuvwxyz
ABCDEFGHIJKLMNOPQRSTUVWXYZ
$1234567890&(.,"";:!?)

10/10

Typography, the major communications advance between the invention of writing and the age of electronic mass co mmunications in the twentieth century, *played a pivotal rol e* in the social, economic, and religious upheavals that occu rred during the fifteenth and sixteenth centuries. The mod ern nation developed as a result of the vigorous spirit of na tionalism that swept over Europe and led to the American and French revolutions of the late eighteenth century. In a ddition to being a powerful vehicle for spreading ideas abo ut human rights and the sovereignty of the people, typogra phic printing stabilized and unified languages. Illiteracy, th e inability to read and write, began a long, steady decline.

12/12

Typography, the major communications advance between the invention of writing and the age of e lectronic mass communications in the twentieth century, *played a pivotal role* in the social, econo mic, and religious upheavals that occurred durin g the fifteenth and sixteenth centuries. The mode rn nation developed as a result of the vigorous sp irit of nationalism that swept over Europe and le d to the American and French revolutions of the late eighteenth century. In addition to being a po

10/11

Typography, the major communications advance between the invention of writing and the age of electronic mass co mmunications in the twentieth century, *played a pivotal rol e* in the social, economic, and religious upheavals that occu rred during the fifteenth and sixteenth centuries. The mod ern nation developed as a result of the vigorous spirit of na tionalism that swept over Europe and led to the American and French revolutions of the late eighteenth century. In a ddition to being a powerful vehicle for spreading ideas abo ut human rights and the sovereignty of the people, typogra phic printing stabilized and unified languages. Illiteracy, th

12/13

Typography, the major communications advance between the invention of writing and the age of e lectronic mass communications in the twentieth century, *played a pivotal role* in the social, econo mic, and religious upheavals that occurred durin g the fifteenth and sixteenth centuries. The mode rn nation developed as a result of the vigorous sp irit of nationalism that swept over Europe and le d to the American and French revolutions of the

10/12

Typography, the major communications advance between the invention of writing and the age of electronic mass co mmunications in the twentieth century, *played a pivotal rol e* in the social, economic, and religious upheavals that occu rred during the fifteenth and sixteenth centuries. The mod ern nation developed as a result of the vigorous spirit of na tionalism that swept over Europe and led to the American and French revolutions of the late eighteenth century. In a ddition to being a powerful vehicle for spreading ideas abo ut human rights and the sovereignty of the people, typogra

12/14

Typography, the major communications advance between the invention of writing and the age of e lectronic mass communications in the twentieth century, *played a pivotal role* in the social, econo mic, and religious upheavals that occurred durin g the fifteenth and sixteenth centuries. The mode rn nation developed as a result of the vigorous sp irit of nationalism that swept over Europe and le d to the American and French revolutions of the

10/13

Typography, the major communications advance between the invention of writing and the age of electronic mass co mmunications in the twentieth century, *played a pivotal rol e* in the social, economic, and religious upheavals that occu rred during the fifteenth and sixteenth centuries. The mod ern nation developed as a result of the vigorous spirit of na tionalism that swept over Europe and led to the American and French revolutions of the late eighteenth century. In a ddition to being a powerful vehicle for spreading ideas abo

12/15

Typography, the major communications advance between the invention of writing and the age of e lectronic mass communications in the twentieth century, *played a pivotal role* in the social, econo mic, and religious upheavals that occurred durin g the fifteenth and sixteenth centuries. The mode rn nation developed as a result of the vigorous sp irit of nationalism that swept over Europe and le

Design: **Sandra Wheeler**

Specimens are set in
**Linotype Neue Helvetica,
Helvetica Condensed,
and Compressed**

In the late 1950s, Max Miedinger collaborated with Edouard Hoffman of the Haas'sche foundry in an effort to improve the Akzidenz-Grotesk fonts. The result was Neue Haas Grotesk. In 1961 this design was produced in Germany by D. Stempel AG and called Helvetica. Helvetica became the predominant typeface of many practitioners of the International Typographic Style, also known as the Swiss Style. This approach, which began during the 1940s, advocated clarity, precision, and objectivity. In design, Helvetica echoes these qualities, for it possesses no formal eccentricities.

Helvetica is a rounded sans-serif typeface with a large x-height. The counterforms within letters such as **O**, **Q**, and **C** are oval. The **C** has a narrow opening and flat terminals; the **G** possesses a spur, and the **R** stands on a curved leg. The dots of the **i** and **j** are square; the **a** is double-storied, and the **Q** has a straight, angled tail.

The family includes a full range of weights, widths, and italics. Other elaborations include outline, double outline, and rounded terminals. Owing to the popularity of Helvetica, in 1983 Linotype introduced an updated version called Neue Helvetica, which comprises abundant variations, including ultrathin and heavy. Neue Helvetica, like Univers, is based on a numerical system that distinguishes one variation from another.

With the advent of desktop publishing, Helvetica has become a household name. It continues to be widely used in publishing and advertising as a face that symbolizes cleanness and simplicity. Given these qualities, Helvetica is seen in abundance in corporate literature and signage.

ABCDEF
GHIJKM
NOPQRS
TUVWXY
Z&(.,"",.;.)

abcdefgh
ijklmnopq
rstuvwxy
z$123456
7890!?

abcdefghijklmnopqrstuvwxyz
ABCDEFGHIJKLMNOPQRSTUVWXYZ
$&1234567890(.,"";:!?)

72

abcdefghijklmn
opqrstuvwxyzA
BCDEFGHIJKL
MNOPQRSTUV
WXYZ$&123456
7890(.,"";:!?)

36

abcdefghijklmnopqrstuvwxyz
ABCDEFGHIJKLMNOPQRSTUV
WXYZ$&1234567890(.,"";:!?)

abcdefghijklmnopqrstuvwxyz
ABCDEFGHIJKLMNOPQRSTUVWXYZ
$&1234567890(.,"";:!?)

abcdefghijklmn
opqrstuvwxyzA
BCDEFGHIJKL
MNOPQRSTUV
WXYZ$&123456
7890(.,"";:!?)

abcdefghijklmnopqrstuvwxyz
ABCDEFGHIJKLMNOPQRSTUV
WXYZ$&1234567890(.,"";:!?)

abcdefghijklmnopqrstuvwxyz
ABCDEFGHIJKLMNOPQRSTUVWXYZ
$&1234567890(.,"";:!?)

72

abcdefghijklmn
opqrstuvwxyz
ABCDEFGHIJK
LMNOPQRSTU
VWXYZ$&12345
67890(.,"";:!?)

36

abcdefghijklmnopqrstuvwxyz
ABCDEFGHIJKLMNOPQRSTUV
WXYZ$&1234567890(.,"";:!?)

abcdefghijklmnopqrstuvwxyz
ABCDEFGHIJKLMNOPQRSTUVWXYZ
$&1234567890(.,"";:!?)

18

72

abcdefghijklmn
opqrstuvwxyz
ABCDEFGHIJK
LMNOPQRSTU
VWXYZ$&12345
67890(.,"";:!?)

36

abcdefghijklmnopqrstuvwxyz
ABCDEFGHIJKLMNOPQRSTUV
WXYZ$1234567890(.,"";:!?)

abcdefghijklmnopqrstuvwxyz
ABCDEFGHIJKLMNOPQRSTUVWXYZ
$&1234567890(.,"";:!?)

72

abcdefghijklm
nopqrstuvwxyz
ABCDEFGHIJ
KLMNOPQRST
UVWXYZ$&123
4567890(.,"";:!?)

36

abcdefghijklmnopqrstuvwxyz
ABCDEFGHIJKLMNOPQRSTU
VWXYZ$&1234567890(.,"";:!?)

abcdefghijklmnopqrstuvwxyz
ABCDEFGHIJKLMNOPQRSTUVWXYZ
$&1234567890(.,"";:!?)

18

72

abcdefghijklm

nopqrstuvwxyz

ABCDEFGHIJ

KLMNOPQRST

UVWXYZ$&123

4567890(.,"";:!?)

36

abcdefghijklmnopqrstuvwxyz
ABCDEFGHIJKLMNOPQRSTU
VWXYZ$&1234567890(.,"";:!?)

abcdefghijklmnopqrstuvwxyz
ABCDEFGHIJKLMNOPQRSTUVWXYZ
$&1234567890(.,"";:!?)

abcdefghijklmnop
qrstuvwxyzABCD
EFGHIJKLMNOPQ
RSTUVWXYZ$&12
34567890(.,"";:!?)

abcdefghijklmnopqrstuvwxyz
ABCDEFGHIJKLMNOPQRSTUVWXYZ
$&1234567890(.,"";:!?)

abcdefghijklmnopqrstuvwxyz
ABCDEFGHIJKLMNOPQRSTUVWXYZ
$&1234567890(.,"";:!?)

18

72

abcdefghijklmnop
qrstuvwxyzABCD
EFGHIJKLMNOPQ
RSTUVWXYZ$&12
34567890(.,"";:!?)

36

abcdefghijklmnopqrstuvwxyz
ABCDEFGHIJKLMNOPQRSTUVWXY
Z$&1234567890(.,"";:!?)

Helvetica Regular Compressed

abcdefghijklmnopqrstuvwxyz
ABCDEFGHIJKLMNOPQRSTUVWXYZ
$&1234567890(.,"";:!?)

abcdefghijklmnop
qrstuvwxyzABCDE
FGHIJKLMNOPQR
STUVWXYZ$&1234
567890(.,"";:!?)

abcdefghijklmnopqrstuvwxyz
ABCDEFGHIJKLMNOPQRSTUVWXYZ
$&1234567890(.,"";:!?)

Helvetica Extra Compressed

abcdefghijklmnopqrstuvwxyz
ABCDEFGHIJKLMNOPQRSTUVWXYZ
$&1234567890(.,"";:!?)

abcdefghijklmnopqrstu
vwxyzABCDEFGHIJKL
MNOPQRSTUVWXYZ$&1
234567890(.,"";:!?)

abcdefghijklmnopqrstuvwxyz
ABCDEFGHIJKLMNOPQRSTUVWXYZ
$&1234567890(.,"";:!?)

Helvetica 55 Roman

abcdefghijklmnopqrstuvwxyz
ABCDEFGHIJKLMNOPQRSTUVWXYZ
$1234567890&(.,"";:!?)

abcdefghijklmnopqrstuvwxyz
ABCDEFGHIJKLMNOPQRSTUVWXYZ
$1234567890&(.,"";:!?)

8/8

Typography, the major communications advance between the invention of writing and the age of electronic mass communications in the twentieth century, *played a pivotal role* in the social, economic, and religious upheavals that occurred during the fifteenth and sixteenth centuries. The modern nation developed as a result of the vigorous spirit of nationalism that swept over Europe and led to the American and French revolutions of the late eighteenth century. In addition to being a powerful vehicle for spreading ideas about human rights and the sovereignty of the people, typographic printing stabilized and unified languages. Illiteracy, the inability to read and write, began a long, steady decline. Typography radically altered education. The medieval classroom had been a scriptorium of sorts, where each student penned his own book. Learning became an increasingly private, rather than communal, process. Human dialog, extended by type, began to take place on a global scale that bridged

9/9

Typography, the major communications advance between the invention of writing and the age of electronic mass communications in the twentieth century, *played a pivotal role* in the social, economic, and religious upheavals that occurred during the fifteenth and sixteenth centuries. The modern nation developed as a result of the vigorous spirit of nationalism that swept over Europe and led to the American and French revolutions of the late eighteenth century. In addition to being a powerful vehicle for spreading ideas about human rights and the sovereignty of the people, typographic printing stabilized and unified languages. Illiteracy, the inability to read and write, began a long, steady decline. Typography radically altered education. The medieval classroom had been

8/9

Typography, the major communications advance between the invention of writing and the age of electronic mass communications in the twentieth century, *played a pivotal role* in the social, economic, and religious upheavals that occurred during the fifteenth and sixteenth centuries. The modern nation developed as a result of the vigorous spirit of nationalism that swept over Europe and led to the American and French revolutions of the late eighteenth century. In addition to being a powerful vehicle for spreading ideas about human rights and the sovereignty of the people, typographic printing stabilized and unified languages. Illiteracy, the inability to read and write, began a long, steady decline. Typography radically altered education. The medieval classroom had been a scriptorium of sorts, where each student penned his own book. Learning became an

9/10

Typography, the major communications advance between the invention of writing and the age of electronic mass communications in the twentieth century, *played a pivotal role* in the social, economic, and religious upheavals that occurred during the fifteenth and sixteenth centuries. The modern nation developed as a result of the vigorous spirit of nationalism that swept over Europe and led to the American and French revolutions of the late eighteenth century. In addition to being a powerful vehicle for spreading ideas about human rights and the sovereignty of the people, typographic printing stabilized and unified languages. Illiteracy, the inability to read and write, began a long, steady decline. Typography

8/10

Typography, the major communications advance between the invention of writing and the age of electronic mass communications in the twentieth century, *played a pivotal role* in the social, economic, and religious upheavals that occurred during the fifteenth and sixteenth centuries. The modern nation developed as a result of the vigorous spirit of nationalism that swept over Europe and led to the American and French revolutions of the late eighteenth century. In addition to being a powerful vehicle for spreading ideas about human rights and the sovereignty of the people, typographic printing stabilized and unified languages. Illiteracy, the inability to read and write, began a long, steady decline. Typography radically altered education. The medieval classroom had been a scriptorium of sorts,

9/11

Typography, the major communications advance between the invention of writing and the age of electronic mass communications in the twentieth century, *played a pivotal role* in the social, economic, and religious upheavals that occurred during the fifteenth and sixteenth centuries. The modern nation developed as a result of the vigorous spirit of nationalism that swept over Europe and led to the American and French revolutions of the late eighteenth century. In addition to being a powerful vehicle for spreading ideas about human rights and the sovereignty of the people, typographic printing stabilized and unified languages. Illiteracy, the inability

8/11

Typography, the major communications advance between the invention of writing and the age of electronic mass communications in the twentieth century, *played a pivotal role* in the social, economic, and religious upheavals that occurred during the fifteenth and sixteenth centuries. The modern nation developed as a result of the vigorous spirit of nationalism that swept over Europe and led to the American and French revolutions of the late eighteenth century. In addition to being a powerful vehicle for spreading ideas about human rights and the sovereignty of the people, typographic printing stabilized and unified languages. Illiteracy, the inability to read and write, began a long, steady decline. Typography radically altered

9/12

Typography, the major communications advance between the invention of writing and the age of electronic mass communications in the twentieth century, *played a pivotal role* in the social, economic, and religious upheavals that occurred during the fifteenth and sixteenth centuries. The modern nation developed as a result of the vigorous spirit of nationalism that swept over Europe and led to the American and French revolutions of the late eighteenth century. In addition to being a powerful vehicle for spreading ideas about human rights and the sovereignty of the people, typographic

abcdefghijklmnopqrstuvwxyz
ABCDEFGHIJKLMNOPQRSTUVWXYZ
$1234567890&(.,"";:!?)

abcdefghijklmnopqrstuvwxyz
ABCDEFGHIJKLMNOPQRSTUVWXYZ
$1234567890&(.,"";:!?)

10/10

Typography, the major communications advance between the invention of writing and the age of electronic mass communications in the twentieth century, *played a pivotal role* in the social, economic, and religious upheavals that occurred during the fifteenth and sixteenth centuries. The modern nation developed as a result of the vigorous spirit of nationalism that swept over Europe and led to the American and French revolutions of the late eighteenth century. In addition to being a powerful vehicle for spreading ideas about human rights and the sovereignty of the people, typographic printing

10/11

Typography, the major communications advance between the invention of writing and the age of electronic mass communications in the twentieth century, *played a pivotal role* in the social, economic, and religious upheavals that occurred during the fifteenth and sixteenth centuries. The modern nation developed as a result of the vigorous spirit of nationalism that swept over Europe and led to the American and French revolutions of the late eighteenth century. In addition to being a powerful vehicle for spreading ideas about human rights and the

10/12

Typography, the major communications advance between the invention of writing and the age of electronic mass communications in the twentieth century, *played a pivotal role* in the social, economic, and religious upheavals that occurred during the fifteenth and sixteenth centuries. The modern nation developed as a result of the vigorous spirit of nationalism that swept over Europe and led to the American and French revolutions of the late eighteenth

10/13

Typography, the major communications advance between the invention of writing and the age of electronic mass communications in the twentieth century, *played a pivotal role* in the social, economic, and religious upheavals that occurred during the fifteenth and sixteenth centuries. The modern nation developed as a result of the vigorous spirit of nationalism that swept over Europe and led to the American and French revolutions of the late eighteenth

12/12

Typography, the major communications advance between the invention of writing and the age of electronic mass communications in the twentieth century, *played a pivotal role* in the social, economic, and religious upheavals that occurred during the fifteenth and sixteenth centuries. The modern nation developed as a result of the vigorous spirit of nationalism that swept over Europe and led to the American and French revolutions of the late eighteenth

12/13

Typography, the major communications advance between the invention of writing and the age of electronic mass communications in the twentieth century, *played a pivotal role* in the social, economic, and religious upheavals that occurred during the fifteenth and sixteenth centuries. The modern nation developed as a result of the vigorous spirit of nationalism that swept over Europe and led to the American

12/14

Typography, the major communications advance between the invention of writing and the age of electronic mass communications in the twentieth century, *played a pivotal role* in the social, economic, and religious upheavals that occurred during the fifteenth and sixteenth centuries. The modern nation developed as a result of the vigorous spirit of nationalism that

12/15

Typography, the major communications advance between the invention of writing and the age of electronic mass communications in the twentieth century, *played a pivotal role* in the social, economic, and religious upheavals that occurred during the fifteenth and sixteenth centuries. The modern nation developed as a result of the vigorous spirit of nationalism that

Nᴀʜɪʟ ᴛᴜʀᴘɪᴜs ǫᴜᴀᴍ
ᴄᴏɢɴɪᴛɪᴏɴᴇᴍ
ᴀssᴇʀᴛɪᴏɴᴇᴍ ᴘʀᴀᴇᴄᴜʀʀᴇʀᴇ.
Cicero 106-43 BC : *A c a d e m i c a*

Nescire quaedum, magna

pars Sapientiae est.

Hugo Grotius 1583-1645:

Docta Ignorantia

Les hommes

prennent souvent

leur imagination

pour leur coeur.

Blaise Pascal 1623-1662: *Pensees*

Ludwig Wittgenstein 1889-1951: *Tractatus Logico-philosophicus*

Ethik und Ästhetik sind Eins.

I

Die Welt und das Leben sind

La gloire

est le soleil

des morts.

Honoré de Balzac 1799-1850

Design: **Christopher Ozubko**
Photograph: **Claudia Meyer-Newman**

Specimens are set in
Linotype Janson Text

Although Janson is a Dutch Old Style type-face, it was designed by the Hungarian punchcutter Nicholas Kis in approximately 1690. Kis acquired instruction in typography and the art of punch-cutting from Dirk Voskens, a well-known Dutch punchcutter. He soon became known as one of the best typographic practitioners in Europe.

Many events led to the renewed interest in Janson as a text face. Among these was the research, writing, and printing of Daniel Berkeley Updike. Using the original Janson fonts he acquired from the Drugulin foundry in 1903, he printed several books at the Merrymount Press beginning about 1918. His finest work is the stunning *Book of Common Prayer*, completed in 1930. In 1937, both the Lanston Monotype Company and the Mergenthaler Linotype Company released their revivals of the typeface. Lino-type, under the direction of C.H. Griffith, carefully copied the original specimens. Linotype released its latest version of Janson in 1985.

Compared to earlier Old Style faces, the Dutch types were more finely cut, less archaic, and exhibited a narrow set width due to the snug fit of the letters. Janson is characterized by a high contrast between the thick and thin strokes; sharply cut, oblique, transitional serifs; a medium x-height; and a vertical stress. The **M** has splayed stems, the **W** has stepped center strokes, and the **G** dons a spur.

The spatial economy, excellent legibility, even texture, and strong color of Janson contributed greatly to its rise in popularity. Janson is one of the most frequently used text types for books, along with Baskerville and Caslon.

ABCDEF
GHIJKL
MNOPQR
STUVWX
YZ&(,""";:)

abcdefghijk
lmnopqrst
uvwxyz$12
34567890!?

abcdefghijklmnopqrstuvwxyz
ABCDEFGHIJKLMNOPQRSTUVWXY
Z$&1234567890(„""";:!?)

72

abcdefghijklmn
opqrstuvwxyzAB
CDEFGHIJKL
MNOPQRSTU
VWXYZ$&1234
567890(„"";:!?)

36

abcdefghijklmnopqrstuvwxyz
ABCDEFGHIJKLMNOPQRST
UVWXYZ$&1234567890(„"";:!?)

abcdefghijklmnopqrstuvwxyz
ABCDEFGHIJKLMNOPQRSTUVWXYZ
$&1234567890(,""::!?)

72

abcdefghijklmnop
qrstuvwxyzABCD
EFGHIJKLMN
OPQRSTUVWX
YZ$&1234567890
(,"";..!?)

36

abcdefghijklmnopqrstuvwxyz
ABCDEFGHIJKLMNOPQRSTU
VWXYZ$&1234567890(,"";:!?)

Janson Roman

abcdefghijklmnopqrstuvwxyz
ABCDEFGHIJKLMNOPQRSTUVWXYZ
$1234567890&(.,""";:!?)

abcdefghijklmnopqrstuvwxyz
ABCDEFGHIJKLMNOPQRSTUVWXYZ
$1234567890&(.,""";:!?)

8/8

Typography, the major communications advance between the invention of writing and the age of electronic mass communications in the twentieth century, *played a pivotal role* in the social, economic, and religious upheavals that occurred during the fifteenth and sixteenth centuries. The modern nation developed as a result of the vigorous spirit of nationalism that swept over Europe and led to the American and French revolutions of the late eighteenth century. In addition to being a powerful vehicle for spreading ideas about human rights and the sovereignty of the people, typographic printing stabilized and unified languages. Illiteracy, the inability to read and write, began a long, steady decline. Typography radically altered education. The medieval classroom had been a scriptorium of sorts, where each student penned his own book. Learning became an increasingly private, rather than communal, process. Human dialog, extended by type, began to take place on a global scale that bridged time and space. Gutenberg's invention was the first mechanization of a skilled handicraft. As such, it set into moti

9/9

Typography, the major communications advance between the invention of writing and the age of electronic mass communications in the twentieth century, *played a pivotal role* in the social, economic, and religious upheavals that occurred during the fifteenth and sixteenth centuries. The modern nation developed as a result of the vigorous spirit of nationalism that swept over Europe and led to the American and French revolutions of the late eighteenth century. In addition to being a powerful vehicle for spreading ideas about human rights and the sovereignty of the people, typographic printing stabilized and unified languages. Illiteracy, the inability to read and write, began a long, steady decline. Typography radically altered education. The medieval classroom had been a scriptorium of sorts, where each student penned his own book. Learning beca

8/9

Typography, the major communications advance between the invention of writing and the age of electronic mass communications in the twentieth century, *played a pivotal role* in the social, economic, and religious upheavals that occurred during the fifteenth and sixteenth centuries. The modern nation developed as a result of the vigorous spirit of nationalism that swept over Europe and led to the American and French revolutions of the late eighteenth century. In addition to being a powerful vehicle for spreading ideas about human rights and the sovereignty of the people, typographic printing stabilized and unified languages. Illiteracy, the inability to read and write, began a long, steady decline. Typography radically altered education. The medieval classroom had been a scriptorium of sorts, where each student penned his own book. Learning became an increasingly private, rather than communal, process. Human dialog, extended by type, began to take

9/10

Typography, the major communications advance between the invention of writing and the age of electronic mass communications in the twentieth century, *played a pivotal role* in the social, economic, and religious upheavals that occurred during the fifteenth and sixteenth centuries. The modern nation developed as a result of the vigorous spirit of nationalism that swept over Europe and led to the American and French revolutions of the late eighteenth century. In addition to being a powerful vehicle for spreading ideas about human rights and the sovereignty of the people, typographic printing stabilized and unified languages. Illiteracy, the inability to read and write, began a long, steady decline. Typography radically altered education. The medieval classroom had been a scriptorium

8/10

Typography, the major communications advance between the invention of writing and the age of electronic mass communications in the twentieth century, *played a pivotal role* in the social, economic, and religious upheavals that occurred during the fifteenth and sixteenth centuries. The modern nation developed as a result of the vigorous spirit of nationalism that swept over Europe and led to the American and French revolutions of the late eighteenth century. In addition to being a powerful vehicle for spreading ideas about human rights and the sovereignty of the people, typographic printing stabilized and unified languages. Illiteracy, the inability to read and write, began a long, steady decline. Typography radically altered education. The medieval classroom had been a scriptorium of sorts, where each student penned his own book. Learning became an increasingly private, rathe

9/11

Typography, the major communications advance between the invention of writing and the age of electronic mass communications in the twentieth century, *played a pivotal role* in the social, economic, and religious upheavals that occurred during the fifteenth and sixteenth centuries. The modern nation developed as a result of the vigorous spirit of nationalism that swept over Europe and led to the American and French revolutions of the late eighteenth century. In addition to being a powerful vehicle for spreading ideas about human rights and the sovereignty of the people, typographic printing stabilized and unified languages. Illiteracy, the inability to read and write, began a long, steady decline. Typography radically a

8/11

Typography, the major communications advance between the invention of writing and the age of electronic mass communications in the twentieth century, *played a pivotal role* in the social, economic, and religious upheavals that occurred during the fifteenth and sixteenth centuries. The modern nation developed as a result of the vigorous spirit of nationalism that swept over Europe and led to the American and French revolutions of the late eighteenth century. In addition to being a powerful vehicle for spreading ideas about human rights and the sovereignty of the people, typographic printing stabilized and unified languages. Illiteracy, the inability to read and write, began a long, steady decline. Typography radically altered education. The medieval classroom had been a scriptorium of sorts, where each stu

9/12

Typography, the major communications advance between the invention of writing and the age of electronic mass communications in the twentieth century, *played a pivotal role* in the social, economic, and religious upheavals that occurred during the fifteenth and sixteenth centuries. The modern nation developed as a result of the vigorous spirit of nationalism that swept over Europe and led to the American and French revolutions of the late eighteenth century. In addition to being a powerful vehicle for spreading ideas about human rights and the sovereignty of the people, typographic printing stabilized and unified languages. Illiteracy, the inability to re

abcdefghijklmnopqrstuvwxyz
ABCDEFGHIJKLMNOPQRSTUVWXYZ
$1234567890&(.,"";:!?)

abcdefghijklmnopqrstuvwxyz
ABCDEFGHIJKLMNOPQRSTUVWXYZ
$1234567890&(.,"";:!?)

10/10

Typography, the major communications advance between the invention of writing and the age of electronic mass com munications in the twentieth century, *played a pivotal role* in the social, economic, and religious upheavals that occurred during the fifteenth and sixteenth centuries. The modern n ation developed as a result of the vigorous spirit of national ism that swept over Europe and led to the American and Fr ench revolutions of the late eighteenth century. In addition to being a powerful vehicle for spreading ideas about huma n rights and the sovereignty of the people, typographic prin ting stabilized and unified languages. Illiteracy, the inability to read and write, began a long, steady decline. Typograp

12/12

Typography, the major communications advance between the invention of writing and the age of ele ctronic mass communications in the twentieth ce ntury, *played a pivotal role* in the social, economic, and religious upheavals that occurred during the fifteenth and sixteenth centuries. The modern na tion developed as a result of the vigorous spirit of nationalism that swept over Europe and led to the American and French revolutions of the late eigh teenth century. In addition to being a powerful ve

10/11

Typography, the major communications advance between the invention of writing and the age of electronic mass com munications in the twentieth century, *played a pivotal role* in the social, economic, and religious upheavals that occurred during the fifteenth and sixteenth centuries. The modern n ation developed as a result of the vigorous spirit of national ism that swept over Europe and led to the American and Fr ench revolutions of the late eighteenth century. In addition to being a powerful vehicle for spreading ideas about huma n rights and the sovereignty of the people, typographic prin

12/13

Typography, the major communications advance between the invention of writing and the age of ele ctronic mass communications in the twentieth ce ntury, *played a pivotal role* in the social, economic, and religious upheavals that occurred during the fifteenth and sixteenth centuries. The modern na tion developed as a result of the vigorous spirit of nationalism that swept over Europe and led to the American and French revolutions of the late eigh

10/12

Typography, the major communications advance between the invention of writing and the age of electronic mass com munications in the twentieth century, *played a pivotal role* in the social, economic, and religious upheavals that occurred during the fifteenth and sixteenth centuries. The modern n ation developed as a result of the vigorous spirit of national ism that swept over Europe and led to the American and Fr ench revolutions of the late eighteenth century. In addition to being a powerful vehicle for spreading ideas about huma n rights and the sovereignty of the people, typographic prin

12/14

Typography, the major communications advance between the invention of writing and the age of ele ctronic mass communications in the twentieth ce ntury, *played a pivotal role* in the social, economic, and religious upheavals that occurred during the fifteenth and sixteenth centuries. The modern na tion developed as a result of the vigorous spirit of nationalism that swept over Europe and led to the American and French revolutions of the late eigh

10/13

Typography, the major communications advance between the invention of writing and the age of electronic mass com munications in the twentieth century, *played a pivotal role* in the social, economic, and religious upheavals that occurred during the fifteenth and sixteenth centuries. The modern n ation developed as a result of the vigorous spirit of national ism that swept over Europe and led to the American and Fr ench revolutions of the late eighteenth century. In addition to being a powerful vehicle for spreading ideas about huma

12/15

Typography, the major communications advance between the invention of writing and the age of ele ctronic mass communications in the twentieth ce ntury, *played a pivotal role* in the social, economic, and religious upheavals that occurred during the fifteenth and sixteenth centuries. The modern na tion developed as a result of the vigorous spirit of nationalism that swept over Europe and led to the

kabel

Ich sage hinfort nicht, daß ihr Knechte seid, denn
ein Knecht weiß nicht, was sein Herr tut. Euch
aber habe ich gesagt, daß ihr Freunde seid, denn
alles, was ich habe von meinem Vater gehört, habe ich euch kundgetan. Ihr habt mich nicht erwählt, sondern ich habe euch erwählt und gesetzt,
daß ihr hingehet und Frucht bringet und eure
Frucht bleibe, auf daß, so ihr den Vater bittet in
meinem Namen, er's euch gebe. Das gebiete ich
euch, daß ihr euch untereinander liebet.
† So euch die Welt haßt, so wisset, daß sie mich
vor euch gehaßt hat. Wäret ihr von der Welt, so
hätte die Welt das Ihre lieb; weil ihr aber nicht
von der Welt seid, sondern ich habe euch von der
Welt erwählt, darum haßt euch die Welt. Ge-
denket an mein Wort, daß ich euch gesagt habe:

Design: **Douglass Scott**

Specimens are set in
ITC Kabel

Rudolf Koch, the celebrated German type designer who designed for the Klingspor Foundry, designed Kabel Light in 1927. His effort coincided with Paul Renner's development of Futura. Both are geometric sans-serif typefaces, designed in response to the call for modernized Gothic types. Unlike Futura, however, Kabel is not strictly geometric; it reflects Koch's preference for spontaneity in letterforms, and evidence of the human hand at work. These qualities can be observed in Koch's earlier German Gothic types, and of course in his famous Neuland.

Indeed, Koch used a compass and straight-edge in the drawing of Kabel, but relaxed the geometry by making many optical decisions as well. He found it difficult to depart entirely from normal roman forms. For example, the **a**, **g**, and **t** are of typical roman origin. The geometry of some of the letters is also softened by slanted stroke endings. A closer look reveals some curious features: the **a** has a truncated terminal, the **e** has a slanted crossbar reminiscent of Venetian forms, and the **m** appears very narrow compared to the rounded letters.

Between the years 1927 and 1929, Koch developed additional variants, including Kabel Medium, Bold, and Heavy. Prisma, also designed by Koch, is a decorative inline version of Kabel.

Over the years, Kabel has been successfully used as both a text and display face. In 1976, the International Typeface Corporation acquired the rights from Berthold AG, who at the time owned Kabel. The family was subsequently revived and made widely available in photo and digital composition formats.

ABCDEFG
HIJKLMN
OPQRSTU
VWXYZ&
(" " . :)

abcdefgh
ijklmnopq
rstuvwxyz
$1234567
890!?

abcdefghijklmnopqrstuvwxyz
ABCDEFGHIJKLMNOPQRSTUVWXYZ
$&1234567890(.,""",;:!?)

abcdefghijklmno
pqrstuvwxyzA
BCDEFGHIJKLMN
OPQRSTUVWXY
Z$&1234567890
(.,"""”;:!?)

abcdefghijklmnopqrstuvwxyz
ABCDEFGHIJKLMNOPQRSTUVWXY
Z$&1234567890(.,"""”;:!?)

abcdefghijklmnopqrstuvwxyz
ABCDEFGHIJKLMNOPQRSTUVWXYZ
$&1234567890(.,"";:!?)

abcdefghijklmno
pqrstuvwxyzAB
CDEFGHIJKLMN
OPQRSTUVWXYZ
$&1234567890
(.,"";:!?)

abcdefghijklmnopqrstuvwxyz
ABCDEFGHIJKLMNOPQRSTUVWXY
Z$&1234567890(.,"";:!?)

abcdefghijklmnopqrstuvwxyz
ABCDEFGHIJKLMNOPQRSTUVWXYZ
$&1234567890(.,""'';:!?)

72

abcdefghijklmn
opqrstuvwxyzA
BCDEFGHIJKLMN
OPQRSTUVWXY
Z$&1234567890
(.,"""";:!?)

36

abcdefghijklmnopqrstuvwxyz
ABCDEFGHIJKLMNOPQRSTUVWXY
Z$&1234567890(.,"""";:!?)

abcdefghijklmnopqrstuvwxyz
ABCDEFGHIJKLMNOPQRSTUVWXYZ
$&1234567890(.,""„;:!?)

18

72

abcdefghijklmn
opqrstuvwxyz
ABCDEFGHIJKLM
NOPQRSTUVW
XYZ$&12345678
90(.,""„;:!?)

36

abcdefghijklmnopqrstuvwxyz
ABCDEFGHIJKLMNOPQRSTUVWX
YZ$&1234567890(.,""„;:!?)

Kabel Book

abcdefghijklmnopqrstuvwxyz
ABCDEFGHIJKLMNOPQRSTUVWXYZ
$1234567890&(.,"";:!?)

abcdefghijklmnopqrstuvwxyz
ABCDEFGHIJKLMNOPQRSTUVWXYZ
$1234567890&(.,"";:!?)

Typography, the major communications advance between the invention of writing and the age of electronic mass communications in the twentieth cent ury, *played a pivotal role* in the social, economic, and religious upheavals tha t occurred during the fifteenth and sixteenth centuries. The modern nation de veloped as a result of the vigorous spirit of nationalism that swept over Europ e and led to the American and French revolutions of the late eighteenth centu ry. In addition to being a powerful vehicle for spreading ideas about human r ights and the sovereignty of the people, typographic printing stabilized and unified languages. Illiteracy, the inability to read and write, began a long, stea dy decline. Typography radically altered education. The medieval classroom had been a scriptorium of sorts, where each student penned his own book. L earning became an increasingly private, rather than communal, process. Hum an dialog, extended by type, began to take place on a global scale that bridg ed time and space. Gutenberg's invention was the first mechanization of a ski lled handicraft. As such, it set into motion, over the next three hundred years,

Typography, the major communications advance between the inve ntion of writing and the age of electronic mass communications in th e twentieth century, *played a pivotal role* in the social, economic, an d religious upheavals that occurred during the fifteenth and sixteenth centuries. The modern nation developed as a result of the vigorous s pirit of nationalism that swept over Europe and led to the American and French revolutions of the late eighteenth century. In addition to being a powerful vehicle for spreading ideas about human rights an d the sovereignty of the people, typographic printing stabilized and unified languages. Illiteracy, the inability to read and write, began a l ong, steady decline. Typography radically altered education. The me dieval classroom had been a scriptorium of sorts, where each stude nt penned his own book. Learning became an increasingly private, ra

Typography, the major communications advance between the invention of writing and the age of electronic mass communications in the twentieth cent ury, *played a pivotal role* in the social, economic, and religious upheavals tha t occurred during the fifteenth and sixteenth centuries. The modern nation de veloped as a result of the vigorous spirit of nationalism that swept over Europ e and led to the American and French revolutions of the late eighteenth centu ry. In addition to being a powerful vehicle for spreading ideas about human r ights and the sovereignty of the people, typographic printing stabilized and unified languages. Illiteracy, the inability to read and write, began a long, stea dy decline. Typography radically altered education. The medieval classroom had been a scriptorium of sorts, where each student penned his own book. L earning became an increasingly private, rather than communal, process. Hum an dialog, extended by type, began to take place on a global scale that bridg

Typography, the major communications advance between the inve ntion of writing and the age of electronic mass communications in th e twentieth century, *played a pivotal role* in the social, economic, an d religious upheavals that occurred during the fifteenth and sixteenth centuries. The modern nation developed as a result of the vigorous s pirit of nationalism that swept over Europe and led to the American and French revolutions of the late eighteenth century. In addition to being a powerful vehicle for spreading ideas about human rights an d the sovereignty of the people, typographic printing stabilized and unified languages. Illiteracy, the inability to read and write, began a l ong, steady decline. Typography radically altered education. The me dieval classroom had been a scriptorium of sorts, where each stude

Typography, the major communications advance between the invention of writing and the age of electronic mass communications in the twentieth cent ury, *played a pivotal role* in the social, economic, and religious upheavals tha t occurred during the fifteenth and sixteenth centuries. The modern nation de veloped as a result of the vigorous spirit of nationalism that swept over Europ e and led to the American and French revolutions of the late eighteenth centu ry. In addition to being a powerful vehicle for spreading ideas about human r ights and the sovereignty of the people, typographic printing stabilized and unified languages. Illiteracy, the inability to read and write, began a long, stea dy decline. Typography radically altered education. The medieval classroom had been a scriptorium of sorts, where each student penned his own book. L earning became an increasingly private, rather than communal, process. Hum

Typography, the major communications advance between the inve ntion of writing and the age of electronic mass communications in th e twentieth century, *played a pivotal role* in the social, economic, an d religious upheavals that occurred during the fifteenth and sixteenth centuries. The modern nation developed as a result of the vigorous s pirit of nationalism that swept over Europe and led to the American and French revolutions of the late eighteenth century. In addition to being a powerful vehicle for spreading ideas about human rights an d the sovereignty of the people, typographic printing stabilized and unified languages. Illiteracy, the inability to read and write, began a l ong, steady decline. Typography radically altered education. The me

Typography, the major communications advance between the invention of writing and the age of electronic mass communications in the twentieth cent ury, *played a pivotal role* in the social, economic, and religious upheavals tha t occurred during the fifteenth and sixteenth centuries. The modern nation de veloped as a result of the vigorous spirit of nationalism that swept over Europ e and led to the American and French revolutions of the late eighteenth centu ry. In addition to being a powerful vehicle for spreading ideas about human r ights and the sovereignty of the people, typographic printing stabilized and unified languages. Illiteracy, the inability to read and write, began a long, stea dy decline. Typography radically altered education. The medieval classroom had been a scriptorium of sorts, where each student penned his own book. L

Typography, the major communications advance between the inve ntion of writing and the age of electronic mass communications in th e twentieth century, *played a pivotal role* in the social, economic, an d religious upheavals that occurred during the fifteenth and sixteenth centuries. The modern nation developed as a result of the vigorous s pirit of nationalism that swept over Europe and led to the American and French revolutions of the late eighteenth century. In addition to being a powerful vehicle for spreading ideas about human rights an d the sovereignty of the people, typographic printing stabilized and unified languages. Illiteracy, the inability to read and write, began a l

abcdefghijklmnopqrstuvwxyz
ABCDEFGHIJKLMNOPQRSTUVWXYZ
$1234567890&(.,"";:!?)

abcdefghijklmnopqrstuvwxyz
ABCDEFGHIJKLMNOPQRSTUVWXYZ
$1234567890&(.,"";:!?)

10/10

Typography, the major communications advance between t he invention of writing and the age of electronic mass commu nications in the twentieth century, *played a pivotal role* in the social, economic, and religious upheavals that occurred durin g the fifteenth and sixteenth centuries. The modern nation dev eloped as a result of the vigorous spirit of nationalism that sw ept over Europe and led to the American and French revoluti ons of the late eighteenth century. In addition to being a pow erful vehicle for spreading ideas about human rights and the sovereignty of the people, typographic printing stabilized an d unified languages. Illiteracy, the inability to read and write, began a long, steady decline. Typography radically altered

12/12

Typography, the major communications advance between the invention of writing and the age of ele ctronic mass communications in the twentieth cent ury, *played a pivotal role* in the social, economic, a nd religious upheavals that occurred during the fifte enth and sixteenth centuries. The modern nation de veloped as a result of the vigorous spirit of nationali sm that swept over Europe and led to the America n and French revolutions of the late eighteenth cent ury. In addition to being a powerful vehicle for

10/11

Typography, the major communications advance between t he invention of writing and the age of electronic mass commu nications in the twentieth century, *played a pivotal role* in the social, economic, and religious upheavals that occurred durin g the fifteenth and sixteenth centuries. The modern nation dev eloped as a result of the vigorous spirit of nationalism that sw ept over Europe and led to the American and French revoluti ons of the late eighteenth century. In addition to being a pow erful vehicle for spreading ideas about human rights and the sovereignty of the people, typographic printing stabilized an d unified languages. Illiteracy, the inability to read and write,

12/13

Typography, the major communications advance between the invention of writing and the age of ele ctronic mass communications in the twentieth cent ury, *played a pivotal role* in the social, economic, a nd religious upheavals that occurred during the fifte enth and sixteenth centuries. The modern nation de veloped as a result of the vigorous spirit of nationali sm that swept over Europe and led to the America n and French revolutions of the late eighteenth cent

10/12

Typography, the major communications advance between t he invention of writing and the age of electronic mass commu nications in the twentieth century, *played a pivotal role* in the social, economic, and religious upheavals that occurred durin g the fifteenth and sixteenth centuries. The modern nation dev eloped as a result of the vigorous spirit of nationalism that sw ept over Europe and led to the American and French revoluti ons of the late eighteenth century. In addition to being a pow erful vehicle for spreading ideas about human rights and the sovereignty of the people, typographic printing stabilized an

12/14

Typography, the major communications advance between the invention of writing and the age of ele ctronic mass communications in the twentieth cent ury, *played a pivotal role* in the social, economic, a nd religious upheavals that occurred during the fifte enth and sixteenth centuries. The modern nation de veloped as a result of the vigorous spirit of nationali sm that swept over Europe and led to the America

10/13

Typography, the major communications advance between t he invention of writing and the age of electronic mass commu nications in the twentieth century, *played a pivotal role* in the social, economic, and religious upheavals that occurred durin g the fifteenth and sixteenth centuries. The modern nation dev eloped as a result of the vigorous spirit of nationalism that sw ept over Europe and led to the American and French revoluti ons of the late eighteenth century. In addition to being a pow erful vehicle for spreading ideas about human rights and the

12/15

Typography, the major communications advance between the invention of writing and the age of ele ctronic mass communications in the twentieth cent ury, *played a pivotal role* in the social, economic, a nd religious upheavals that occurred during the fifte enth and sixteenth centuries. The modern nation de veloped as a result of the vigorous spirit of nationali sm that swept over Europe and led to the America

Design: **Jeff Barnes**

Specimens are set in
Adobe News Gothic

News Gothic is a slightly condensed, medial weight sans serif, designed by Morris F. Benton for American Type Founders and released in 1908. It was originally issued in regular, condensed, and extra condensed versions, but without accompanying bold or italic fonts. As the name suggests, the News Gothics were initially designed for news-paper headlines and subheads, and they were widely accepted for routine advertising display work. News Gothic was systemati-cally designed, for the three versions were coordinated by having the same optical stroke weight and consistent alignment of the base line, x-height, and capital height. American Type Founders's companion Mono-tone Gothic had a lighter stroke weight and is slightly expanded; their Franklin Gothics provided bold counterparts.

Akzidenz-Grotesk influenced News Gothic, which has a slightly lighter stroke weight and more condensed letterforms. The **c** has a larger aperture; **g** is two-storied. Circular letters such as **c** and **o** are drawn as slightly compressed ovals; the **b**, **d**, **p**, and **q** were designed by combining an oval form with a straight line. **B**, **P**, and **R** are slightly con-densed in News Gothic, but expanded in Akzidenz-Grotesk.

The invention of keyboard composition in the 1880s expanded the number and size of publications, and advertising increased sharply. Instead of ending handset metal typography, typesetting machines created an expanded need for handset display type for headlines and advertising work. News Gothic was one of American Type Founders's early 20th century "workhorse Gothics." After World War II, new bold and italic fonts enabled News Gothic to emerge as a sans-serif family of subtle distinction.

ABCDEFG
HIJKLMN
OPQRST
UVWXYZ
&(.,""";.)

abcdefgh
ijklmnopq
rstuvwxyz
$123456
7890!?

abcdefghijklmnopqrstuvwxyz
ABCDEFGHIJKLMNOPQRSTUVWXYZ
$&1234567890(.,"";:!?)

72

abcdefghijklmno
pqrstuvwxyzABC
DEFGHIJKLMNOP
QRSTUVWXYZ$&
1234567890
(.,"";:!?)

36

abcdefghijklmnopqrstuvwxyz
ABCDEFGHIJKLMNOPQRSTUVWXYZ
$&1234567890(.,"";:!?)

18

abcdefghijklmnopqrstuvwxyz
ABCDEFGHIJKLMNOPQRSTUVWXYZ
$&1234567890(.,"";:!?)

72

abcdefghijklmnop
qrstuvwxyzABC
DEFGHIJKLMNOP
QRSTUVWXYZ$&
1234567890
(.,"";:·!?)

36

abcdefghijklmnopqrstuvwxyz
ABCDEFGHIJKLMNOPQRSTUVWXYZ
$&1234567890(.,"";:!?)

abcdefghijklmnopqrstuvwxyz
ABCDEFGHIJKLMNOPQRSTUVWXYZ
$&1234567890(.,"";:!?)

abcdefghijklmn
opqrstuvwxyz
ABCDEFGHIJKL
MNOPQRSTUV
WXYZ$&12345
67890(.,"";:-!?)

abcdefghijklmnopqrstuvwxyz
ABCDEFGHIJKLMNOPQRSTUV
WXYZ$&1234567890(.,"";:-!?)

abcdefghijklmnopqrstuvwxyz
ABCDEFGHIJKLMNOPQRSTUVWXYZ
$&1234567890(.,"";:!?)

18

72

abcdefghijklmn
opqrstuvwxyz
ABCDEFGHIJKL
MNOPQRSTUV
WXYZ$&12345
67890(.,"";:!?)

36

abcdefghijklmnopqrstuvwxyz
ABCDEFGHIJKLMNOPQRSTUV
WXYZ$&1234567890(.,"";:!?)

News Gothic

abcdefghijklmnopqrstuvwxyz
ABCDEFGHIJKLMNOPQRSTUVWXYZ
$1234567890&(.,"";:!?)

abcdefghijklmnopqrstuvwxyz
ABCDEFGHIJKLMNOPQRSTUVWXYZ
$1234567890&(.,"";:!?)

Typography, the major communications advance between the invention of writing and the age of electronic mass communications in the twentieth century, *played a pivotal role* in the social, economic, and religious upheavals that occurred during the fifteenth and sixteenth centuries. The modern nation developed as a result of the vigorous spirit of nationalism that swept over Europe and led to the American and French revolutions of the late eighteenth century. In addition to being a powerful vehicle for spreading ideas about human rights and the sovereignty of the people, typographic printing stabilized and unified languages. Illiteracy, the inability to read and write, began a long, steady decline. Typography radically altered education. The medieval classroom had been a scriptorium of sorts, where each student penned his own book. Learning became an increasingly private, rather than communal, process.Human dialog, extended by type, began to take place on a global scale that bridged time and space. Gutenberg's invention was the first mechanization of a skilled handicraft. As such, it set into mot

Typography, the major communications advance between the invention of writing and the age of electronic mass communications in the twentieth century, *played a pivotal role* in the social, economic, and religious upheavals that occurred during the fifteenth and sixteenth centuries. The modern nation developed as a result of the vigorous spirit of nationalism that swept over Europe and led to the American and French revolutions of the late eighteenth century. In addition to being a powerful vehicle for spreading ideas about human rights and the sovereignty of the people, typographic printing stabilized and unified languages. Illiteracy, the inability to read and write, began a long, steady decline. Typography radically altered education. The medieval class room had been a scriptorium of sorts, where each student penned his own book. Learning became an increasingly private, rather than

Typography, the major communications advance between the invention of writing and the age of electronic mass communications in the twentieth century, *played a pivotal role* in the social, economic, and religious upheavals that occurred during the fifteenth and sixteenth centuries. The modern nation developed as a result of the vigorous spirit of nationalism that swept over Europe and led to the American and French revolutions of the late eighteenth century. In addition to being a powerful vehicle for spreading ideas about human rights and the sovereignty of the people, typographic printing stabilized and unified languages. Illiteracy, the inability to read and write, began a long, steady decline. Typography radically altered education. The medieval classroom had been a scriptorium of sorts,where each student penned his own book. Learning became an increasingly private, rather than communal, process.Human dialog, extended by type, began to take

Typography, the major communications advance between the invention of writing and the age of electronic mass communications in the twentieth century, *played a pivotal role* in the social, economic, and religious upheavals that occurred during the fifteenth and sixteenth centuries. The modern nation developed as a result of the vigorous spirit of nationalism that swept over Europe and led to the American and French revolutions of the late eighteenth century. In addition to being a powerful vehicle for spreading ideas about human rights and the sovereignty of the people, typographic printing stabilized and unified languages. Illiteracy, the inability to read and write, began a long, steady decline. Typography radically altered education. The medieval class room had been a scriptorium of sorts, where each student penned

Typography, the major communications advance between the invention of writing and the age of electronic mass communications in the twentieth century, *played a pivotal role* in the social, economic, and religious upheavals that occurred during the fifteenth and sixteenth centuries. The modern nation developed as a result of the vigorous spirit of nationalism that swept over Europe and led to the American and French revolutions of the late eighteenth century. In addition to being a powerful vehicle for spreading ideas about human rights and the sovereignty of the people, typographic printing stabilized and unified languages. Illiteracy, the inability to read and write, began a long, steady decline. Typography radically altered education. The medieval classroom had been a scriptorium of sorts,where each student penned his own book. Learning became an increasingly private, rath

Typography, the major communications advance between the invention of writing and the age of electronic mass communications in the twentieth century, *played a pivotal role* in the social, economic, and religious upheavals that occurred during the fifteenth and sixteenth centuries. The modern nation developed as a result of the vigorous spirit of nationalism that swept over Europe and led to the American and French revolutions of the late eighteenth century. In addition to being a powerful vehicle for spreading ideas about human rights and the sovereignty of the people, typographic printing stabilized and unified languages. Illiteracy, the inability to read and write, began a long, steady decline. Typography radically altered education. The medieval class

Typography, the major communications advance between the invention of writing and the age of electronic mass communications in the twentieth century, *played a pivotal role* in the social, economic, and religious upheavals that occurred during the fifteenth and sixteenth centuries. The modern nation developed as a result of the vigorous spirit of nationalism that swept over Europe and led to the American and French revolutions of the late eighteenth century. In addition to being a powerful vehicle for spreading ideas about human rights and the sovereignty of the people, typographic printing stabilized and unified languages. Illiteracy, the inability to read and write, began a long, steady decline. Typography radically altered education. The medieval classroom had been a scriptorium of sorts,where each stu

Typography, the major communications advance between the invention of writing and the age of electronic mass communications in the twentieth century, *played a pivotal role* in the social, economic, and religious upheavals that occurred during the fifteenth and sixteenth centuries. The modern nation developed as a result of the vigorous spirit of nationalism that swept over Europe and led to the American and French revolutions of the late eighteenth century. In addition to being a powerful vehicle for spreading ideas about human rights and the sovereignty of the people, typographic printing stabilized and unified languages. Illiteracy, the inability to read and write, began a long, steady

abcdefghijklmnopqrstuvwxyz
ABCDEFGHIJKLMNOPQRSTUVWXYZ
$1234567890&(.,"";:!?)

abcdefghijklmnopqrstuvwxyz
ABCDEFGHIJKLMNOPQRSTUVWXYZ
$1234567890&(.,"";:!?)

10/10

Typography, the major communications advance between the invention of writing and the age of electronic mass com munications in the twentieth century, *played a pivotal role* in the social, economic, and religious upheavals that occurred during the fifteenth and sixteenth centuries. The modern nation dev eloped as a result of the vigorous spirit of nationalism that swe pt over Europe and led to the American and French revolutions of the late eighteenth century. In addition to being a powerful veh icle for spreading ideas about human rights and the sovereignty of the people, typographic printing stabilized and unified lan guages. Illiteracy, the inability to read and write, began a long, ste ady decline. Typography radically altered education. The medieval

10/11

Typography, the major communications advance between the invention of writing and the age of electronic mass com munications in the twentieth century, *played a pivotal role* in the social, economic, and religious upheavals that occurred during the fifteenth and sixteenth centuries. The modern nation dev eloped as a result of the vigorous spirit of nationalism that swe pt over Europe and led to the American and French revolutions of the late eighteenth century. In addition to being a powerful veh icle for spreading ideas about human rights and the sovereignty of the people, typographic printing stabilized and unified lan guages. Illiteracy, the inability to read and write, began a long, ste

10/12

Typography, the major communications advance between the invention of writing and the age of electronic mass com munications in the twentieth century, *played a pivotal role* in the social, economic, and religious upheavals that occurred during the fifteenth and sixteenth centuries. The modern nation dev eloped as a result of the vigorous spirit of nationalism that swe pt over Europe and led to the American and French revolutions of the late eighteenth century. In addition to being a powerful veh icle for spreading ideas about human rights and the sovereignty

10/13

Typography, the major communications advance between the invention of writing and the age of electronic mass com munications in the twentieth century, *played a pivotal role* in the social, economic, and religious upheavals that occurred during the fifteenth and sixteenth centuries. The modern nation dev eloped as a result of the vigorous spirit of nationalism that swe pt over Europe and led to the American and French revolutions of the late eighteenth century. In addition to being a powerful veh icle for spreading ideas about human rights and the sovereignty

12/12

Typography, the major communications advance be tween the invention of writing and the age of electro nic mass communications in the twentieth century, *played a pivotal role* in the social, economic, and reli gious upheavals that occurred during the fifteenth and sixteenth centuries. The modern nation develop ed as a result of the vigorous spirit of nationalism that swept over Europe and led to the American and Fre nch revolutions of the late eighteenth century. In add ition to being a powerful vehicle for spreading ideas ab

12/13

Typography, the major communications advance be tween the invention of writing and the age of electro nic mass communications in the twentieth century, *played a pivotal role* in the social, economic, and reli gious upheavals that occurred during the fifteenth and sixteenth centuries. The modern nation develop ed as a result of the vigorous spirit of nationalism that swept over Europe and led to the American and Fre nch revolutions of the late eighteenth century. In add

12/14

Typography, the major communications advance be tween the invention of writing and the age of electro nic mass communications in the twentieth century, *played a pivotal role* in the social, economic, and reli gious upheavals that occurred during the fifteenth and sixteenth centuries. The modern nation develop ed as a result of the vigorous spirit of nationalism that swept over Europe and led to the American and Fre

12/15

Typography, the major communications advance be tween the invention of writing and the age of electro nic mass communications in the twentieth century, *played a pivotal role* in the social, economic, and reli gious upheavals that occurred during the fifteenth and sixteenth centuries. The modern nation develop ed as a result of the vigorous spirit of nationalism that swept over Europe and led to the American and Fre

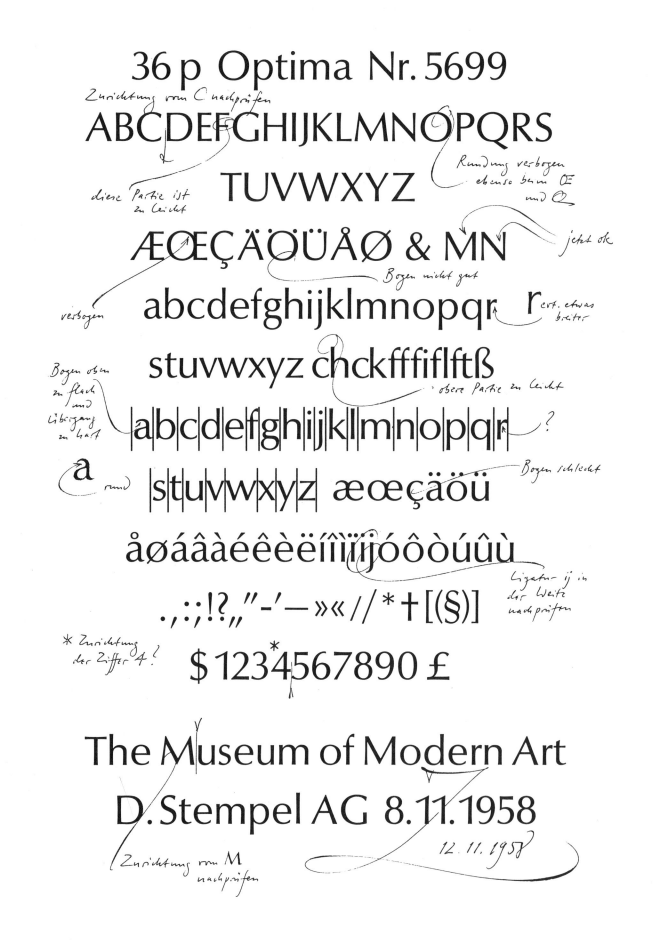

Foundry proof sheet with correction notes for the casting, 1958

Design: **Hermann Zapf**

Specimens are set in
Linotype Optima

When Optima was released by the Stempel foundry as hand-set metal type and by Linotype for machine composition in 1958, this design by Hermann Zapf transcended the chasm separating serif and sans-serif typefaces. Although Optima lacks serifs, its strokes have a slight taper – swelling at the terminals – and a decisive thick-and-thin contrast. Its letters have the proportional relationships of traditional old style types, and the capitals are closely modelled upon the 115 A.D. inscriptions on Trajan's Column in Rome. Zapf succeeded in mingling the traditional letterforms of Renaissance typography with the contemporary simplicity of sans-serif type; the result is a humanist sans-serif typeface.

Settings of Optima project openness and light, combining the textural uniformity of sans serif with the variety of shapes found in old style type. The **g** has a loop and ear; the bowls of curved lowercase letters such as **b** and **e** are open and wide. The apertures of **C** and **G** are open. Curved letters such as **D** and **O** are very wide, while **E**, **F**, and **L** are very narrow in the manner of the Roman inscriptional models. Zapf designed Optima with the harmonious proportions of the Golden Section; the ratio of the lowercase x-height to the ascenders and descenders is in the 3-to-5 ratio dating from classical Greek geometry.

Optima has broad application in graphic design as sans-serif running text and when the resonance of traditional typography combined with the clean simplicity of sans serif is desired. Other attempts to blend these attributes include R. Hunter Middleton's 1929 Stellar and Warren Chappel's 1938 Lydian, which has a pronounced pen-stroke appearance.

ABCDEF
GHIJKLM
NOPQRS
TUVWXY
Z&(.,""";:)

abcdefghi
jklmnopq
rstuvwxy
z$123456
7890!?

abcdefghijklmnopqrstuvwxyz
ABCDEFGHIJKLMNOPQRSTUVWXYZ
$&1234567890(.,"";:!?)

72

abcdefghijklmno
pqrstuvwxyzABC
DEFGHIJKLMNO
PQRSTUVWXYZ
$&1234567890
(.,"";:!?)

36

abcdefghijklmnopqrstuvwxyz
ABCDEFGHIJKLMNOPQRSTUV
WXYZ$&1234567890(.,"";:!?)

abcdefghijklmnopqrstuvwxyz
ABCDEFGHIJKLMNOPQRSTUVWXYZ
$&1234567890(.,"";:!?)

18

72

abcdefghijklmno
pqrstuvwxyzABC
DEFGHIJKLMNO
PQRSTUVWXYZ
$&1234567890
(.,"";:!?)

36

abcdefghijklmnopqrstuvwxyz
ABCDEFGHIJKLMNOPQRSTUV
WXYZ$&1234567890(.,"";:!?)

abcdefghijklmnopqrstuvwxyz
ABCDEFGHIJKLMNOPQRSTUVWXYZ
$&1234567890(.,""";:!?)

72

abcdefghijklmno
pqrstuvwxyzAB
CDEFGHIJKLM
NOPQRSTUVW
XYZ$&12345678
90(.,"";:!?)

36

abcdefghijklmnopqrstuvwxyz
ABCDEFGHIJKLMNOPQRSTUV
WXYZ$&1234567890(.,"";:!?)

Optima Semibold Italic

abcdefghijklmnopqrstuvwxyz
ABCDEFGHIJKLMNOPQRSTUVWXYZ
$&1234567890(.,"";:!?)

18

72

abcdefghijklmn
opqrstuvwxyz
ABCDEFGHIJKL
MNOPQRSTUV
WXYZ$&12345
67890(.,"";:!?)

36

abcdefghijklmnopqrstuvwxyz
ABCDEFGHIJKLMNOPQRSTUV
WXYZ$&1234567890(.,"";:!?)

Optima

abcdefghijklmnopqrstuvwxyz
ABCDEFGHIJKLMNOPQRSTUVWXYZ
1234567890&(.,"";:!?)

abcdefghijklmnopqrstuvwxyz
ABCDEFGHIJKLMNOPQRSTUVWXYZ
1234567890&(.,"";:!?)

8/8

Typography, the major communications advance between the invention of writing and the age of electronic mass communications in the twentieth century, *played a pivotal role* in the social, economic, and religious up heavals that occurred during the fifteenth and sixteenth centuries. The mo dern nation developed as a result of the vigorous spirit of nationalism that swept over Europe and led to the American and French revolutions of the late eighteenth century. In addition to being a powerful vehicle for spre ading ideas about human rights and the sovereignty of the people, typo graphic printing stabilized and unified languages. Illiteracy, the inability to read and write, began a long, steady decline. Typography radically altered education. The medieval classroom had been a scriptorium of sorts, where each student penned his own book. Learning became an increasingly pri vate, rather than communal, process. Human dialog, extended by type, be gan to take place on a global scale that bridged time and space. Gut enberg's invention was the first mechanization of a skilled handicraft. As

9/9

Typography, the major communications advance between the inv ention of writing and the age of electronic mass communications in the twentieth century, *played a pivotal role* in the social, econ omic, and religious upheavals that occurred during the fifteenth and sixteenth centuries. The modern nation developed as a result of the vigorous spirit of nationalism that swept over Europe and led to the American and French revolutions of the late eighteenth cen tury. In addition to being a powerful vehicle for spreading ideas about human rights and the sovereignty of the people, typogra phic printing stabilized and unified languages. Illiteracy, the inabi lity to read and write, began a long, steady decline. Typography rad ically altered education. The medieval classroom had been a scrip torium of sorts, where each student penned his own book. Learn ing became an increasingly private, rather than communal, proc

8/9

Typography, the major communications advance between the invention of writing and the age of electronic mass communications in the twentieth century, *played a pivotal role* in the social, economic, and religious up heavals that occurred during the fifteenth and sixteenth centuries. The mo dern nation developed as a result of the vigorous spirit of nationalism that swept over Europe and led to the American and French revolutions of the late eighteenth century. In addition to being a powerful vehicle for spre ading ideas about human rights and the sovereignty of the people, typo graphic printing stabilized and unified languages. Illiteracy, the inability to read and write, began a long, steady decline. Typography radically altered education. The medieval classroom had been a scriptorium of sorts, where each student penned his own book. Learning became an increasingly pri vate, rather than communal, process. Human dialog, extended by type, be

9/10

Typography, the major communications advance between the inv ention of writing and the age of electronic mass communications in the twentieth century, *played a pivotal role* in the social, econ omic, and religious upheavals that occurred during the fifteenth and sixteenth centuries. The modern nation developed as a result of the vigorous spirit of nationalism that swept over Europe and led to the American and French revolutions of the late eighteenth cen tury. In addition to being a powerful vehicle for spreading ideas about human rights and the sovereignty of the people, typogra phic printing stabilized and unified languages. Illiteracy, the inabi lity to read and write, began a long, steady decline. Typography rad ically altered education. The medieval classroom had been a scrip

8/10

Typography, the major communications advance between the invention of writing and the age of electronic mass communications in the twentieth century, *played a pivotal role* in the social, economic, and religious up heavals that occurred during the fifteenth and sixteenth centuries. The mo dern nation developed as a result of the vigorous spirit of nationalism that swept over Europe and led to the American and French revolutions of the late eighteenth century. In addition to being a powerful vehicle for spre ading ideas about human rights and the sovereignty of the people, typo graphic printing stabilized and unified languages. Illiteracy, the inability to read and write, began a long, steady decline. Typography radically altered education. The medieval classroom had been a scriptorium of sorts, where each student penned his own book. Learning became an increasingly pri

9/11

Typography, the major communications advance between the inv ention of writing and the age of electronic mass communications in the twentieth century, *played a pivotal role* in the social, econ omic, and religious upheavals that occurred during the fifteenth and sixteenth centuries. The modern nation developed as a result of the vigorous spirit of nationalism that swept over Europe and led to the American and French revolutions of the late eighteenth cen tury. In addition to being a powerful vehicle for spreading ideas about human rights and the sovereignty of the people, typogra phic printing stabilized and unified languages. Illiteracy, the inabi lity to read and write, began a long, steady decline. Typography rad

8/11

Typography, the major communications advance between the invention of writing and the age of electronic mass communications in the twentieth century, *played a pivotal role* in the social, economic, and religious up heavals that occurred during the fifteenth and sixteenth centuries. The mo dern nation developed as a result of the vigorous spirit of nationalism that swept over Europe and led to the American and French revolutions of the late eighteenth century. In addition to being a powerful vehicle for spre ading ideas about human rights and the sovereignty of the people, typo graphic printing stabilized and unified languages. Illiteracy, the inability to read and write, began a long, steady decline. Typography radically altered education. The medieval classroom had been a scriptorium of sorts, where

9/12

Typography, the major communications advance between the inv ention of writing and the age of electronic mass communications in the twentieth century, *played a pivotal role* in the social, econ omic, and religious upheavals that occurred during the fifteenth and sixteenth centuries. The modern nation developed as a result of the vigorous spirit of nationalism that swept over Europe and led to the American and French revolutions of the late eighteenth cen tury. In addition to being a powerful vehicle for spreading ideas about human rights and the sovereignty of the people, typogra phic printing stabilized and unified languages. Illiteracy, the inabi

abcdefghijklmnopqrstuvwxyz
ABCDEFGHIJKLMNOPQRSTUVWXYZ
1234567890&(.,"";:!?)

abcdefghijklmnopqrstuvwxyz
ABCDEFGHIJKLMNOPQRSTUVWXYZ
1234567890&(.,"";:!?)

10/10

Typography, the major communications advance between the invention of writing and the age of electronic mass commu nications in the twentieth century, *played a pivotal role* in the soc ial, economic, and religious upheavals that occurred during the fift eenth and sixteenth centuries. The modern nation developed as a result of the vigorous spirit of nationalism that swept over Europe and led to the American and French revolutions of the late eight eenth century. In addition to being a powerful vehicle for spre ading ideas about human rights and the sovereignty of the people, typographic printing stabilized and unified languages. Illiteracy, the inability to read and write, began a long, steady decline. Typogra phy radically altered education. The medieval classroom had been a

---

10/11

Typography, the major communications advance between the invention of writing and the age of electronic mass commu nications in the twentieth century, *played a pivotal role* in the soc ial, economic, and religious upheavals that occurred during the fift eenth and sixteenth centuries. The modern nation developed as a result of the vigorous spirit of nationalism that swept over Europe and led to the American and French revolutions of the late eight eenth century. In addition to being a powerful vehicle for spre ading ideas about human rights and the sovereignty of the people, typographic printing stabilized and unified languages. Illiteracy, the

---

10/12

Typography, the major communications advance between the invention of writing and the age of electronic mass commu nications in the twentieth century, *played a pivotal role* in the soc ial, economic, and religious upheavals that occurred during the fift eenth and sixteenth centuries. The modern nation developed as a result of the vigorous spirit of nationalism that swept over Europe and led to the American and French revolutions of the late eight eenth century. In addition to being a powerful vehicle for spre ading ideas about human rights and the sovereignty of the people,

---

10/13

Typography, the major communications advance between the invention of writing and the age of electronic mass commu nications in the twentieth century, *played a pivotal role* in the soc ial, economic, and religious upheavals that occurred during the fift eenth and sixteenth centuries. The modern nation developed as a result of the vigorous spirit of nationalism that swept over Europe and led to the American and French revolutions of the late eight eenth century. In addition to being a powerful vehicle for spre ading ideas about human rights and the sovereignty of the people,

---

12/12

Typography, the major communications advance be tween the invention of writing and the age of electr onic mass communications in the twentieth cent ury, *played a pivotal role* in the social, economic, and religious upheavals that occurred during the fifteenth and sixteenth centuries. The modern nation developed as a result of the vigorous spirit of nation alism that swept over Europe and led to the Amer ican and French revolutions of the late eighteenth cen tury. In addition to being a powerful vehicle for spread

---

12/13

Typography, the major communications advance be tween the invention of writing and the age of electr onic mass communications in the twentieth cent ury, *played a pivotal role* in the social, economic, and religious upheavals that occurred during the fifteenth and sixteenth centuries. The modern nation developed as a result of the vigorous spirit of nation alism that swept over Europe and led to the Amer ican and French revolutions of the late eighteenth cen

---

12/14

Typography, the major communications advance be tween the invention of writing and the age of electr onic mass communications in the twentieth cent ury, *played a pivotal role* in the social, economic, and religious upheavals that occurred during the fifteenth and sixteenth centuries. The modern nation developed as a result of the vigorous spirit of nation alism that swept over Europe and led to the Amer

---

12/15

Typography, the major communications advance be tween the invention of writing and the age of electr onic mass communications in the twentieth cent ury, *played a pivotal role* in the social, economic, and religious upheavals that occurred during the fifteenth and sixteenth centuries. The modern nation developed as a result of the vigorous spirit of nation alism that swept over Europe and led to the Amer

Palatino väterlich gewichtig und namensgleich mit dem italienischen Schreibmeister des 16. Jahrhunderts, bestimmt die Schrift-Familie, welche unter der Bezeichnung Palatino zusammengefaßt ist. Lebendig, als eine typische Kursiv, steht daneben die *Palatino-Kursiv* Für die Linotype gibt es dazu eine identische Kursiv und Halbfette in den Werkschriftgraden. Die **Halbfette Palatino** ein robustes Familienmitglied, ist nützlich überall, wo es gilt, eine Titelzeile durchzusetzen oder eine Anzeige lautstark zu machen. Anmutig zeigen sich die PALATINO-KAPITÄLCHEN in Kapitelüberschriften. *Schwungfiguren* zur Palatino-Kursiv dagegen sind vorwiegend im Akzidenzbereich verwendbar, wo ihr graziöses und bisweilen kapriziöses Wesen begrüßt wird. Bei Arbeiten, wo eine monumentale Wirkung erstrebt wird, ist die MICHELANGELO willkommen. Versalien dieser Art sind von zeitloser Gültigkeit, ernsthaft und festlich zugleich. Die stattlich wirkende Schwester **SISTINA** vermag sich mit ihrer kräftigeren Stimme auch im Marktwirbel der lauten Akzidenzschriften zu behaupten. PHIDIAS [ΦΕΙΔΙΑΣ] der griechische Vetter der Michelangelo, zeigt die geistige Verwandschaft des Griechischen mit dem Römischen. Auch die **Heraklit** (Ἡρακλειτου) als griechische Auszeichnungsschrift paßt gut zur Palatino. Ein wichtiger Zweig innerhalb der Palatino-Familie ist die **Linotype-Aldus-Buchschrift** *mit Kursiv,* und neuerdings die **Enge Linotype Aldus-Antiqua** *mit Kursiv,* welche überall als Werkschriften die Palatino ergänzen, wo ein leichteres und schmaleres Buchstabenbild erforderlich ist. Nicht vergessen den kraftvollen Schwager **Kompakt** denn er bewältigt oft die schwierigsten Probleme, ohne dabei plump oder derb vorzugehen. Den lieblichsten Kontrast dazu bilden die zarte *Virtuosa I & II* zwei Schwestern, die eine stiller, die andere bewegter im Ausdruck. Die griechische Kusine dieser Virtuosa-Schwestern *Frederika (Φρειδερίκης)* steht an Liebreiz ihren Verwandten nicht nach. Kein Familienjubiläum, kein Geburtstag ohne die SAPHIR stets ist der Entwerfer beglückt von ihren festlichen Buchstaben. Schließlich sei die Frakturschrift Gilgengart nicht vergessen. Zwar gehört sie zum deutschen Schriftzweig, neben mancher Type der Palatino-Familie steht sie aber so gut, daß man sie gern zur Verwandten ernennen möchte.

Design: **Hermann Zapf**

Specimens are set in
Linotype Palatino

Palatino was designed by Hermann Zapf, a master calligrapher and then art director of the Stempel foundry in Frankfurt, Germany. It was released by Stempel in 1950. Zapf considers design, printing production, and typographic manufacturing processes when designing his typefaces. To compensate for the problems of mediocre paper in Germany after the war, as well as the nature of widely-used lithographic and gravure printing presses, Zapf gave Palatino open counters and a stroke weight slightly heavier than most roman fonts. Zapf intended Palatino to be a display face for commercial work.

The design of Palatino was inspired by letterforms of the Italian Renaissance and inscriptions carved during the Roman Empire. There is a pronounced calligraphic quality to some letters, such as **R**, **S**, **X**, and **Y**; this is particularly true of the *lowercase italic*. Lowercase letters are fairly wide and have large counters. The capital **E**, **F**, and **L** are narrow as they are in Roman inscriptions. The right stroke of **h**, **m**, and **n** has a serif on the right side only. Ascenders, notably the **t**, are tall.

Zapf received international acclaim after Palatino's release, and it became one of the most widely used typefaces. Its frequent use as a book face became controversial, for some designers believed its calligraphic touches made it less readable in large amounts of text than traditional Old Style faces. These mild criticisms never diminished Palatino's wide use in all areas of graphic design. The page at left, designed by Zapf in 1953, shows Palatino with italics, semibold, and several Zapf display faces, including Palatino's companion titling faces – Michelangelo and Sistina.

ABCDEF
GHIJKLM
NOPQRS
TUVWX
YZ&(("''""..)

abcdefghi
jklmnopq
rstuvwxy
z$1234567
890!?

abcdefghijklmnopqrstuvwxyz
ABCDEFGHIJKLMNOPQRSTU
VWXYZ$&1234567890(.,""";:!?)

abcdefghijklmno
pqrstuvwxyz
ABCDEFGHIJKL
MNOPQRSTU
VWXYZ$&12345
67890(.,""";:!?)

abcdefghijklmnopqrstuvwxyz
ABCDEFGHIJKLMNOPQRSTU
VWXYZ$&1234567890(.,""";:!?)

18

72

abcdefghijklmnopq
rstuvwxyz
ABCDEFGHIJKL
MNOPQRSTU
VWXYZ$&12345
67890(.,"";:!?)

36

abcdefghijklmnopqrstuvwxyz
ABCDEFGHIJKLMNOPQRSTU
VWXYZ$&1234567890(.,"";:!?)

abcdefghijklmnopqrstuvwxyz
ABCDEFGHIJKLMNOPQRSTU
VWXYZ$&1234567890(.,"";:!?)

72

abcdefghijklm
nopqrstuvwxyz
ABCDEFGHIJK
LMNOPQRSTU
VWXYZ$&1234
567890(.,"";:!?)

36

abcdefghijklmnopqrstuvwxyz
ABCDEFGHIJKLMNOPQRSTU
VWXYZ$&1234567890(.,"";:!?)

abcdefghijklmnopqrstuvwxyz
ABCDEFGHIJKLMNOPQRSTU
VWXYZ$&1234567890(.,"";:!?)

18

72

abcdefghijklmno
pqrstuvwxyzAB
CDEFGHIJKLM
NOPQRSTUVW
XYZ$&123456789
0(.,"";:!?)

36

abcdefghijklmnopqrstuvwxyz
ABCDEFGHIJKLMNOPQRSTU
VWXYZ$&1234567890(.,"";:!?)

Palatino

abcdefghijklmnopqrstuvwxyz
ABCDEFGHIJKLMNOPQRSTUVWXYZ
$1234567890&(.,"";:!?)

abcdefghijklmnopqrstuvwxyz
ABCDEFGHIJKLMNOPQRSTUVWXYZ
$1234567890&(.,"";:!?)

Typography, the major communications advance between the invention of writing and the age of electronic mass communications in the twentieth century, *played a pivotal role* in the social, economic, and religious upheavals that occurred during the fifteenth and sixteenth centuries. The modern nation developed as a result of the vigorous spirit of nationalism that swept over Europe and led to the American and French revolutions of the late eighteenth century. In addition to being a powerful vehicle for spreading ideas about human rights and the sovereignty of the people, typographic printing stabilized and unified languages. Illiteracy, the inability to read and write, began a long, steady decline. Typography radically altered education. The medieval classroom had been a scriptorium of sorts, where each student penned his own book. Learning became an increasingly private, rather than communal, process. Human dialog, extended by type, began to take place on a global scale that

Typography, the major communications advance between the invention of writing and the age of electronic mass communications in the twentieth century, *played a pivotal role* in the social, economic, and religious upheavals that occurred during the fifteenth and sixteenth centuries. The modern nation developed as a result of the vigorous spirit of nationalism that swept over Europe and led to the American and French revolutions of the late eighteenth century. In addition to being a powerful vehicle for spreading ideas about human rights and the sovereignty of the people, typographic printing stabilized and unified languages.Illiteracy, the inability to read and write, began a long, steady decline. Typography radically altered education. The medieval classroom had been a scriptorium of sorts, where each student penned his

Typography, the major communications advance between the invention of writing and the age of electronic mass communications in the twentieth century, *played a pivotal role* in the social, economic, and religious upheavals that occurred during the fifteenth and sixteenth centuries. The modern nation developed as a result of the vigorous spirit of nationalism that swept over Europe and led to the American and French revolutions of the late eighteenth century. In addition to being a powerful vehicle for spreading ideas about human rights and the sovereignty of the people, typographic printing stabilized and unified languages. Illiteracy, the inability to read and write, began a long, steady decline. Typography radically altered education. The medieval classroom had been a scriptorium of sorts, where each student penned his own book. Learning became an increasingly private, rather than communal, process. Hu

Typography, the major communications advance between the invention of writing and the age of electronic mass communications in the twentieth century, *played a pivotal role* in the social, economic, and religious upheavals that occurred during the fifteenth and sixteenth centuries. The modern nation developed as a result of the vigorous spirit of nationalism that swept over Europe and led to the American and French revolutions of the late eighteenth century. In addition to being a powerful vehicle for spreading ideas about human rights and the sovereignty of the people, typographic printing stabilized and unified languages.Illiteracy, the inability to read and write, began a long, steady decline.Typography radically altered education. The medieval classroom

Typography, the major communications advance between the invention of writing and the age of electronic mass communications in the twentieth century, *played a pivotal role* in the social, economic, and religious upheavals that occurred during the fifteenth and sixteenth centuries. The modern nation developed as a result of the vigorous spirit of nationalism that swept over Europe and led to the American and French revolutions of the late eighteenth century. In addition to being a powerful vehicle for spreading ideas about human rights and the sovereignty of the people, typographic printing stabilized and unified languages. Illiteracy, the inability to read and write, began a long, steady decline. Typography radically altered education. The medieval classroom had been a scriptorium of sorts, where each student penned his own book. Learn

Typography, the major communications advance between the invention of writing and the age of electronic mass communications in the twentieth century, *played a pivotal role* in the social, economic, and religious upheavals that occurred during the fifteenth and sixteenth centuries. The modern nation developed as a result of the vigorous spirit of nationalism that swept over Europe and led to the American and French revolutions of the late eighteenth century. In addition to being a powerful vehicle for spreading ideas about human rights and the sovereignty of the people, typographic printing stabilized and unified languages.Illiteracy, the inability to read and write, began a long, steady decline.Ty

Typography, the major communications advance between the invention of writing and the age of electronic mass communications in the twentieth century, *played a pivotal role* in the social, economic, and religious upheavals that occurred during the fifteenth and sixteenth centuries. The modern nation developed as a result of the vigorous spirit of nationalism that swept over Europe and led to the American and French revolutions of the late eighteenth century. In addition to being a powerful vehicle for spreading ideas about human rights and the sovereignty of the people, typographic printing stabilized and unified languages. Illiteracy, the inability to read and write, began a long, steady decline. Typography radically altered education. The medieval classroom had been a

Typography, the major communications advance between the invention of writing and the age of electronic mass communications in the twentieth century, *played a pivotal role* in the social, economic, and religious upheavals that occurred during the fifteenth and sixteenth centuries. The modern nation developed as a result of the vigorous spirit of nationalism that swept over Europe and led to the American and French revolutions of the late eighteenth century. In addition to being a powerful vehicle for spreading ideas about human rights and the sovereignty of the people, typographic printing stabilized and unified languages.Illitera

abcdefghijklmnopqrstuvwxyz
ABCDEFGHIJKLMNOPQRSTUVWXYZ
$1234567890&(.,""";:!?)

abcdefghijklmnopqrstuvwxyz
ABCDEFGHIJKLMNOPQRSTUVWXYZ
$1234567890&(.,""";:!?)

10/10

Typography, the major communications advance between the invention of writing and the age of electronic mass com munications in the twentieth century, *played a pivotal role* in the social, economic, and religious upheavals that occurred during the fifteenth and sixteenth centuries. The modern na tion developed as a result of the vigorous spirit of national ism that swept over Europe and led to the American and French revolutions of the late eighteenth century. In add ition to being a powerful vehicle for spreading ideas about human rights and the sovereignty of the people, typogra phic printing stabilized and unified languages. Illiteracy, the

12/12

Typography, the major communications advance between the invention of writing and the age of electronic mass communications in the twentieth century, *played a pivotal role* in the social, econo mic, and religious upheavals that occurred dur ing the fifteenth and sixteenth centuries. The mo dern nation developed as a result of the vigorous spirit of nationalism that swept over Europe and led to the American and French revolutions of the

10/11

Typography, the major communications advance between the invention of writing and the age of electronic mass com munications in the twentieth century, *played a pivotal role* in the social, economic, and religious upheavals that occurred during the fifteenth and sixteenth centuries. The modern na tion developed as a result of the vigorous spirit of national ism that swept over Europe and led to the American and French revolutions of the late eighteenth century. In add ition to being a powerful vehicle for spreading ideas about human rights and the sovereignty of the people, typogra

12/13

Typography, the major communications advance between the invention of writing and the age of electronic mass communications in the twentieth century, *played a pivotal role* in the social, econo mic, and religious upheavals that occurred dur ing the fifteenth and sixteenth centuries. The mo dern nation developed as a result of the vigorous spirit of nationalism that swept over Europe and led to the American and French revolutions of the

10/12

Typography, the major communications advance between the invention of writing and the age of electronic mass com munications in the twentieth century, *played a pivotal role* in the social, economic, and religious upheavals that occurred during the fifteenth and sixteenth centuries. The modern na tion developed as a result of the vigorous spirit of national ism that swept over Europe and led to the American and French revolutions of the late eighteenth century. In add ition to being a powerful vehicle for spreading ideas about

12/14

Typography, the major communications advance between the invention of writing and the age of electronic mass communications in the twentieth century, *played a pivotal role* in the social, econo mic, and religious upheavals that occurred dur ing the fifteenth and sixteenth centuries. The mo dern nation developed as a result of the vigorous spirit of nationalism that swept over Europe and

10/13

Typography, the major communications advance between the invention of writing and the age of electronic mass com munications in the twentieth century, *played a pivotal role* in the social, economic, and religious upheavals that occurred during the fifteenth and sixteenth centuries. The modern na tion developed as a result of the vigorous spirit of national ism that swept over Europe and led to the American and French revolutions of the late eighteenth century. In add ition to being a powerful vehicle for spreading ideas about

12/15

Typography, the major communications advance between the invention of writing and the age of electronic mass communications in the twentieth century, *played a pivotal role* in the social, econo mic, and religious upheavals that occurred dur ing the fifteenth and sixteenth centuries. The mo dern nation developed as a result of the vigorous spirit of nationalism that swept over Europe and

Now there were apprehended the young catechumens, Revocatus and Felicity his fellow-servant, Saturninus and Secundulus. With them also was Vibia Perpetua, nobly born, reared in a liberal manner, wedded honourably; having a father and two brothers, one of them a catechumen likewise, and a child at breast; and she herself was about twenty-two years of age…it was in the camp games that [they] were to fight; and the time was the birthday of Geta Ceasar… Now dawned the day of their victory, and they went forth from the prison into the amphitheatre as it were into heaven, cheerful and bright of countenance; if they trembled at all, it was for joy, not for fear. Perpetua followed behind, glorious of presence, as a true spouse of Christ and darling of God; at whose piercing look all cast down their eyes.

Mr. Gill's serifs, even when pen drawn, are never fumbled

And when they had been brought to the gate and were being compelled to put on, the men the dress of the priest of Saturn and the women of the priestesses of Ceres, the noble Perpetua remained to the end of like firmness and would not…But for the women the devil had made ready a most savage cow, prepared for this purpose against

or self-conscious because the incised letter, that structure

all custom…Perpetua was first thrown, and fell upon her loins, and her tunic being rent at the side, from where she sat she drew it down to cover her thigh, being mindful rather of her shame than of her pain… So she stood up; and when she saw Felicity smit-

of light and shade, taught him exactly why and how a

ten down, she went up and gave her her hand, and raised her up…And when the people besought that they should be brought forward, that when the sword pierced through their bodies their eyes might be joined thereto as witnesses to the slaughter, they

stroke should be finished– long and exquisitely sharpened

rose of themselves and moved whither the people willed them, first kissing one another that they might accomplish their martyrdom with the rites of peace… But Perpetua, that she might have some taste of pain, was pierced between the bones and

from shallow brackets. *Paul Beaujon (Beatrice Ward) 1930*

shrieked out; and when the swordsman's hand wandered still (for he was a novice), herself set it upon her own neck. Perchance so great a woman could not else have been slain (being feared of the unclean spirit), had she not herself so willed it.

Perpetua and Felicity are two Saints who have been celebrated in the Roman Catholic church since 203AD, the year of their martyrdom. They are the only African saints in the catholic church, having been from Carthage. A full translation of their Passio was completed by W. H. Shewring and first published in the 7th volume of The Fleuron *in 1930. This printing introduced the new typeface, Perpetua, designed by Eric Gill and cut by the Langston Monotype Corporation.*

Gill's initial letter wood engraving from Luke v. 3-7 of *The Four Gospels*

PERPETUA

Felicity was originally Gill's italic to accompany Perpetua roman and was cut in 1926. It was actually a sloped roman and was later replaced by his Perpetua italic in the more traditional calligraphic style.

Example of Gill's carving on a gravestone of 1924 compared with Adobe's Perpetua font

aAbBcCdDeEfFgGhHiIjJkKlLmMnNoOpPqQrRsStTuUvV

aAbBcCdDeEfFgGhHiIjJkKlLmMnNoOpPqQrRsStTuUvV

Design: **Eve Faulkes**

Specimens are set in
Monotype Perpetua

Perpetua is one of two of the best-known type designs by Eric Gill. Initial sketches of the design were begun in 1925, and it was first published in 1928 in a private printing by Gill of *The Passion of Perpetua and Felicity*. The driving force behind the design was Stanley Morison, typographical advisor to Monotype Corporation. Morison had previously been responsible for reviving several classical typefaces for the company, and was determined to release an original serif typeface by a contemporary designer. Gill was chosen for the task, and the result of his effort was Perpetua. After many delays, Monotype issued the face between 1929 and 1930. The italic version of Perpetua, named Felicity, was one of the first major italics to be based on a sloped roman rather than the traditional cursive form.

An Old Style face having the visual qualities of stone-incised letters, Perpetua has horizontal serifs that are very short and razor sharp, a left-slanting stress, and medium contrast between thick-and-thin strokes within letters. The x-height, which is extremely short, combined with long ascenders and descenders, requires that Perpetua be set with very generous leading for acceptable readability. Particularly notable earmarks are an **E** with a heavy middle bar; an **M** with flaired stems; a **j** with a sharp, hooked tail; and terminals in the letters **c** and **e**, and the numerals **2** and **3** that terminate with a point. The **g** in Perpetua Italic — designed later to replace Felicity — is decidedly calligraphic.

Perpetua has been widely used as a text and titling face for books, and as a display face for various applications when a crisp, noble, and confident typeface is needed.

ABCDEFG

HIJKLMN

OPQRSTU

VWXYZ&

(" " ., ;:)

abcdefghijk
lmnopqrstu
vwxyz$123
4567890!?

abcdefghijklmnopqrstuvwxyz
ABCDEFGHIJKLMNOPQRSTUVWXYZ
$&1234567890(.,"";:!?)

72

abcdefghijklmnopqr
stuvwxyzABCDEF
GHIJKLMNOPQRS
TUVWXYZ$&123
4567890(.,"";:!?)

36

abcdefghijklmnopqrstuvwxyz
ABCDEFGHIJKLMNOPQRSTUVWXY
Z$&1234567890(.,"";:!?)

abcdefghijklmnopqrstuvwxyz
ABCDEFGHIJKLMNOPQRSTUVWXYZ
$&1234567890(.,"";:!?)

18

72

abcdefghijklmnopqrstu
vwxyzABCDEFGHIJ
KLMNOPQRSTUVWX
YZ$&1234567890
(.,"";:!?)

36

abcdefghijklmnopqrstuvwxyz
ABCDEFGHIJKLMNOPQRSTUVWXYZ
$&1234567890(.,"";:!?)

abcdefghijklmnopqrstuvwxyz
ABCDEFGHIJKLMNOPQRSTUVWXYZ
$&1234567890(„""•;:!?)

abcdefghijklmno
pqrstuvwxyzAB
CDEFGHIJKLMN
OPQRSTUVWX
YZ$&1234567890
(„"";:!?)

abcdefghijklmnopqrstuvwxyz
ABCDEFGHIJKLMNOPQRSTUVW
XYZ$&1234567890(„"";:!?)

abcdefghijklmnopqrstuvwxyz
ABCDEFGHIJKLMNOPQRSTUVWXYZ
$&1234567890(.,""";:!?)

18

72

abcdefghijklmnopq
rstuvwxyz*ABCDE*
FGHIJKLMNOPQ
RSTUVWXYZ$&12
34567890(.,"";:!?)

36

abcdefghijklmnopqrstuvwxyz
ABCDEFGHIJKLMNOPQRSTUVWX
YZ$&1234567890(.,""";:!?)

Perpetua Regular

abcdefghijklmnopqrstuvwxyz
ABCDEFGHIJKLMNOPQRSTUVWXYZ
$1234567890&(.,"";:!?)

abcdefghijklmnopqrstuvwxyz
ABCDEFGHIJKLMNOPQRSTUVWXYZ
$1234567890&(.,"";:!?)

Typography, the major communications advance between the invention of writing and the age of electronic mass communications in the twentieth century, *played a pivotal role* in the social, economic, and religious upheavals that occurred during the fifteenth and sixteenth centuries. The modern nation developed as a result of the vigorous spirit of nationalism that swept over Europe and led to the American and French revolutions of the late eighteenth century. In addition to being a powerful vehicle for spreading ideas about human rights and the sovereignty of the people, typographic printing stabilized and unified languages. Illiteracy, the inability to read and write, began a long, steady decline. Typography radically altered education. The medieval classroom had been a scriptorium of sorts, where each student penned his own book. Learning became an increasingly private, rather than communal, process. Human dialog, extended by type, began to take place on a global scale that bridged time and space. Gutenberg's invention was the first mechanization of a skilled handicraft. As such, it set into motion, over the next three hundred years, the mach inations that

Typography, the major communications advance between the invention of writing and the age of electronic mass communications in the twentieth century, *played a pivotal role* in the social, economic, and religious upheavals that occurred during the fifteenth and sixteenth centuries. The modern nation dev eloped as a result of the vigorous spirit of nationalism that swept over Europe and led to the American and French revolutions of the late eighteenth century. In addition to being a powerful vehicle for spreading ideas about human rights and the sovereignty of the people, typographic printing stab ilized and unified languages. Illiteracy, the inability to read and write, began a long, steady decline. Typography radically altered education. The medieval classroom had been a scriptorium of sorts, where each student penned his own book. Learning became an increasingly private, rather than communal, process. Human dialog, extended by type, began to take place on a global

Typography, the major communications advance between the invention of writing and the age of electronic mass communications in the twentieth century, *played a pivotal role* in the social, economic, and religious upheavals that occurred during the fifteenth and sixteenth centuries. The modern nation developed as a result of the vigorous spirit of nationalism that swept over Europe and led to the American and French revolutions of the late eighteenth century. In addition to being a powerful vehicle for spreading ideas about human rights and the sovereignty of the people, typographic printing stabilized and unified languages. Illiteracy, the inability to read and write, began a long, steady decline. Typography radically altered education. The medieval classroom had been a scriptorium of sorts, where each student penned his own book. Learning became an increasingly private, rather than communal, process. Human dialog, extended by type, began to take place on a global scale that bridged time and space. Gutenberg's invention was the first mechanization of a skilled handicraft.

Typography, the major communications advance between the invention of writing and the age of electronic mass communications in the twentieth century, *played a pivotal role* in the social, economic, and religious upheavals that occurred during the fifteenth and sixteenth centuries. The modern nation dev eloped as a result of the vigorous spirit of nationalism that swept over Europe and led to the American and French revolutions of the late eighteenth century. In addition to being a powerful vehicle for spreading ideas about human rights and the sovereignty of the people, typographic printing stab ilized and unified languages. Illiteracy, the inability to read and write, began a long, steady decline. Typography radically altered education. The medieval classroom had been a scriptorium of sorts, where each student penned his own book. Learning became an increasingly private, rather than communal,

Typography, the major communications advance between the invention of writing and the age of electronic mass communications in the twentieth century, *played a pivotal role* in the social, economic, and religious upheavals that occurred during the fifteenth and sixteenth centuries. The modern nation developed as a result of the vigorous spirit of nationalism that swept over Europe and led to the American and French revolutions of the late eighteenth century. In addition to being a powerful vehicle for spreading ideas about human rights and the sovereignty of the people, typographic printing stabilized and unified languages. Illiteracy, the inability to read and write, began a long, steady decline. Typography radically altered education. The medieval classroom had been a scriptorium of sorts, where each student penned his own book. Learning became an increasingly private, rather than communal, process. Human dialog, extended by type, began to take place on a global scale that bridged ti

Typography, the major communications advance between the invention of writing and the age of electronic mass communications in the twentieth cen tury, *played a pivotal role* in the social, economic, and religious upheavals that occurred during the fifteenth and sixteenth centuries. The modern nation dev eloped as a result of the vigorous spirit of nationalism that swept over Europe and led to the American and French revolutions of the late eighteenth century. In addition to being a powerful vehicle for spreading ideas about human rights and the sovereignty of the people, typographic printing stab ilized and unified languages. Illiteracy, the inability to read and write, began a long, steady decline. Typography radically altered education. The medieval classroom had been a scriptorium of sorts, where each student penned his

Typography, the major communications advance between the invention of writing and the age of electronic mass communications in the twentieth century, *played a pivotal role* in the social, economic, and religious upheavals that occurred during the fifteenth and sixteenth centuries. The modern nation developed as a result of the vigorous spirit of nationalism that swept over Europe and led to the American and French revolutions of the late eighteenth century. In addition to being a powerful vehicle for spreading ideas about human rights and the sovereignty of the people, typographic printing stabilized and unified languages. Illiteracy, the inability to read and write, began a long, steady decline. Typography radically altered education. The medieval classroom had been a scriptorium of sorts, where each student penned his own book. Learning became an increasingly private, rather than communal, process.

Typography, the major communications advance between the invention of writing and the age of electronic mass communications in the twentieth cen tury, *played a pivotal role* in the social, economic, and religious upheavals that occurred during the fifteenth and sixteenth centuries. The modern nation dev eloped as a result of the vigorous spirit of nationalism that swept over Europe and led to the American and French revolutions of the late eighteenth century. In addition to being a powerful vehicle for spreading ideas about human rights and the sovereignty of the people, typographic printing stab ilized and unified languages. Illiteracy, the inability to read and write, began a long, steady decline. Typography radically altered education. The medieval

abcdefghijklmnopqrstuvwxyz
ABCDEFGHIJKLMNOPQRSTUVWXYZ
$1234567890&(.,"";:!?)

abcdefghijklmnopqrstuvwxyz
ABCDEFGHIJKLMNOPQRSTUVWXYZ
$1234567890&(.,"";:!?)

10/10

Typography, the major communications advance between the inve ntion of writing and the age of electronic mass communications in the twentieth century, *played a pivotal role* in the social, economic, and re ligious upheavals that occurred during the fifteenth and sixteenth ce nturies. The modern nation developed as a result of the vigorous spir it of nationalism that swept over Europe and led to the American and French revolutions of the late eighteenth century. In addition to being a powerful vehicle for spreading ideas about human rights and the so vereignty of the people, typographic printing stabilized and unified languages. Illiteracy, the inability to read and write, began a long, ste ady decline. Typography radically altered education. The medieval cl assroom had been a scriptorium of sorts, where each student penned

12/12

Typography, the major communications advance betwe en the invention of writing and the age of electronic mass communications in the twentieth century, *played a pivotal role* in the social, economic, and religious upheavals that o ccurred during the fifteenth and sixteenth centuries. The modern nation developed as a result of the vigorous spirit of nationalism that swept over Europe and led to the Ame rican and French revolutions of the late eighteenth cent ury. In addition to being a powerful vehicle for spreading i deas about human rights and the sovereignty of the peop

10/11

Typography, the major communications advance between the inve ntion of writing and the age of electronic mass communications in the twentieth century, *played a pivotal role* in the social, economic, and re ligious upheavals that occurred during the fifteenth and sixteenth ce nturies. The modern nation developed as a result of the vigorous spir it of nationalism that swept over Europe and led to the American and French revolutions of the late eighteenth century. In addition to being a powerful vehicle for spreading ideas about human rights and the so vereignty of the people, typographic printing stabilized and unified languages. Illiteracy, the inability to read and write, began a long, ste ady decline. Typography radically altered education. The medieval cl

12/13

Typography, the major communications advance betwe en the invention of writing and the age of electronic mass communications in the twentieth century, *played a pivotal role* in the social, economic, and religious upheavals that o ccurred during the fifteenth and sixteenth centuries. The modern nation developed as a result of the vigorous spirit of nationalism that swept over Europe and led to the Ame rican and French revolutions of the late eighteenth cent ury. In addition to being a powerful vehicle for spreading i

10/12

Typography, the major communications advance between the inve ntion of writing and the age of electronic mass communications in the twentieth century, *played a pivotal role* in the social, economic, and re ligious upheavals that occurred during the fifteenth and sixteenth ce nturies. The modern nation developed as a result of the vigorous spir it of nationalism that swept over Europe and led to the American and French revolutions of the late eighteenth century. In addition to being a powerful vehicle for spreading ideas about human rights and the so vereignty of the people, typographic printing stabilized and unified languages. Illiteracy, the inability to read and write, began a long, ste

12/14

Typography, the major communications advance betwe en the invention of writing and the age of electronic mass communications in the twentieth century, *played a pivotal role* in the social, economic, and religious upheavals that o ccurred during the fifteenth and sixteenth centuries. The modern nation developed as a result of the vigorous spirit of nationalism that swept over Europe and led to the Ame rican and French revolutions of the late eighteenth cent ury. In addition to being a powerful vehicle for spreading i

10/13

Typography, the major communications advance between the inve ntion of writing and the age of electronic mass communications in the twentieth century, *played a pivotal role* in the social, economic, and re ligious upheavals that occurred during the fifteenth and sixteenth ce nturies. The modern nation developed as a result of the vigorous spir it of nationalism that swept over Europe and led to the American and French revolutions of the late eighteenth century. In addition to being a powerful vehicle for spreading ideas about human rights and the so vereignty of the people, typographic printing stabilized and unified

12/15

Typography, the major communications advance betwe en the invention of writing and the age of electronic mass communications in the twentieth century, *played a pivotal role* in the social, economic, and religious upheavals that o ccurred during the fifteenth and sixteenth centuries. The modern nation developed as a result of the vigorous spirit of nationalism that swept over Europe and led to the Ame rican and French revolutions of the late eighteenth cent

know

the conduct and handLing

of mAtters arising

within [your] life time But

alsO...*understand* things

which aRE past in order to

p a s s t h e m dOwn to those who

should **survive** [you] and

to **portray** them as they arE To [*your*]

*succ*c*essors,* whO by this meaNS

can *See* afTer a

t h o u s AN d years the Things

whIch were done as if they hAd been

present. "

Design: **Banu Berker**

Specimens are set in
Monotype Plantin

In 1913, the Monotype Corporation issued a revival based on Robert Granjon's 16th-century Gros Cicero typeface and named it Plantin. In the text about Garamond on page 209, it was noted that many 20th century Garamond italics are copies of typefaces cut by Granjon. Revivals of Granjon roman fonts are named Plantin after the renowned Antwerp printer Christophe Plantin. Granjon's designs, still used today, are named after a fellow punchcutter and a printer. Ironically, a 1928 Linotype face named Granjon is closely modelled after one of Garamond's fonts.

Monotype Plantin's designer, F.H. Pierpont, deviated from the 16th century prototype to meet the legibility and production needs of early 20th century periodicals. To increase legibility in small text, it was given shorter ascenders and descenders, a larger x-height, and a slightly condensed width. To improve reproduction, thin strokes were thickened to a weight closer to the thick strokes. The **A** has a flat top; the **M** is splayed. The top serifs on lowercase letters such as **b** and **r** have a triangular or wedge-shaped appearance; this is especially pronounced in bold variations. The **a** has a larger bowl than most old style faces; the **j** has but a slight hook, and the **t** is very narrow. The italic capital *J* is cursive.

The value of Pierpont's revisions was affirmed when Monotype Plantin 113 was chosen as the prototype for Times New Roman in the early 1930s. Plantin has been widely used in promotional and advertising text for its distinctive appearance. Plantin Bold, including many variations in weight and width, has been a very popular typeface for advertising headlines.

ABCDEF
GHIJKL
MNOPQR
STUVWX
YZ&(.,""'';:)

abcdefghij
klmnopqr
stuvwxyz
$12345678
90!?

abcdefghijklmnopqrstuvwxyz
ABCDEFGHIJKLMNOPQRSTUV
WXYZ$&1234567890(.,""";:!?)

72

abcdefghijklmno
pqrstuvwxyzABC
DEFGHIJKLM
NOPQRSTUV
WXYZ$&12345
67890(.,"";:!?)

36

abcdefghijklmnopqrstuvwxyz
ABCDEFGHIJKLMNOPQRST
UVWXYZ$&1234567890(.,""";:!?)

abcdefghijklmnopqrstuvwxyz
ABCDEFGHIJKLMNOPQRSTUV
WXYZ$&1234567890(.,""";:!?)

18

72

abcdefghijklmnop
qrstuvwxyzABCD
EFGHIJKLMN
OPQRSTUVWX
YZ$&1234567890
(.,""";:!?)

36

abcdefghijklmnopqrstuvwxyz
ABCDEFGHIJKLMNOPQRSTU
VWXYZ$&1234567890(.,""";:!?)

abcdefghijklmnopqrstuvwxyz
ABCDEFGHIJKLMNOPQRSTU
VWXYZ$&1234567890(.,""";:!?)

72

abcdefghijklmn

opqrstuvwxyzA

BCDEFGHIJK

LMNOPQRST

UVWXYZ$&12

34567890(.,""";:!?)

36

abcdefghijklmnopqrstuvwxyz
ABCDEFGHIJKLMNOPQRST
UVWXYZ$&1234567890(.,""";:!?)

abcdefghijklmnopqrstuvwxyz
ABCDEFGHIJKLMNOPQRSTUV
WXYZ$&1234567890(.,"";:!?)

18

72

abcdefghijklmn

opqrstuvwxyz

ABCDEFGHIJK

LMNOPQRST

UVWXYZ$&123

4567890(.,"";:!?)

36

abcdefghijklmnopqrstuvwxyz
ABCDEFGHIJKLMNOPQRST
UVWXYZ$&1234567890(.,"";:!?)

Plantin

abcdefghijklmnopqrstuvwxyz
ABCDEFGHIJKLMNOPQRSTUVWXYZ
$1234567890&(.,"";:!?)

abcdefghijklmnopqrstuvwxyz
ABCDEFGHIJKLMNOPQRSTUVWXYZ
$1234567890&(.,"";:!?)

8/8

Typography, the major communications advance between the inven tion of writing and the age of electronic mass communications in the tw entieth century, *played a pivotal role* in the social, economic, and relig ious upheavals that occurred during the fifteenth and sixteenth centu ries. The modern nation developed as a result of the vigorous spirit of nationalism that swept over Europe and led to the American and French revolutions of the late eighteenth century. In addition to being a pow erful vehicle for spreading ideas about human rights and the sovereign ty of the people, typographic printing stabilized and unified languages. Il literacy, the inability to read and write, began a long, steady decline. Ty pography radically altered education. The medieval classroom had been a scriptorium of sorts, where each student penned his own book. Learning became an increasingly private, rather than communal, process. Human dialog, extended by type, began to take place on a global scale that brid ged time and space. Gutenberg's invention was the first mechanization of

---

9/9

Typography, the major communications advance between the in vention of writing and the age of electronic mass communications in the twentieth century, *played a pivotal role* in the social, econo mic, and religious upheavals that occurred during the fifteenth and sixteenth centuries. The modern nation developed as a result of the vigorous spirit of nationalism that swept over Europe and led to the American and French revolutions of the late eighteenth century. In addition to being a powerful vehicle for spreading ideas about hum an rights and the sovereignty of the people, typographic printing sta bilized and unified languages. Illiteracy, the inability to read and write, began a long, steady decline. Typography radically altered edu cation. The medieval classroom had been a scriptorium of sorts, whe re each student penned his own book. Learning became an increa

---

8/9

Typography, the major communications advance between the inven tion of writing and the age of electronic mass communications in the tw entieth century, *played a pivotal role* in the social, economic, and relig ious upheavals that occurred during the fifteenth and sixteenth centu ries. The modern nation developed as a result of the vigorous spirit of nationalism that swept over Europe and led to the American and French revolutions of the late eighteenth century. In addition to being a pow erful vehicle for spreading ideas about human rights and the sovereign ty of the people, typographic printing stabilized and unified languages. Il literacy, the inability to read and write, began a long, steady decline. Ty pography radically altered education. The medieval classroom had been a scriptorium of sorts, where each student penned his own book. Learning became an increasingly private, rather than communal, process. Human

---

9/10

Typography, the major communications advance between the in vention of writing and the age of electronic mass communications in the twentieth century, *played a pivotal role* in the social, econo mic, and religious upheavals that occurred during the fifteenth and sixteenth centuries. The modern nation developed as a result of the vigorous spirit of nationalism that swept over Europe and led to the American and French revolutions of the late eighteenth century. In addition to being a powerful vehicle for spreading ideas about hum an rights and the sovereignty of the people, typographic printing sta bilized and unified languages. Illiteracy, the inability to read and write, began a long, steady decline. Typography radically altered edu cation. The medieval classroom had been a scriptorium of sorts, whe

---

8/10

Typography, the major communications advance between the inven tion of writing and the age of electronic mass communications in the tw entieth century, *played a pivotal role* in the social, economic, and relig ious upheavals that occurred during the fifteenth and sixteenth centu ries. The modern nation developed as a result of the vigorous spirit of nationalism that swept over Europe and led to the American and French revolutions of the late eighteenth century. In addition to being a pow erful vehicle for spreading ideas about human rights and the sovereign ty of the people, typographic printing stabilized and unified languages. Il literacy, the inability to read and write, began a long, steady decline. Ty pography radically altered education. The medieval classroom had been a scriptorium of sorts, where each student penned his own book. Learning

---

9/11

Typography, the major communications advance between the in vention of writing and the age of electronic mass communications in the twentieth century, *played a pivotal role* in the social, econo mic, and religious upheavals that occurred during the fifteenth and sixteenth centuries. The modern nation developed as a result of the vigorous spirit of nationalism that swept over Europe and led to the American and French revolutions of the late eighteenth century. In addition to being a powerful vehicle for spreading ideas about hum an rights and the sovereignty of the people, typographic printing sta bilized and unified languages. Illiteracy, the inability to read and write, began a long, steady decline. Typography radically altered edu

---

8/11

Typography, the major communications advance between the inven tion of writing and the age of electronic mass communications in the tw entieth century, *played a pivotal role* in the social, economic, and relig ious upheavals that occurred during the fifteenth and sixteenth centu ries. The modern nation developed as a result of the vigorous spirit of nationalism that swept over Europe and led to the American and French revolutions of the late eighteenth century. In addition to being a pow erful vehicle for spreading ideas about human rights and the sovereign ty of the people, typographic printing stabilized and unified languages. Il literacy, the inability to read and write, began a long, steady decline. Ty pography radically altered education. The medieval classroom had been a

---

9/12

Typography, the major communications advance between the in vention of writing and the age of electronic mass communications in the twentieth century, *played a pivotal role* in the social, econo mic, and religious upheavals that occurred during the fifteenth and sixteenth centuries. The modern nation developed as a result of the vigorous spirit of nationalism that swept over Europe and led to the American and French revolutions of the late eighteenth century. In addition to being a powerful vehicle for spreading ideas about human rights and the sovereignty of the people, typographic printing stabilized and unified languages. Illiteracy, the inability to

abcdefghijklmnopqrstuvwxyz
ABCDEFGHIJKLMNOPQRSTUVWXYZ
$1234567890&(.,"";:!?)

abcdefghijklmnopqrstuvwxyz
ABCDEFGHIJKLMNOPQRSTUVWXYZ
$1234567890&(.,"";:!?)

10/10

Typography, the major communications advance between the invention of writing and the age of electronic mass com munications in the twentieth century, *played a pivotal role* in the social, economic, and religious upheavals that occurred during the fifteenth and sixteenth centuries. The modern na tion developed as a result of the vigorous spirit of nation alism that swept over Europe and led to the American and French revolutions of the late eighteenth century. In add ition to being a powerful vehicle for spreading ideas about hum an rights and the sovereignty of the people, typogra phic printing stabilized and unified languages. Illiteracy, the inability to read and write, began a long, steady decline. Typ

12/12

Typography, the major communications advance between the invention of writing and the age of ele ctronic mass communications in the twentieth cen tury, *played a pivotal role* in the social, economic, and religious upheavals that occurred during the fif teenth and sixteenth centuries. The modern nation developed as a result of the vigorous spirit of nat ionalism that swept over Europe and led to the Ame rican and French revolutions of the late eighteenth century. In addition to being a powerful vehicle for

10/11

Typography, the major communications advance between the invention of writing and the age of electronic mass com munications in the twentieth century, *played a pivotal role* in the social, economic, and religious upheavals that occurred during the fifteenth and sixteenth centuries. The modern na tion developed as a result of the vigorous spirit of nation alism that swept over Europe and led to the American and French revolutions of the late eighteenth century. In add ition to being a powerful vehicle for spreading ideas about hum an rights and the sovereignty of the people, typogra phic printing stabilized and unified languages. Illiteracy, the

12/13

Typography, the major communications advance between the invention of writing and the age of ele ctronic mass communications in the twentieth cen tury, *played a pivotal role* in the social, economic, and religious upheavals that occurred during the fif teenth and sixteenth centuries. The modern nat ion developed as a result of the vigorous spirit of nat ionalism that swept over Europe and led to the Ame rican and French revolutions of the late eighteenth

10/12

Typography, the major communications advance between the invention of writing and the age of electronic mass com munications in the twentieth century, *played a pivotal role* in the social, economic, and religious upheavals that occurred during the fifteenth and sixteenth centuries. The modern na tion developed as a result of the vigorous spirit of nation alism that swept over Europe and led to the American and French revolutions of the late eighteenth century. In add ition to being a powerful vehicle for spreading ideas about

12/14

Typography, the major communications advance between the invention of writing and the age of ele ctronic mass communications in the twentieth cen tury, *played a pivotal role* in the social, economic, and religious upheavals that occurred during the fif teenth and sixteenth centuries. The modern nat ion developed as a result of the vigorous spirit of nat ionalism that swept over Europe and led to the Ame

10/13

Typography, the major communications advance between the invention of writing and the age of electronic mass com munications in the twentieth century, *played a pivotal role* in the social, economic, and religious upheavals that occurred during the fifteenth and sixteenth centuries. The modern na tion developed as a result of the vigorous spirit of nation alism that swept over Europe and led to the American and French revolutions of the late eighteenth century. In add ition to being a powerful vehicle for spreading ideas about

12/15

Typography, the major communications advance between the invention of writing and the age of ele ctronic mass communications in the twentieth cen tury, *played a pivotal role* in the social, economic, and religious upheavals that occurred during the fif teenth and sixteenth centuries. The modern nation developed as a result of the vigorous spirit of nat ionalism that swept over Europe and led to the Ame

S

Tschichold

1 9 6 7

— 1641 —

MEDITATIONS

RENÉ DESCARTES

MEDITATION I.

*Of the things which may be brought within
the sphere of the doubtful.*

It is now some years since I detected how many were the false beliefs that I had from my earliest youth admitted as true, and how doubtful was everything I had since constructed on this basis; and from that time I was convinced that I must once for all seriously undertake to rid myself of all the opinions which I had formerly accepted, and commence to build anew from the foundation, if I wanted to establish any firm and permanent structure in the sciences. But as this enterprise appeared to be a very great one, I waited until I had attained an age so mature that I could not hope that at any later date I should be better fitted to execute my design. This reason caused me to delay so long that I should feel that I was doing wrong were I to occupy in deliberation the time that yet remains to me for action. To-day, then, since very opportunely for the plan I have in view I have delivered my mind from every care [and am happily agitated by no passions] and since I have procured for myself an assured leisure in a peaceable retirement, I shall at last seriously and freely address myself to the general upheaval of all my former opinions.

Now for this object it is not necessary that I should show that all of these are false — I shall perhaps never arrive at this end. But inasmuch as reason already persuades me that I ought no less carefully to withhold my assent from matters which are not entirely certain and indubitable than from those which appear

6

All

typography

implies

T R A D I T I O N

& ———.

conventions.

Design: **Stephen Chovanec**

Specimens are set in
Linotype Sabon

In 1960, a committee of German master printers asked the type industry to develop a new Old Style typeface based on Garamond. They needed fonts that would be identical in appearance on the page whether hand-set, Linotype, or Monotype composition was used. The Stempel type foundry joined Linotype and Monotype in accepting the challenge. Jan Tschichold, who played a major role in defining 1920s modern typography before turning to the humanist book design tradition, was commissioned to design the new fonts. Tschichold selected a fourteen point roman – named Saint Augustine and attributed to Garamond on a 1592 specimen sheet from the Egenolff-Berner foundry – as his model. He selected an italic attributed to Robert Granjon on the same specimen sheet. To avoid confusion with other Garamond fonts, the new typeface was named Sabon after the 16th century punchcutter, Jacque Sabon.

Tschichold was asked to condense the set width by five percent compared to other Garamond revivals and meet the technical requirements of three technologies. The most difficult restriction was the Linotype machine's lack of kerning. Sabon's f has a short hook on its ascender, since it cannot overhang other characters. Linotype typesetters require the same set width for the two fonts whose matrices are in the typesetting machine at the same time; thus Sabon's italic has the same set width as the roman. More traditional Garamond italics have a considerably shorter set width.

Sabon's design excellence enabled it to become one of Europe's leading text faces. Limited availability in the United States restricted its use until recent years, when Sabon has become more widely available.

ABCDEF
GHIJKLM
NOPQRS
TUVWX
YZ&-(„ "" ;:)

abcdefghij
klmnopqrs
tuvwxyz
$1234567 8
90!?

abcdefghijklmnopqrstuvwxyz
ABCDEFGHIJKLMNOPQRSTU
VWXYZ$&1234567890(.,""::!?)

abcdefghijklmnop
qrstuvwxyzABC
DEFGHIJKLMN
OPQRSTUVWX
YZ$&123456789
0(.,"";:!?)

abcdefghijklmnopqrstuvwxyz
ABCDEFGHIJKLMNOPQRSTU
VWXYZ$&1234567890(.,"";:!?)

abcdefghijklmnopqrstuvwxyz
ABCDEFGHIJKLMNOPQRSTU
VWXYZ$&1234567890(.,""";:!?)

18

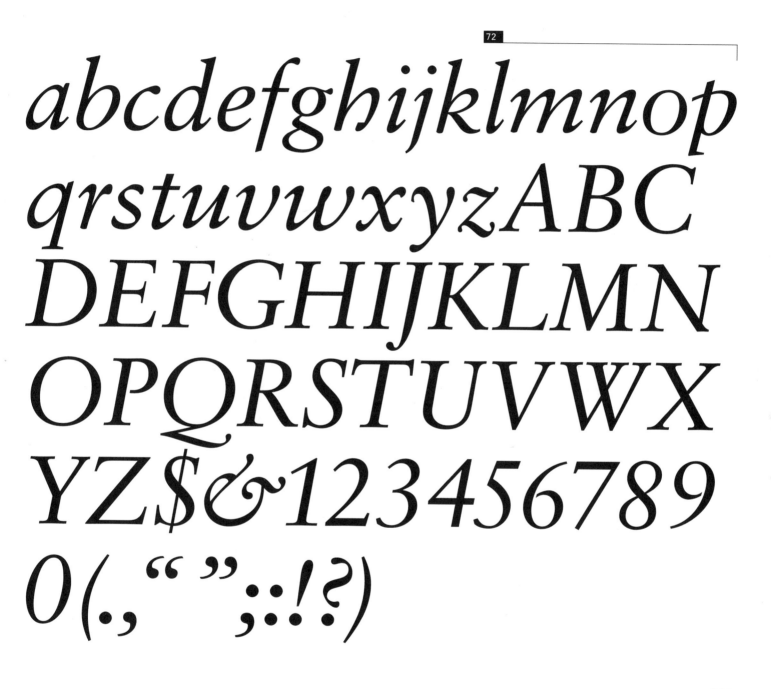

72

36

abcdefghijklmnopqrstuvwxyz
ABCDEFGHIJKLMNOPQRSTU
VWXYZ$&1234567890(.,""";:!?)

abcdefghijklmnopqrstuvwxyz
ABCDEFGHIJKLMNOPQRSTU
VWXYZ$&1234567890(.,"";:!?)

abcdefghijklmno
pqrstuvwxyzAB
CDEFGHIJKLM
NOPQRSTUVW
XYZ$&1234567
890(.,"";:!?)

abcdefghijklmnopqrstuvwxyz
ABCDEFGHIJKLMNOPQRSTU
VWXYZ$&1234567890(.,"";:!?)

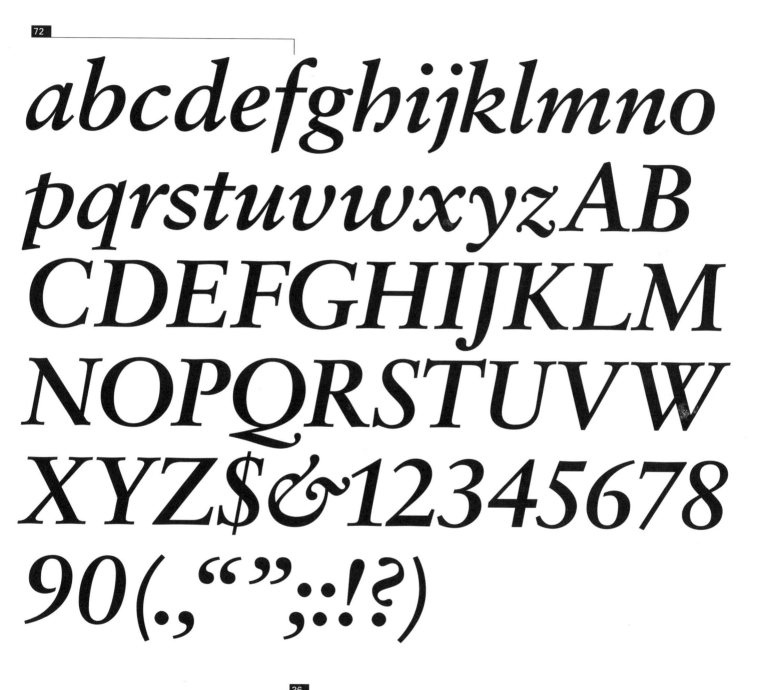

72

abcdefghijklmno
pqrstuvwxyzAB
CDEFGHIJKLM
NOPQRSTUVW
XYZ$&12345678
90(.,"";:!?)

36

abcdefghijklmnopqrstuvwxyz
ABCDEFGHIJKLMNOPQRSTU
VWXYZ$&1234567890(.,""";:!?)

Sabon

abcdefghijklmnopqrstuvwxyz
ABCDEFGHIJKLMNOPQRSTUVWXYZ
$1234567890&(.,"";:!?)

abcdefghijklmnopqrstuvwxyz
ABCDEFGHIJKLMNOPQRSTUVWXYZ
$1234567890&(.,"";:!?)

8/8

Typography, the major communications advance between the invention of writing and the age of electronic mass communications in the twentieth century, *played a pivotal role* in the social, economic, and religious upheavals that occurred during the fifteenth and sixteenth centuries. The modern nation developed as a result of the vigorous spirit of nationalism that swept over Europe and led to the American and French revolutions of the late eighteenth century. In addition to being a powerful vehicle for spreading ideas about human rights and the sover eignty of the people, typographic printing stabilized and unified languages. Illiteracy, the inability to read and write, began a long, steady decline. Typography rad ically altered education. The medieval classroom had been a scriptorium of sorts, where each student penned his own book. Learning became an increasingly private, rather than communal, process. Human dialog, extended by type, began to take place on a global scale that bridged time

9/9

Typography, the major communications advance between the inven tion of writing and the age of electronic mass communications in the twentieth century, *played a pivotal role* in the social, economic, and re ligious upheavals that occurred during the fifteenth and sixteenth cen turies. The modern nation developed as a result of the vigorous spirit of nationalism that swept over Europe and led to the American and French revolutions of the late eighteenth century. In addition to being a powerful vehicle for spreading ideas about human rights and the so vereignty of the people, typographic printing stabilized and unified languages. Illiteracy, the inability to read and write, began a long, ste ady decline. Typography radically altered education. The medieval cla ssroom had been a scriptorium of sorts, where each student penned his own book. Learning became an increasingly private, rather than communal,

8/9

Typography, the major communications advance between the invention of writing and the age of electronic mass communications in the twen tieth century, *played a pivotal role* in the social, economic, and religious upheavals that occurred during the fifteenth and sixteenth centuries. The modern nation developed as a result of the vigorous spirit of nationalism that swept over Europe and led to the American and French revolutions of the late eighteenth century. In addition to being a powerful vehicle for spreading ideas about human rights and the sover eignty of the people, typographic printing stabilized and unified languages. Illiteracy, the inability to read and write, began a long, steady decline. Typography rad ically altered education. The medieval classroom had been a scriptorium of sorts, where each student penned his own book. Learning became an increasingly private, rather than communal, process. Human dialog,

9/10

Typography, the major communications advance between the inven tion of writing and the age of electronic mass communications in the twentieth century, *played a pivotal role* in the social, economic, and re ligious upheavals that occurred during the fifteenth and sixteenth cen turies. The modern nation developed as a result of the vigorous spirit of nationalism that swept over Europe and led to the American and French revolutions of the late eighteenth century. In addition to being a powerful vehicle for spreading ideas about human rights and the so vereignty of the people, typographic printing stabilized and unified languages. Illiteracy, the inability to read and write, began a long, ste ady decline. Typography radically altered education. The medieval cla ssroom had been a scriptorium of sorts, where each student penned his own

8/10

Typography, the major communications advance between the invention of writing and the age of electronic mass communications in the twen tieth century, *played a pivotal role* in the social, economic, and religious upheavals that occurred during the fifteenth and sixteenth centuries. The modern nation developed as a result of the vigorous spirit of nationalism that swept over Europe and led to the American and French revolutions of the late eighteenth century. In addition to being a powerful vehicle for spreading ideas about human rights and the sover eignty of the people, typographic printing stabilized and unified languages. Illiteracy, the inability to read and write, began a long, steady decline. Typography rad ically altered education. The medieval classroom had been a scriptorium of sorts, where each student penned his own book. Learning became an

9/11

Typography, the major communications advance between the inven tion of writing and the age of electronic mass communications in the twentieth century, *played a pivotal role* in the social, economic, and re ligious upheavals that occurred during the fifteenth and sixteenth cen turies. The modern nation developed as a result of the vigorous spirit of nationalism that swept over Europe and led to the American and French revolutions of the late eighteenth century. In addition to being a powerful vehicle for spreading ideas about human rights and the so vereignty of the people, typographic printing stabilized and unified languages. Illiteracy, the inability to read and write, began a long, ste ady decline. Typography radically altered education. The medieval cla

8/11

Typography, the major communications advance between the invention of writing and the age of electronic mass communications in the twen tieth century, *played a pivotal role* in the social, economic, and religious upheavals that occurred during the fifteenth and sixteenth centuries. The modern nation developed as a result of the vigorous spirit of nationalism that swept over Europe and led to the American and French revolutions of the late eighteenth century. In addition to being a powerful vehicle for spreading ideas about human rights and the sover eignty of the people, typographic printing stabilized and unified languages. Illiteracy, the inability to read and write, began a long, steady decline. Typography rad ically altered education. The medieval classroom had been a scriptorium

9/12

Typography, the major communications advance between the inven tion of writing and the age of electronic mass communications in the twentieth century, *played a pivotal role* in the social, economic, and re ligious upheavals that occurred during the fifteenth and sixteenth cen turies. The modern nation developed as a result of the vigorous spirit of nationalism that swept over Europe and led to the American and French revolutions of the late eighteenth century. In addition to being a powerful vehicle for spreading ideas about human rights and the so vereignty of the people, typographic printing stabilized and unified languages. Illiteracy, the inability to read and write, began a long, ste

abcdefghijklmnopqrstuvwxyz
ABCDEFGHIJKLMNOPQRSTUVWXYZ
$1234567890&(.,""";:!?)

abcdefghijklmnopqrstuvwxyz
ABCDEFGHIJKLMNOPQRSTUVWXYZ
$1234567890&(.,""";:!?)

10/10

Typography, the major communications advance between the invention of writing and the age of electronic mass com munications in the twentieth century, *played a pivotal role* in the social, economic, and religious upheavals that occur red during the fifteenth and sixteenth centuries. The modern nation developed as a result of the vigorous spirit of nation alism that swept over Europe and led to the American and French revolutions of the late eighteenth century. In addi tion to being a powerful vehicle for spreading ideas about human rights and the sovereignty of the people, typographic printing stabilized and unified languages. Illiteracy, the

12/12

Typography, the major communications advance be tween the invention of writing and the age of electro nic mass communications in the twentieth century, *played a pivotal role* in the social, economic, and reli gious upheavals that occurred during the fifteenth and sixteenth centuries. The modern nation develop ed as a result of the vigorous spirit of nationalism that swept over Europe and led to the American and Fre nch revolutions of the late eighteenth century. In

10/11

Typography, the major communications advance between the invention of writing and the age of electronic mass com munications in the twentieth century, *played a pivotal role* in the social, economic, and religious upheavals that occur red during the fifteenth and sixteenth centuries. The modern nation developed as a result of the vigorous spirit of nation alism that swept over Europe and led to the American and French revolutions of the late eighteenth century. In addi tion to being a powerful vehicle for spreading ideas about human rights and the sovereignty of the people, typographic

12/13

Typography, the major communications advance be tween the invention of writing and the age of electro nic mass communications in the twentieth century, *played a pivotal role* in the social, economic, and reli gious upheavals that occurred during the fifteenth and sixteenth centuries. The modern nation develop ed as a result of the vigorous spirit of nationalism that swept over Europe and led to the American and Fre nch revolutions of the late eighteenth century. In

10/12

Typography, the major communications advance between the invention of writing and the age of electronic mass com munications in the twentieth century, *played a pivotal role* in the social, economic, and religious upheavals that occur red during the fifteenth and sixteenth centuries. The modern nation developed as a result of the vigorous spirit of nation alism that swept over Europe and led to the American and French revolutions of the late eighteenth century. In addi tion to being a powerful vehicle for spreading ideas about

12/14

Typography, the major communications advance be tween the invention of writing and the age of electro nic mass communications in the twentieth century, *played a pivotal role* in the social, economic, and reli gious upheavals that occurred during the fifteenth and sixteenth centuries. The modern nation develop ed as a result of the vigorous spirit of nationalism that swept over Europe and led to the American and Fre

10/13

Typography, the major communications advance between the invention of writing and the age of electronic mass com munications in the twentieth century, *played a pivotal role* in the social, economic, and religious upheavals that occur red during the fifteenth and sixteenth centuries. The modern nation developed as a result of the vigorous spirit of nation alism that swept over Europe and led to the American and French revolutions of the late eighteenth century. In addi tion to being a powerful vehicle for spreading ideas about

12/15

Typography, the major communications advance be tween the invention of writing and the age of electro nic mass communications in the twentieth century, *played a pivotal role* in the social, economic, and reli gious upheavals that occurred during the fifteenth and sixteenth centuries. The modern nation develop ed as a result of the vigorous spirit of nationalism that swept over Europe and led to the American and Fre

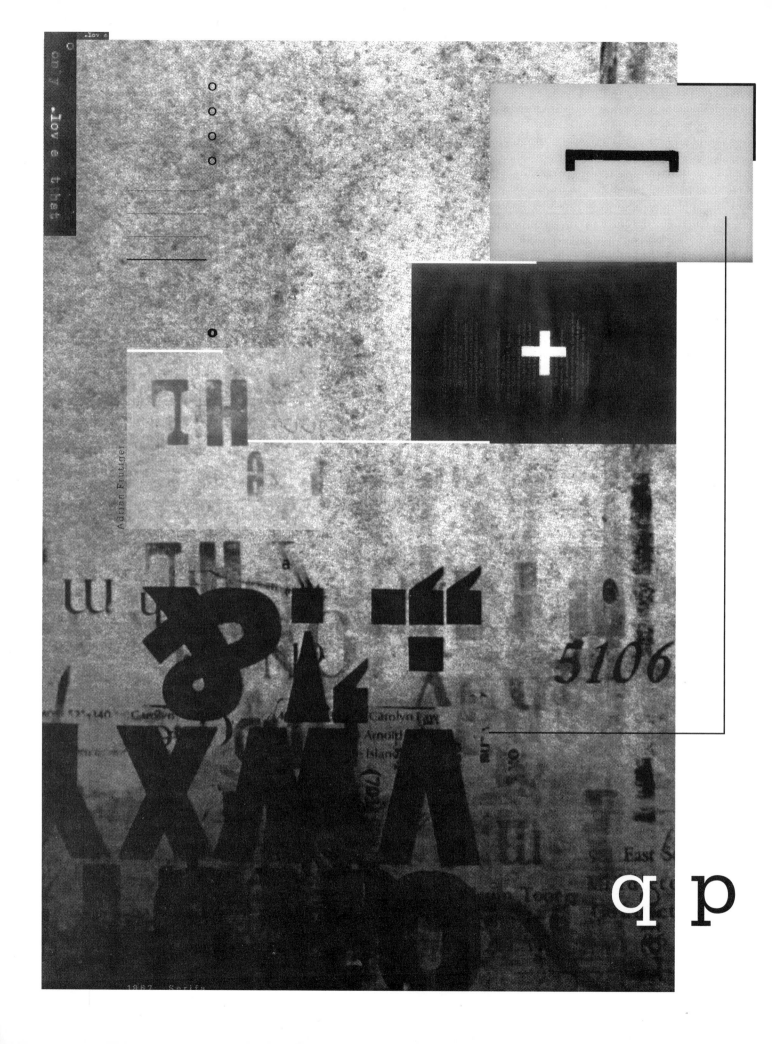

Design: **Katie Salen**

The Swiss type designer Adrian Frutiger has described Serifa as Univers with serifs. It was designed for the Bauer Foundry in 1967. Unlike Univers, however, Frutiger did not use a numerical coding system to distinguish one variant of the type family from another; instead he used traditional terminology. The Serifa family consists of the following variations: thin, thin italic, light, light italic, medium, medium italic, bold, black, and bold condensed.

A comparison of Serifa and Univers reveals striking similarities in form and structure. However, a fundamental difference lies in the width of the letters; Serifa's letters are more extended and open than those of Univers. Some Serifa letters differ from corresponding Univers letters to more effectively accommodate serifs. For example, the Serifa lowercase **k** has a stepped joint which enables the foot serifs to appear optically correct. Serifa's slab serifs are the same width as the main strokes of the letters; the face has an extra tall x-height, and a vertical stress. The **C** does not have a bottom serif; a spur is attached to the **G**; the tail of the **Q** extends horizontally along the baseline; and the **W** does not have a middle serif. Serifa italic is a slanted roman face.

Specimens are set in
Bauer Serifa

Serifa has all of the optical characteristics that make Univers readable as a sans-serif face, but the addition of serifs further enhances this quality. It is used as a text and display face for wide-ranging applications, and since its release, has become available from several manufacturers, including Adobe, Berthold, Bitstream, Compugraphic, and Linotype.

ABCDEF
GHIJKLM
NOPQRS
TUVWXY
Z&₰(.,""";.)

abcdefgh
ijklmnopq
rstuvwxy
z$123456
7890!?

abcdefghijklmnopqrstuvwxyz
ABCDEFGHIJKLMNOPQRSTUVWXYZ
$&1234567890(.,"";:!?)

72

abcdefghijklmn
opqrstuvwxyz
ABCDEFGHIJK
LMNOPQRSTU
VWXYZ$&1234
567890(.,"";:!?)

36

abcdefghijklmnopqrstuvwxyz
ABCDEFGHIJKLMNOPQRSTU
VWXYZ$&1234567890(.,"";:!?)

abcdefghijklmnopqrstuvwxyz
ABCDEFGHIJKLMNOPQRSTUVWXYZ
$&1234567890(.,""::!?)

18

72

abcdefghijklmn
opqrstuvwxyz
ABCDEFGHIJK
LMNOPQRSTU
VWXYZ$&1234
567890(.,"";:!?)

36

abcdefghijklmnopqrstuvwxyz
ABCDEFGHIJKLMNOPQRSTU
VWXYZ$&1234567890(.,"";:!?)

abcdefghijklmnopqrstuvwxyz
ABCDEFGHIJKLMNOPQRSTUVWXYZ
$&1234567890(.,"'"';:!?)

abcdefghijklmn
opqrstuvwxyz
ABCDEFGHIJK
LMNOPQRSTU
VWXYZ$&1234
567890(.,"'"';:!?)

abcdefghijklmnopqrstuvwxyz
ABCDEFGHIJKLMNOPQRSTUVW
XYZ$&1234567890(.,"'"';:!?)

abcdefghijklmnopqrstuvwxyz
ABCDEFGHIJKLMNOPQRSTUVWXYZ
$&1234567890(.,"";:!?)

18

70

abcdefghijklm
nopqrstuvwxy
zABCDEFGHIJ
KLMNOPQRST
UVWXYZ$&123
4567890(.,"";:!?)

32

abcdefghijklmnopqrstuvwxyz
ABCDEFGHIJKLMNOPQRSTUVW
XYZ$&1234567890(.,"";:!?)

Serifa Roman

abcdefghijklmnopqrstuvwxyz
ABCDEFGHIJKLMNOPQRSTUVWXYZ
$1234567890&(.,"";:!?)

abcdefghijklmnopqrstuvwxyz
ABCDEFGHIJKLMNOPQRSTUVWXYZ
$1234567890&(.,"";:!?)

8/8

Typography, the major communications advance between the i nvention of writing and the age of electronic mass communica tions in the twentieth century, *played a pivotal role* in the social, economic, and religious upheavals that occurred during the fifteenth and sixteenth centuries. The modern nation developed as a result of the vigorous spirit of nationalism that swept over Europe and led to the American and French revolutions of the late eighteenth century. In addition to being a powerful vehicle for spreading ideas about human rights and the sovereignty of the p eople, typographic printing stabilized and unified languages. Il literacy, the inability to read and write, began a long, steady dec line. Typography radically altered education. The medieval classr oom had been a scriptorium of sorts, where each student penned his own book. Learning became an increasingly private, rather th an communal, process. Human dialog, extended by type, began to

9/9

Typography, the major communications advance between the invention of writing and the age of electronic mass communications in the twentieth century, *played a pivotal role* in the social, economic, and religious upheavals that occurred during the fifteenth and sixteenth centuries. The modern nation developed as a result of the vigorous spirit of nationalism that swept over Europe and led to the Am erican and French revolutions of the late eighteenth centu ry. In addition to being a powerful vehicle for spreading ideas about human rights and the sovereignty of the peo ple, typographic printing stabilized and unified languages. Illiteracy, the inability to read and write, began a long, st eady decline. Typography radically altered education. The

8/9

Typography, the major communications advance between the i nvention of writing and the age of electronic mass communica tions in the twentieth century, *played a pivotal role* in the social, economic, and religious upheavals that occurred during the fifteenth and sixteenth centuries. The modern nation developed as a result of the vigorous spirit of nationalism that swept over Europe and led to the American and French revolutions of the late eighteenth century. In addition to being a powerful vehicle for spreading ideas about human rights and the sovereignty of the p eople, typographic printing stabilized and unified languages. Il literacy, the inability to read and write, began a long, steady dec line. Typography radically altered education. The medieval classr oom had been a scriptorium of sorts, where each student penned

9/10

Typography, the major communications advance between the invention of writing and the age of electronic mass communications in the twentieth century, *played a pivotal role* in the social, economic, and religious upheavals that occurred during the fifteenth and sixteenth centuries. The modern nation developed as a result of the vigorous spirit of nationalism that swept over Europe and led to the Am erican and French revolutions of the late eighteenth centu ry. In addition to being a powerful vehicle for spreading ideas about human rights and the sovereignty of the peo ple, typographic printing stabilized and unified languages. Illiteracy, the inability to read and write, began a long, st

8/10

Typography, the major communications advance between the i nvention of writing and the age of electronic mass communica tions in the twentieth century, *played a pivotal role* in the social, economic, and religious upheavals that occurred during the fifteenth and sixteenth centuries. The modern nation developed as a result of the vigorous spirit of nationalism that swept over Europe and led to the American and French revolutions of the late eighteenth century. In addition to being a powerful vehicle for spreading ideas about human rights and the sovereignty of the p eople, typographic printing stabilized and unified languages. Il literacy, the inability to read and write, began a long, steady dec line. Typography radically altered education. The medieval classr

9/11

Typography, the major communications advance between the invention of writing and the age of electronic mass communications in the twentieth century, *played a pivotal role* in the social, economic, and religious upheavals that occurred during the fifteenth and sixteenth centuries. The modern nation developed as a result of the vigorous spirit of nationalism that swept over Europe and led to the Am erican and French revolutions of the late eighteenth centu ry. In addition to being a powerful vehicle for spreading ideas about human rights and the sovereignty of the peo ple, typographic printing stabilized and unified languages.

8/11

Typography, the major communications advance between the i nvention of writing and the age of electronic mass communica tions in the twentieth century, *played a pivotal role* in the social, economic, and religious upheavals that occurred during the fifteenth and sixteenth centuries. The modern nation developed as a result of the vigorous spirit of nationalism that swept over Europe and led to the American and French revolutions of the late eighteenth century. In addition to being a powerful vehicle for spreading ideas about human rights and the sovereignty of the p eople, typographic printing stabilized and unified languages. Il literacy, the inability to read and write, began a long, steady dec

9/12

Typography, the major communications advance between the invention of writing and the age of electronic mass communications in the twentieth century, *played a pivotal role* in the social, economic, and religious upheavals that occurred during the fifteenth and sixteenth centuries. The modern nation developed as a result of the vigorous spirit of nationalism that swept over Europe and led to the Am erican and French revolutions of the late eighteenth centu ry. In addition to being a powerful vehicle for spreading ideas about human rights and the sovereignty of the peo

abcdefghijklmnopqrstuvwxyz
ABCDEFGHIJKLMNOPQRSTUVWXYZ
$1234567890&(.,“”;:!?)

abcdefghijklmnopqrstuvwxyz
ABCDEFGHIJKLMNOPQRSTUVWXYZ
$1234567890&(.,“”;:!?)

10/10

Typography, the major communications advance be
tween the invention of writing and the age of elec
tronic mass communications in the twentieth centur
y, *played a pivotal role* in the social, economic, and re
ligious upheavals that occurred during the fifteenth
and sixteenth centuries. The modern nation develop
ed as a result of the vigorous spirit of nationalism th
at swept over Europe and led to the American and Fr
ench revolutions of the late eighteenth century. In ad
dition to being a powerful vehicle for spreading ideas
about human rights and the sovereignty of the peop
le, typographic printing stabilized and unified lan

12/12

Typography, the major communications ad
vance between the invention of writing an
d the age of electronic mass communicatio
ns in the twentieth century, *played a pivotal
role* in the social, economic, and religious up
heavals that occurred during the fifteenth a
nd sixteenth centuries. The modern nation
developed as a result of the vigorous spirit o
f nationalism that swept over Europe and le
d to the American and French revolutions of

10/11

Typography, the major communications advance be
tween the invention of writing and the age of elec
tronic mass communications in the twentieth centur
y, *played a pivotal role* in the social, economic, and re
ligious upheavals that occurred during the fifteenth
and sixteenth centuries. The modern nation develop
ed as a result of the vigorous spirit of nationalism th
at swept over Europe and led to the American and Fr
ench revolutions of the late eighteenth century. In ad
dition to being a powerful vehicle for spreading ideas
about human rights and the sovereignty of the peop

12/13

Typography, the major communications ad
vance between the invention of writing an
d the age of electronic mass communicatio
ns in the twentieth century, *played a pivotal
role* in the social, economic, and religious up
heavals that occurred during the fifteenth a
nd sixteenth centuries. The modern nation
developed as a result of the vigorous spirit o
f nationalism that swept over Europe and le

10/12

Typography, the major communications advance be
tween the invention of writing and the age of elec
tronic mass communications in the twentieth centur
y, *played a pivotal role* in the social, economic, and re
ligious upheavals that occurred during the fifteenth
and sixteenth centuries. The modern nation develop
ed as a result of the vigorous spirit of nationalism th
at swept over Europe and led to the American and Fr
ench revolutions of the late eighteenth century. In ad
dition to being a powerful vehicle for spreading ideas

12/14

Typography, the major communications ad
vance between the invention of writing an
d the age of electronic mass communicatio
ns in the twentieth century, *played a pivotal
role* in the social, economic, and religious up
heavals that occurred during the fifteenth a
nd sixteenth centuries. The modern nation
developed as a result of the vigorous spirit o
f nationalism that swept over Europe and le

10/13

Typography, the major communications advance be
tween the invention of writing and the age of elec
tronic mass communications in the twentieth centur
y, *played a pivotal role* in the social, economic, and re
ligious upheavals that occurred during the fifteenth
and sixteenth centuries. The modern nation develop
ed as a result of the vigorous spirit of nationalism th
at swept over Europe and led to the American and Fr
ench revolutions of the late eighteenth century. In ad

12/15

Typography, the major communications ad
vance between the invention of writing an
d the age of electronic mass communicatio
ns in the twentieth century, *played a pivotal
role* in the social, economic, and religious up
heavals that occurred during the fifteenth a
nd sixteenth centuries. The modern nation
developed as a result of the vigorous spirit o

Design: **Brian Wu**

Specimens are set in
Adobe Stone Sans

Stone Sans was designed by Sumner Stone and released by Adobe Systems in 1987. It is a type family of three weights: medium, semibold, and bold; with three matching italic fonts. Stone Sans is fully compatible – in cap heights, lowercase x-height, stroke weights, and letterform proportions – with Stone Serif and Stone Informal, two companion type families designed in the same three weights plus italics. The resulting integrated type family of eighteen typefaces can be intermixed due to their full compatibility. All eighteen of the Stone types were designed to enable good definition when output on coarse resolution output devices, such as the 300 dot-per-inch laser printers, as well as high resolution devices. There are no light or book weights in the Stone family; this ensures full compatibility with the technical limitations of low resolution laser printers.

Stone Sans is a sturdy sans serif whose proportions are based on classical letterforms; the capitals have the structure of ancient Roman inscriptions, and the lowercase letters are modelled on old style fonts. The **C** and **S** are slightly condensed and open in design. The apertures of **G**, **a**, **e**, and **g** are quite wide.

The Stone family has been widely used since its introduction, due to its outstanding legibility and good reproduction from low resolution output devices. The integrated structure of the 18-font Stone family brings to mind the revolutionary integrated structure of the 21-font Univers type family; but while Univers permits the mixing of sans-serif fonts, Stone enables the integration of sans-serif, serif, and informal fonts.

abcdefgh
ijklmnop
qrstuvwx
yz$12345
67890!?

abcdefghijklmnopqrstuvwxyz
ABCDEFGHIJKLMNOPQRSTUVWXYZ
$&1234567890(.,"";:!?)

72

abcdefghijklmno
pqrstuvwxyzABC
DEFGHIJKLMNO
PQRSTUVWXYZ$
&1234567890
(.,"";:!?)

36

abcdefghijklmnopqrstuvwxyz
ABCDEFGHIJKLMNOPQRSTUVW
XYZ$&1234567890(.,"";:!?)

abcdefghijklmnopqrstuvwxyz
ABCDEFGHIJKLMNOPQRSTUVWXYZ
$&1234567890(.,""";:!?)

18

72

abcdefghijklmnop
qrstuvwxyzABC
DEFGHIJKLMNOP
QRSTUVWXYZ$&
1234567890
(.,"";:!?)

36

abcdefghijklmnopqrstuvwxyz
ABCDEFGHIJKLMNOPQRSTUVW
XYZ$&1234567890(.,"";:!?)

abcdefghijklmnopqrstuvwxyz
ABCDEFGHIJKLMNOPQRSTUVWXYZ
$&1234567890(.,"''";:!?)

72

abcdefghijklm
nopqrstuvwxy
zABCDEFGHIJK
LMNOPQRSTU
VWXYZ$&1234
567890(.,""'";:!?)

36

abcdefghijklmnopqrstuvwxy
zABCDEFGHIJKLMNOPQRSTU
VWXYZ$&1234567890(.,""'";:!?)

Stone Sans Bold Italic

abcdefghijklmnopqrstuvwxyz
ABCDEFGHIJKLMNOPQRSTUVWXYZ
§&1234567890(.,"";:!?)

abcdefghijklm
nopqrstuvwxyz
ABCDEFGHIJKL
MNOPQRSTUV
WXYZ§&12345
67890(.,"";:!?)

abcdefghijklmnopqrstuvwxyz
ABCDEFGHIJKLMNOPQRSTUVW
XYZ§&1234567890(.,"";:!?)

Stone Sans Medium

abcdefghijklmnopqrstuvwxyz
ABCDEFGHIJKLMNOPQRSTUVWXYZ
1234567890&(.,"";:!?)

abcdefghijklmnopqrstuvwxyz
ABCDEFGHIJKLMNOPQRSTUVWXYZ
1234567890&(.,"";:!?)

Typography, the major communications advance between the inven
tion of writing and the age of electronic mass communications in the
twentieth century, *played a pivotal role* in the social, economic, and relig
ious upheavals that occurred during the fifteenth and sixteenth cen
turies. The modern nation developed as a result of the vigorous spirit of
nationalism that swept over Europe and led to the American and French
revolutions of the late eighteenth century. In addition to being a pow
erful vehicle for spreading ideas about human rights and the sover
eignty of the people, typographic printing stabilized and unified langu
ages. Illiteracy, the inability to read and write, began a long, steady decl
ine. Typography radically altered education. The medieval classroom had
been a scriptorium of sorts, where each student penned his own book.
Learning became an increasingly private, rather than communal, pro
cess. Human dialog, extended by type, began to take place on a global
scale that bridged time and space. Gutenberg's invention was the first

Typography, the major communications advance between
the invention of writing and the age of electronic mass commu
nications in the twentieth century, *played a pivotal role* in the so
cial, economic, and religious upheavals that occurred during
the fifteenth and sixteenth centuries. The modern nation devel
oped as a result of the vigorous spirit of nationalism that swept
over Europe and led to the American and French revolutions of
the late eighteenth century. In addition to being a powerful veh
icle for spreading ideas about human rights and the sover
eignty of the people, typographic printing stabilized and unified
languages. Illiteracy, the inability to read and write, began a long,
steady decline. Typography radically altered education. The
medieval classroom had been a scriptorium of sorts, where each

Typography, the major communications advance between the inven
tion of writing and the age of electronic mass communications in the
twentieth century, *played a pivotal role* in the social, economic, and relig
ious upheavals that occurred during the fifteenth and sixteenth cen
turies. The modern nation developed as a result of the vigorous spirit of
nationalism that swept over Europe and led to the American and French
revolutions of the late eighteenth century. In addition to being a pow
erful vehicle for spreading ideas about human rights and the sover
eignty of the people, typographic printing stabilized and unified langu
ages. Illiteracy, the inability to read and write, began a long, steady decl
ine. Typography radically altered education. The medieval classroom had
been a scriptorium of sorts, where each student penned his own book.
Learning became an increasingly private, rather than communal, pro

Typography, the major communications advance between
the invention of writing and the age of electronic mass commu
nications in the twentieth century, *played a pivotal role* in the so
cial, economic, and religious upheavals that occurred during
the fifteenth and sixteenth centuries. The modern nation devel
oped as a result of the vigorous spirit of nationalism that swept
over Europe and led to the American and French revolutions of
the late eighteenth century. In addition to being a powerful veh
icle for spreading ideas about human rights and the sover
eignty of the people, typographic printing stabilized and unified
languages. Illiteracy, the inability to read and write, began a long,
steady decline. Typography radically altered education. The

Typography, the major communications advance between the inven
tion of writing and the age of electronic mass communications in the
twentieth century, *played a pivotal role* in the social, economic, and relig
ious upheavals that occurred during the fifteenth and sixteenth cen
turies. The modern nation developed as a result of the vigorous spirit of
nationalism that swept over Europe and led to the American and French
revolutions of the late eighteenth century. In addition to being a pow
erful vehicle for spreading ideas about human rights and the sover
eignty of the people, typographic printing stabilized and unified langu
ages. Illiteracy, the inability to read and write, began a long, steady decl
ine. Typography radically altered education. The medieval classroom had
been a scriptorium of sorts, where each student penned his own book.

Typography, the major communications advance between
the invention of writing and the age of electronic mass commu
nications in the twentieth century, *played a pivotal role* in the so
cial, economic, and religious upheavals that occurred during
the fifteenth and sixteenth centuries. The modern nation devel
oped as a result of the vigorous spirit of nationalism that swept
over Europe and led to the American and French revolutions of
the late eighteenth century. In addition to being a powerful veh
icle for spreading ideas about human rights and the sover
eignty of the people, typographic printing stabilized and unified
languages. Illiteracy, the inability to read and write, began a long,

Typography, the major communications advance between the inven
tion of writing and the age of electronic mass communications in the
twentieth century, *played a pivotal role* in the social, economic, and relig
ious upheavals that occurred during the fifteenth and sixteenth cen
turies. The modern nation developed as a result of the vigorous spirit of
nationalism that swept over Europe and led to the American and French
revolutions of the late eighteenth century. In addition to being a pow
erful vehicle for spreading ideas about human rights and the sover
eignty of the people, typographic printing stabilized and unified langu
ages. Illiteracy, the inability to read and write, began a long, steady decl
ine. Typography radically altered education. The medieval classroom had

Typography, the major communications advance between
the invention of writing and the age of electronic mass commu
nications in the twentieth century, *played a pivotal role* in the so
cial, economic, and religious upheavals that occurred during
the fifteenth and sixteenth centuries. The modern nation devel
oped as a result of the vigorous spirit of nationalism that swept
over Europe and led to the American and French revolutions of
the late eighteenth century. In addition to being a powerful veh
icle for spreading ideas about human rights and the sover
eignty of the people, typographic printing stabilized and unified

abcdefghijklmnopqrstuvwxyz
ABCDEFGHIJKLMNOPQRSTUVWXYZ
1234567890&(.,"";:!?)

abcdefghijklmnopqrstuvwxyz
ABCDEFGHIJKLMNOPQRSTUVWXYZ
1234567890&(.,"";:!?)

10/10

Typography, the major communications advance betwe en the invention of writing and the age of electronic mass communications in the twentieth century, *played a pivotal role* in the social, economic, and religious upheavals that occurred during the fifteenth and sixteenth centuries. The modern nation developed as a result of the vigorous spirit of nationalism that swept over Europe and led to the Ame rican and French revolutions of the late eighteenth cen tury. In addition to being a powerful vehicle for spreading ideas about human rights and the sovereignty of the peo ple, typographic printing stabilized and unified languages. Illiteracy, the inability to read and write, began a long, ste

12/12

Typography, the major communications advan ce between the invention of writing and the age of electronic mass communications in the twentieth century, *played a pivotal role* in the social, econo mic, and religious upheavals that occurred during the fifteenth and sixteenth centuries. The modern nation developed as a result of the vigorous spirit of nationalism that swept over Europe and led to the American and French revolutions of the late eighteenth century. In addition to being a power

10/11

Typography, the major communications advance betwe en the invention of writing and the age of electronic mass communications in the twentieth century, *played a pivotal role* in the social, economic, and religious upheavals that occurred during the fifteenth and sixteenth centuries. The modern nation developed as a result of the vigorous spirit of nationalism that swept over Europe and led to the Ame rican and French revolutions of the late eighteenth cen tury. In addition to being a powerful vehicle for spreading ideas about human rights and the sovereignty of the peo ple, typographic printing stabilized and unified languages.

12/13

Typography, the major communications advan ce between the invention of writing and the age of electronic mass communications in the twentieth century, *played a pivotal role* in the social, econo mic, and religious upheavals that occurred during the fifteenth and sixteenth centuries. The modern nation developed as a result of the vigorous spirit of nationalism that swept over Europe and led to the American and French revolutions of the late

10/12

Typography, the major communications advance betwe en the invention of writing and the age of electronic mass communications in the twentieth century, *played a pivotal role* in the social, economic, and religious upheavals that occurred during the fifteenth and sixteenth centuries. The modern nation developed as a result of the vigorous spirit of nationalism that swept over Europe and led to the Ame rican and French revolutions of the late eighteenth cen tury. In addition to being a powerful vehicle for spreading

12/14

Typography, the major communications advan ce between the invention of writing and the age of electronic mass communications in the twentieth century, *played a pivotal role* in the social, econo mic, and religious upheavals that occurred during the fifteenth and sixteenth centuries. The modern nation developed as a result of the vigorous spirit of nationalism that swept over Europe and led to

10/13

Typography, the major communications advance betwe en the invention of writing and the age of electronic mass communications in the twentieth century, *played a pivotal role* in the social, economic, and religious upheavals that occurred during the fifteenth and sixteenth centuries. The modern nation developed as a result of the vigorous spirit of nationalism that swept over Europe and led to the Ame rican and French revolutions of the late eighteenth cen tury. In addition to being a powerful vehicle for spreading

12/15

Typography, the major communications advan ce between the invention of writing and the age of electronic mass communications in the twentieth century, *played a pivotal role* in the social, econo mic, and religious upheavals that occurred during the fifteenth and sixteenth centuries. The modern nation developed as a result of the vigorous spirit of nationalism that swept over Europe and led to

Design: **Brian Wu**

Stone Serif was designed by Sumner Stone and released by Adobe Systems in 1987. It is a type family of three weights: medium, semibold, and bold; with three matching italic fonts. As discussed in the text for Stone Sans, it is fully compatible with Stone Sans and Stone Informal.

Stone Serif is a hybrid typeface, integrating features from a number of influences. General letterform proportions and structure are similar to traditional old style faces; however, the thin strokes are considerably thicker than their companion elements in old style fonts, and letters such as **a** and **e** are more conventional and lack the enlarged counters of true old style fonts. The design of the foot serifs fall between Baskerville and Clarendon, resulting in good reproduction at small sizes and from low resolution printers. The crossbar on the **t** does not connect to the stem with a bracket. The top serifs on such letters as **a**, **c**, and **f** have the appearance of a softly rounded trapezoid. The **k** has a thin top serif and no foot serif. The italic fonts have a moderate slant and follow the basic design of the roman letters, but the *a* becomes one storied, the *f* has a cursive descender, and the *y* has a calligraphic sweep to its descender.

Specimens are set in
Adobe Stone Serif

The heavy strokes of Stone Sans and Stone Serif are the exact same weight, but the thin strokes of Stone Serif are much thinner. The set widths are similar, although the set width of Stone Sans is slightly smaller. Stone Informal integrates features of Stone Sans and Stone Serif; stroke weights are closer to Stone Sans, and the serifs are similar yet thicker than those on Stone Serif.

ABCDEF
GHIJKLM
NOPQRS
TUVWX
YZ&("";:)

abcdefgh
ijklmnop
qrstuvwx
yz$12345
67890!?

abcdefghijklmnopqrstuvwxyz
ABCDEFGHIJKLMNOPQRSTUVWXYZ
$&1234567890(.,"";:!?)

72

abcdefghijklmn
opqrstuvwxyz
ABCDEFGHIJKL
MNOPQRSTUV
WXYZ$&123456
7890(.,"";:!?)

36

abcdefghijklmnopqrstuvwxyz
ABCDEFGHIJKLMNOPQRSTUV
WXYZ$&1234567890(.,"";:!?)

abcdefghijklmnopqrstuvwxyz
ABCDEFGHIJKLMNOPQRSTUVWXYZ
$&1234567890(.,""::!?)

18

72

abcdefghijklmnop
qrstuvwxyzABC
DEFGHIJKLMNO
PQRSTUVWXYZ
$&1234567890
(.,"";::!?)

36

abcdefghijklmnopqrstuvwxyz
ABCDEFGHIJKLMNOPQRSTUV
WXYZ$&1234567890(.,"";::!?)

abcdefghijklmnopqrstuvwxyz
ABCDEFGHIJKLMNOPQRSTUVWXYZ
$&1234567890(.,""::!?)

abcdefghijklm
nopqrstuvwxy
zABCDEFGHIJ
KLMNOPQRST
UVWXYZ$&123
4567890(.,"";:!?)

abcdefghijklmnopqrstuvwxyz
ABCDEFGHIJKLMNOPQRSTU
VWXYZ$&1234567890(.,"";:!?)

abcdefghijklmnopqrstuvw
xyzABCDEFGHIJKLMNOPQRSTUV
WXYZ$&1234567890(.,""";:!?)

18

70

abcdefghijklm
nopqrstuvwxy
zABCDEFGHIJ
KLMNOPQRST
UVWXYZ$&12
34567890(.,"";:!?)

32

abcdefghijklmnopqrstuvwx
yzABCDEFGHIJKLMNOPQRST
UVWXYZ$&1234567890(.,"";:!?)

Stone Serif Medium

abcdefghijklmnopqrstuvwxyz
ABCDEFGHIJKLMNOPQRSTUVWXYZ
$1234567890&(.,"";:!?)

abcdefghijklmnopqrstuvwxyz
ABCDEFGHIJKLMNOPQRSTUVWXYZ
$1234567890&(.,"";:!?)

8/8

Typography, the major communications advance between the invention of writing and the age of electronic mass communications in the twentieth century, *played a pivotal role* in the social, economic, and religious upheavals that occurred during the fifteenth and sixteenth centuries. The modern nation developed as a result of the vigorous spirit of nationalism that swept over Europe and led to the American and French revolutions of the late eighteenth century. In addition to being a powerful vehicle for spreading ideas about human rights and the sovereignty of the people, typographic printing stabilized and unified languages. Illiteracy, the inability to read and write, began a long, steady decline. Typography radically altered education. The medieval classroom had been a scriptorium of sorts, where each student penned his own book. Learning became an increasingly private, rather than communal, process. Human dialog, extended

9/9

Typography, the major communications advance between the invention of writing and the age of electronic mass communications in the twentieth century, *played a pivotal role* in the social, economic, and religious upheavals that occurred during the fifteenth and sixteenth centuries. The modern nation developed as a result of the vigorous spirit of nationalism that swept over Europe and led to the American and French revolutions of the late eighteenth century. In addition to being a powerful vehicle for spreading ideas about human rights and the sovereignty of the people, typographic printing stabilized and unified languages. Illiteracy, the inability to read and write, began a long, steady decline. Typography radically altered

8/9

Typography, the major communications advance between the invention of writing and the age of electronic mass communications in the twentieth century, *played a pivotal role* in the social, economic, and religious upheavals that occurred during the fifteenth and sixteenth centuries. The modern nation developed as a result of the vigorous spirit of nationalism that swept over Europe and led to the American and French revolutions of the late eighteenth century. In addition to being a powerful vehicle for spreading ideas about human rights and the sovereignty of the people, typographic printing stabilized and unified languages. Illiteracy, the inability to read and write, began a long, steady decline. Typography radically altered education. The medieval classroom had been a scriptorium of sorts, where each

9/10

Typography, the major communications advance between the invention of writing and the age of electronic mass communications in the twentieth century, *played a pivotal role* in the social, economic, and religious upheavals that occurred during the fifteenth and sixteenth centuries. The modern nation developed as a result of the vigorous spirit of nationalism that swept over Europe and led to the American and French revolutions of the late eighteenth century. In addition to being a powerful vehicle for spreading ideas about human rights and the sovereignty of the people, typographic printing stabilized and unified languages. Illiteracy, the inability to read and write, began a

8/10

Typography, the major communications advance between the invention of writing and the age of electronic mass communications in the twentieth century, *played a pivotal role* in the social, economic, and religious upheavals that occurred during the fifteenth and sixteenth centuries. The modern nation developed as a result of the vigorous spirit of nationalism that swept over Europe and led to the American and French revolutions of the late eighteenth century. In addition to being a powerful vehicle for spreading ideas about human rights and the sovereignty of the people, typographic printing stabilized and unified languages. Illiteracy, the inability to read and write, began a long, steady decline. Typography radically altered education. The

9/11

Typography, the major communications advance between the invention of writing and the age of electronic mass communications in the twentieth century, *played a pivotal role* in the social, economic, and religious upheavals that occurred during the fifteenth and sixteenth centuries. The modern nation developed as a result of the vigorous spirit of nationalism that swept over Europe and led to the American and French revolutions of the late eighteenth century. In addition to being a powerful vehicle for spreading ideas about human rights and the sovereignty of the people, typographic printing stabilized and unified

8/11

Typography, the major communications advance between the invention of writing and the age of electronic mass communications in the twentieth century, *played a pivotal role* in the social, economic, and religious upheavals that occurred during the fifteenth and sixteenth centuries. The modern nation developed as a result of the vigorous spirit of nationalism that swept over Europe and led to the American and French revolutions of the late eighteenth century. In addition to being a powerful vehicle for spreading ideas about human rights and the sovereignty of the people, typographic printing stabilized and unified languages. Illiteracy, the inability to read and write, began

9/12

Typography, the major communications advance between the invention of writing and the age of electronic mass communications in the twentieth century, *played a pivotal role* in the social, economic, and religious upheavals that occurred during the fifteenth and sixteenth centuries. The modern nation developed as a result of the vigorous spirit of nationalism that swept over Europe and led to the American and French revolutions of the late eighteenth century. In addition to being a powerful vehicle for spreading ideas about human rights and the sovereignty of

abcdefghijklmnopqrstuvwxyz
ABCDEFGHIJKLMNOPQRSTUVWXYZ
$1234567890&(.,"";:!?)

abcdefghijklmnopqrstuvwxyz
ABCDEFGHIJKLMNOPQRSTUVWXYZ
$1234567890&(.,"";:!?)

10/10

Typography, the major communications advance between the invention of writing and the age of electronic mass communications in the twentieth century, *played a pivotal role* in the social, economic, and religious upheavals that occurred during the fifteenth and sixteenth centuries. The modern nation developed as a result of the vigorous spirit of nationalism that swept over Europe and led to the American and French revolutions of the late eighteenth century. In addition to being a powerful vehicle for spreading ideas about human rights and the sovereignty of the people, typographic printing

---

12/12

Typography, the major communications adv ance between the invention of writing and the age of electronic mass communications in the tw entieth century, *played a pivotal role* in the soci al, economic, and religious upheavals that occ urred during the fifteenth and sixteenth centu ries. The modern nation developed as a result of the vigorous spirit of nationalism that swe pt over Europe and led to the American and Fre nch revolutions of the late eighteenth century. In

---

10/11

Typography, the major communications advance between the invention of writing and the age of electronic mass communications in the twentieth century, *played a pivotal role* in the social, economic, and religious upheavals that occurred during the fifteenth and sixteenth centuries. The modern nation developed as a result of the vigorous spirit of nationalism that swept over Europe and led to the American and French revolutions of the late eighteenth century. In addition to being a powerful vehicle for spreading ideas about human rights and

---

12/13

Typography, the major communications adv ance between the invention of writing and the age of electronic mass communications in the tw entieth century, *played a pivotal role* in the soci al, economic, and religious upheavals that occ urred during the fifteenth and sixteenth centu ries. The modern nation developed as a result of the vigorous spirit of nationalism that swe pt over Europe and led to the American and Fre

---

10/12

Typography, the major communications advance between the invention of writing and the age of electronic mass communications in the twentieth century, *played a pivotal role* in the social, economic, and religious upheavals that occurred during the fifteenth and sixteenth centuries. The modern nation developed as a result of the vigorous spirit of nationalism that swept over Europe and led to the American and French revolutions of the late

---

12/14

Typography, the major communications adv ance between the invention of writing and the age of electronic mass communications in the tw entieth century, *played a pivotal role* in the soci al, economic, and religious upheavals that occ urred during the fifteenth and sixteenth centu ries. The modern nation developed as a result of the vigorous spirit of nationalism that swe

---

10/13

Typography, the major communications advance between the invention of writing and the age of electronic mass communications in the twentieth century, *played a pivotal role* in the social, economic, and religious upheavals that occurred during the fifteenth and sixteenth centuries. The modern nation developed as a result of the vigorous spirit of nationalism that swept over Europe and led to the American and French revolutions of the late

---

12/15

Typography, the major communications adv ance between the invention of writing and the age of electronic mass communications in the tw entieth century, *played a pivotal role* in the soci al, economic, and religious upheavals that occ urred during the fifteenth and sixteenth centu ries. The modern nation developed as a result of the vigorous spirit of nationalism that swe

IF

YOU CAN

SPEC THIS

TYPE, YOU CAN

GET A GOOD JOB

Design: **Louise Fili**

Morris F. Benton designed Stymie for American Type Founders, and it was first released in 1931. Stymie is a slab serif or Egyptian family with geometric forms and light, medium, bold, and black weights. Actually, Stymie Medium is a reissue of Litho Antique, an American Type Founders face designed before 1912, with some characters redrawn in a more geometric manner.

When geometric sans-serif faces such as Futura and Kabel were designed in the late 1920s, type designers and manufacturers became interested in developing Egyptian fonts with monoline strokes, geometric forms, and a range of stroke weights from light to very bold. These fonts differ from Clarendons, which have optically adjusted thick-and-thin strokes and subtle bracketing of the serifs. One might almost say that foundries raced to add square serifs to the widely emulated Futura. Memphis, designed by Rudolf Wolf for Stempel in 1929, was the first version to reach the market. Other similar competitors include Beton, designed by Heinrich Jost for Bauer and Intertype in 1931; Karnak, designed by R.H. Middleton for Ludlow in 1931; and Rockwell, issued by Monotype in 1934.

Stymie's round characters such as **C**, **O**, and **Q** are based on a perfect circle. The **A** has a horizontal top serif extending to both the left and right. The **G** has a straight vertical spur. The **e** is a perfect circle divided by a horizontal cross bar and has a very small aperture. Unlike some geometric Egyptians, the **a** is two-storied.

Specimens are set in
Bitstream Stymie

Stymie and other similar faces are most frequently used in advertising and publicity. The rigorous geometry of Futura is combined with the complex texture of the serifs.

abcdefgh
ijklmnop
qrstuvwx
yz$12345
67890!?

abcdefghijklmnopqrstuvwxyz
ABCDEFGHIJKLMNOPQRSTUVWXYZ
$&1234567890(.,"";:!?)

72

abcdefghijklmno
pqrstuvwxyzAB
CDEFGHIJKLMN
OPQRSTUVWX
YZ$&1234567890
(.,"";:!?)

36

abcdefghijklmnopqrstuvwxyz
ABCDEFGHIJKLMNOPQRSTUV
WXYZ$&1234567890(.,"";:!?)

abcdefghijklmnopqrstuvwxyz
ABCDEFGHIJKLMNOPQRSTUVW
XYZ$&1234567890(.,"";:!?)

18

72

abcdefghijklmno
pqrstuvwxyzAB
CDEFGHIJKLMN
OPQRSTUVWXY
Z$&1234567890
(.,"";:!?)

36

abcdefghijklmnopqrstuvwxyz
ABCDEFGHIJKLMNOPQRSTUV
WXYZ$&1234567890(.,"";:!?)

abcdefghijklmnopqrstuvwxyz
ABCDEFGHIJKLMNOPQRSTUVWXYZ
$&1234567890(.,"";:!?)

`72`

abcdefghijklmno
pqrstuvwxyzABC
DEFGHIJKLMNO
PQRSTUVWXYZ
$&1234567890
(.,"";:!?)

`36`

abcdefghijklmnopqrstuvwxyz
ABCDEFGHIJKLMNOPQRSTU
VWXYZ$&1234567890(.,"";:!?)

abcdefghijklmnopqrstuvwxyz
ABCDEFGHIJKLMNOPQRSTUVWXYZ
$&1234567890(.,"";:!?)

18

72

abcdefghijklmnopqr
stuvwxyzABCDEFGHI
JKLMNOPQRSTUVW
XYZ$&1234567890
(.,"";:!?)

36

abcdefghijklmnopqrstuvwxyz
ABCDEFGHIJKLMNOPQRSTUVWXYZ
$&1234567890(.,"";:!?)

Stymie Medium

abcdefghijklmnopqrstuvwxyz
ABCDEFGHIJKLMNOPQRSTUVWXYZ
$1234567890&(.,"";:!?)

abcdefghijklmnopqrstuvwxyz
ABCDEFGHIJKLMNOPQRSTUVWXYZ
$1234567890&(.,"";:!?)

8/8

Typography, the major communications advance between the invention of writing and the age of electronic mass communications in the twentieth century, *played a pivotal role* in the social, economic, and religious upheavals that occurred during the fifteenth and sixteenth centuries. The modern nation developed as a result of the vigorous spirit of nationalism that swept over Europe and led to the American and French revolutions of the late eighteenth century. In addition to being a powerful vehicle for spreading ideas about human rights and the sovereignty of the people, typographic printing stabilized and unified languages. Illiteracy, the inability to read and write, began a long, steady decline. Typography radically altered education. The medieval classroom had been a scriptorium of sorts, where each student penned his own book. Learning became an increasingly private, rather than communal, process. Human dialog,

9/9

Typography, the major communications advance between the invention of writing and the age of electronic mass communications in the twentieth century, *played a pivotal role* in the social, economic, and religious upheavals that occurred during the fifteenth and sixteenth centuries. The modern nation developed as a result of the vigorous spirit of nationalism that swept over Europe and led to the American and French revolutions of the late eighteenth century. In addition to being a powerful vehicle for spreading ideas about human rights and the sovereignty of the people, typographic printing stabilized and unified languages. Illiteracy, the inability to read and write, began a long, steady decline. Typography radically altered education. The medieval class room had been a

8/9

Typography, the major communications advance between the invention of writing and the age of electronic mass communications in the twentieth century, *played a pivotal role* in the social, economic, and religious upheavals that occurred during the fifteenth and sixteenth centuries. The modern nation developed as a result of the vigorous spirit of nationalism that swept over Europe and led to the American and French revolutions of the late eighteenth century. In addition to being a powerful vehicle for spreading ideas about human rights and the sovereignty of the people, typographic printing stabilized and unified languages. Illiteracy, the inability to read and write, began a long, steady decline. Typography radically altered education. The medieval classroom had been a scriptorium of sorts, where each student penned his own book. Learning became an in

9/10

Typography, the major communications advance between the invention of writing and the age of electronic mass communications in the twentieth century, *played a pivotal role* in the social, economic, and religious upheavals that occurred during the fifteenth and sixteenth centuries. The modern nation developed as a result of the vigorous spirit of nationalism that swept over Europe and led to the American and French revolutions of the late eighteenth century. In addition to being a powerful vehicle for spreading ideas about human rights and the sovereignty of the people, typographic printing stabilized and unified languages. Illiteracy, the inability to read and write, began a long, steady decline. Typography rad

8/10

Typography, the major communications advance between the invention of writing and the age of electronic mass communications in the twentieth century, *played a pivotal role* in the social, economic, and religious upheavals that occurred during the fifteenth and sixteenth centuries. The modern nation developed as a result of the vigorous spirit of nationalism that swept over Europe and led to the American and French revolutions of the late eighteenth century. In addition to being a powerful vehicle for spreading ideas about human rights and the sovereignty of the people, typographic printing stabilized and unified languages. Illiteracy, the inability to read and write, began a long, steady decline. Typography radically altered education. The medieval classroom had been a scriptorium of sorts,

9/11

Typography, the major communications advance between the invention of writing and the age of electronic mass communications in the twentieth century, *played a pivotal role* in the social, economic, and religious upheavals that occurred during the fifteenth and sixteenth centuries. The modern nation developed as a result of the vigorous spirit of nationalism that swept over Europe and led to the American and French revolutions of the late eighteenth century. In addition to being a powerful vehicle for spreading ideas about human rights and the sovereignty of the people, typographic printing stabilized and unified languages. Illiteracy, the inability to

8/11

Typography, the major communications advance between the invention of writing and the age of electronic mass communications in the twentieth century, *played a pivotal role* in the social, economic, and religious upheavals that occurred during the fifteenth and sixteenth centuries. The modern nation developed as a result of the vigorous spirit of nationalism that swept over Europe and led to the American and French revolutions of the late eighteenth century. In addition to being a powerful vehicle for spreading ideas about human rights and the sovereignty of the people, typographic printing stabilized and unified languages. Illiteracy, the inability to read and write, began a long, steady decline. Typography radically altered

9/12

Typography, the major communications advance between the invention of writing and the age of electronic mass communications in the twentieth century, *played a pivotal role* in the social, economic, and religious upheavals that occurred during the fifteenth and sixteenth centuries. The modern nation developed as a result of the vigorous spirit of nationalism that swept over Europe and led to the American and French revolutions of the late eighteenth century. In addition to being a powerful vehicle for spreading ideas about human rights and the sovereignty of the people, typographic printing

abcdefghijklmnopqrstuvwxyz
ABCDEFGHIJKLMNOPQRSTUVWXYZ
$1234567890&(.,"";:!?)

abcdefghijklmnopqrstuvwxyz
ABCDEFGHIJKLMNOPQRSTUVWXYZ
$1234567890&(.,"";:!?)

10/10

Typography, the major communications advance bet ween the invention of writing and the age of elec tronic mass communications in the twentieth century, *played a pivotal role* in the social, economic, and relig ious upheavals that occurred during the fifteenth and sixteenth centuries. The modern nation developed as a result of the vigorous spirit of nationalism that swe pt over Europe and led to the American and French re volutions of the late eighteenth century. In addition to being a powerful vehicle for spreading ideas about hu man rights and the sovereignty of the people, typogra

---

10/11

Typography, the major communications advance bet ween the invention of writing and the age of elec tronic mass communications in the twentieth century, *played a pivotal role* in the social, economic, and relig ious upheavals that occurred during the fifteenth and sixteenth centuries. The modern nation developed as a result of the vigorous spirit of nationalism that swe pt over Europe and led to the American and French re volutions of the late eighteenth century. In addition to being a powerful vehicle for spreading ideas about hu man rights and the sovereignty of the people, typogra

---

10/12

Typography, the major communications advance bet ween the invention of writing and the age of elec tronic mass communications in the twentieth century, *played a pivotal role* in the social, economic, and relig ious upheavals that occurred during the fifteenth and sixteenth centuries. The modern nation developed as a result of the vigorous spirit of nationalism that swe pt over Europe and led to the American and French re volutions of the late eighteenth century. In addition to

---

10/13

Typography, the major communications advance bet ween the invention of writing and the age of elec tronic mass communications in the twentieth century, *played a pivotal role* in the social, economic, and relig ious upheavals that occurred during the fifteenth and sixteenth centuries. The modern nation developed as a result of the vigorous spirit of nationalism that swe pt over Europe and led to the American and French re volutions of the late eighteenth century. In addition to

---

12/12

Typography, the major communications advan ce between the invention of writing and the age of electronic mass communications in the twen tieth century, *played a pivotal role* in the social, economic, and religious upheavals that occurr ed during the fifteenth and sixteenth centuries. The modern nation developed as a result of the vigorous spirit of nationalism that swept over Europe and led to the American and French rev olutions of the late eighteenth century. In addit

---

12/13

Typography, the major communications advan ce between the invention of writing and the age of electronic mass communications in the twen tieth century, *played a pivotal role* in the social, economic, and religious upheavals that occurr ed during the fifteenth and sixteenth centuries. The modern nation developed as a result of the vigorous spirit of nationalism that swept over Europe and led to the American and French rev

---

12/14

Typography, the major communications advan ce between the invention of writing and the age of electronic mass communications in the twen tieth century, *played a pivotal role* in the social, economic, and religious upheavals that occurr ed during the fifteenth and sixteenth centuries. The modern nation developed as a result of the vigorous spirit of nationalism that swept over

---

12/15

Typography, the major communications advan ce between the invention of writing and the age of electronic mass communications in the twen tieth century, *played a pivotal role* in the social, economic, and religious upheavals that occurr ed during the fifteenth and sixteenth centuries. The modern nation developed as a result of the vigorous spirit of nationalism that swept over

Times
New Roman

Design: **David Colley**

Specimens are set in
Monotype Times New Roman

In 1932, the English typographer and type historian Stanley Morison was commissioned by *The Times* of London to redesign the newspaper's text typeface. In collaboration with Victor Lardent, who was the artist for the project, Morison designed this new typeface using Monotype Plantin 113 as the model. With this source, Lardent designed a prototype face that was later revised by Morison. The resulting text face was very similar to Plantin, but the serifs were sharper and there was a higher degree of contrast in the strokes of the letters. The new design met Morison's expectations which were to create a highly legible text face that was both spatially economic and true to the needs of modern newspaper printing and production methods.

Times New Roman is an Old Style face void of affectations. Its visual character is defined by sound proportions, short ascenders and descenders, sharp bracketed serifs, and an oblique stress. The counters are very open as exemplified by the large bowl of the lowercase **a**, and the rounded uppercase letters, such as the **C** and **G**, are comfortably wide. The numerous weights, widths, italics, and other font variations make it a highly desirable and practical text face for most kinds of publications.

A year after the typeface was designed, it was made available by Monotype for general distribution. Later, versions released in the United States were called Times Roman. There has never been a more popular text face than Times Roman. It continues to be used in all facets of printed communication, from books and magazines to advertising, and it is pervasive in the emerging world of desktop publishing.

ABCDEF
GHIJKL
MNOPQR
STUVWX
YZ&(.,""„;:)

abcdefghij
klmnopqrs
tuvwxyz$1
234567890
!?

abcdefghijklmnopqrstuvwxyz
ABCDEFGHIJKLMNOPQRSTUVWXYZ
$&1234567890(.,""";:!?)

72

abcdefghijklmn
opqrstuvwxyzAB
CDEFGHIJKL
MNOPQRSTUV
WXYZ$&123456
7890(.,"";:!?)

36

abcdefghijklmnopqrstuvwxyz
ABCDEFGHIJKLMNOPQRST
UVWXYZ$&1234567890(.,"";:!?)

abcdefghijklmnopqrstuvwxyz
ABCDEFGHIJKLMNOPQRSTUVWXYZ
$&1234567890(.,""";:!?)

18

72

abcdefghijklmno
pqrstuvwxyz ABC
DEFGHIJKLM
NOPQRSTUVW
XYZ$&1234567
890(.,""";:!?)

36

abcdefghijklmnopqrstuvwxyz
ABCDEFGHIJKLMNOPQRSTUV
WXYZ$&1234567890(.,""";:!?)

abcdefghijklmnopqrstuvwxyz
ABCDEFGHIJKLMNOPQRSTUVWXYZ
$&1234567890(.,""";:!?)

72

abcdefghijklmno
pqrstuvwxyzABC
DEFGHIJKLM
NOPQRSTUV
WXYZ$&123456
7890(.,"";:!?)

36

abcdefghijklmnopqrstuvwxyz
ABCDEFGHIJKLMNOPQRSTU
VWXYZ$&1234567890(.,"";:!?)

abcdefghijklmnopqrstuvwxyz
ABCDEFGHIJKLMNOPQRSTUVWXYZ
$&1234567890(.,""";:!?)

18

72

abcdefghijklmnop
qrstuvwxyzABC
DEFGHIJKLMN
OPQRSTUVW
XYZ$&12345678
90(.,"";:!?)

36

abcdefghijklmnopqrstuvwxyz
ABCDEFGHIJKLMNOPQRSTUV
WXYZ$&1234567890(.,"";:!?)

Times New Roman Regular

abcdefghijklmnopqrstuvwxyz
ABCDEFGHIJKLMNOPQRSTUVWXYZ
$1234567890&(.,"";:!?)

abcdefghijklmnopqrstuvwxyz
ABCDEFGHIJKLMNOPQRSTUVWXYZ
$1234567890&(.,"";:!?)

8/8

Typography, the major communications advance between the invention of writing and the age of electronic mass communications in the twentieth ce ntury, *played a pivotal role* in the social, economic, and religious upheav als that occurred during the fifteenth and sixteenth centuries. The modern nation developed as a result of the vigorous spirit of nationalism that swept over Europe and led to the American and French revolutions of the late eighteenth century. In addition to being a powerful vehicle for spre ading ideas about human rights and the sovereignty of the people, typogr aphic printing stabilized and unified languages. Illiteracy, the inability to r ead and write, began a long, steady decline. Typography radically altered education. The medieval classroom had been a scriptorium of sorts, where each student penned his own book. Learning became an increasingly priv ate, rather than communal, process. Human dialog, extended by type, beg an to take place on a global scale that bridged time and space. Gutenber g's invention was the first mechanization of a skilled handicraft. As such, i

9/9

Typography, the major communications advance between the inv ention of writing and the age of electronic mass communications i n the twentieth century, *played a pivotal role* in the social, econom ic, and religious upheavals that occurred during the fifteenth and sixteenth centuries. The modern nation developed as a result of th e vigorous spirit of nationalism that swept over Europe and led to the American and French revolutions of the late eighteenth centu ry. In addition to being a powerful vehicle for spreading ideas abo ut human rights and the sovereignty of the people, typographic p rinting stabilized and unified languages. Illiteracy, the inability to read and write, began a long, steady decline. Typography radicall y altered education. The medieval classroom had been a scriptori um of sorts, where each student penned his own book. Learning b

8/9

Typography, the major communications advance between the invention of writing and the age of electronic mass communications in the twentieth ce ntury, *played a pivotal role* in the social, economic, and religious upheav als that occurred during the fifteenth and sixteenth centuries. The modern nation developed as a result of the vigorous spirit of nationalism that swept over Europe and led to the American and French revolutions of the late eighteenth century. In addition to being a powerful vehicle for spre ading ideas about human rights and the sovereignty of the people, typogr aphic printing stabilized and unified languages. Illiteracy, the inability to r ead and write, began a long, steady decline. Typography radically altered education. The medieval classroom had been a scriptorium of sorts, where each student penned his own book. Learning became an increasingly priv ate, rather than communal, process. Human dialog, extended by type, beg

9/10

Typography, the major communications advance between the inv ention of writing and the age of electronic mass communications i n the twentieth century, *played a pivotal role* in the social, econom ic, and religious upheavals that occurred during the fifteenth and sixteenth centuries. The modern nation developed as a result of th e vigorous spirit of nationalism that swept over Europe and led to the American and French revolutions of the late eighteenth centu ry. In addition to being a powerful vehicle for spreading ideas abo ut human rights and the sovereignty of the people, typographic p rinting stabilized and unified languages. Illiteracy, the inability to read and write, began a long, steady decline. Typography radicall y altered education. The medieval classroom had been a scriptori

8/10

Typography, the major communications advance between the invention of writing and the age of electronic mass communications in the twentieth ce ntury, *played a pivotal role* in the social, economic, and religious upheav als that occurred during the fifteenth and sixteenth centuries. The modern nation developed as a result of the vigorous spirit of nationalism that swept over Europe and led to the American and French revolutions of the late eighteenth century. In addition to being a powerful vehicle for spre ading ideas about human rights and the sovereignty of the people, typogr aphic printing stabilized and unified languages. Illiteracy, the inability to r ead and write, began a long, steady decline. Typography radically altered education. The medieval classroom had been a scriptorium of sorts, where each student penned his own book. Learning became an increasingly priv

9/11

Typography, the major communications advance between the inv ention of writing and the age of electronic mass communications i n the twentieth century, *played a pivotal role* in the social, econom ic, and religious upheavals that occurred during the fifteenth and sixteenth centuries. The modern nation developed as a result of th e vigorous spirit of nationalism that swept over Europe and led to the American and French revolutions of the late eighteenth centu ry. In addition to being a powerful vehicle for spreading ideas abo ut human rights and the sovereignty of the people, typographic p rinting stabilized and unified languages. Illiteracy, the inability to read and write, began a long, steady decline. Typography radicall

8/11

Typography, the major communications advance between the invention of writing and the age of electronic mass communications in the twentieth ce ntury, *played a pivotal role* in the social, economic, and religious upheav als that occurred during the fifteenth and sixteenth centuries. The modern nation developed as a result of the vigorous spirit of nationalism that swept over Europe and led to the American and French revolutions of the late eighteenth century. In addition to being a powerful vehicle for spre ading ideas about human rights and the sovereignty of the people, typogr aphic printing stabilized and unified languages. Illiteracy, the inability to r ead and write, began a long, steady decline. Typography radically altered education. The medieval classroom had been a scriptorium of sorts, where

9/12

Typography, the major communications advance between the inv ention of writing and the age of electronic mass communications i n the twentieth century, *played a pivotal role* in the social, econom ic, and religious upheavals that occurred during the fifteenth and sixteenth centuries. The modern nation developed as a result of th e vigorous spirit of nationalism that swept over Europe and led to the American and French revolutions of the late eighteenth centu ry. In addition to being a powerful vehicle for spreading ideas abo ut human rights and the sovereignty of the people, typographic p rinting stabilized and unified languages. Illiteracy, the inability to

abcdefghijklmnopqrstuvwxyz
ABCDEFGHIJKLMNOPQRSTUVWXYZ
$1234567890&(.,"";:!?)

abcdefghijklmnopqrstuvwxyz
ABCDEFGHIJKLMNOPQRSTUVWXYZ
$1234567890&(.,"";:!?)

10/10

Typography, the major communications advance between t he invention of writing and the age of electronic mass com munications in the twentieth century, *played a pivotal role* i n the social, economic, and religious upheavals that occurr ed during the fifteenth and sixteenth centuries. The modern nation developed as a result of the vigorous spirit of nation alism that swept over Europe and led to the American and French revolutions of the late eighteenth century. In additi on to being a powerful vehicle for spreading ideas about h uman rights and the sovereignty of the people, typographic printing stabilized and unified languages. Illiteracy, the ina bility to read and write, began a long, steady decline. Typo

---

12/12

Typography, the major communications advance between the invention of writing and the age of el ectronic mass communications in the twentieth ce ntury, *played a pivotal role* in the social, economi c, and religious upheavals that occurred during the fifteenth and sixteenth centuries. The modern nation developed as a result of the vigorous spirit of nationalism that swept over Europe and led to the American and French revolutions of the late e ighteenth century. In addition to being a powerfu

---

10/11

Typography, the major communications advance between t he invention of writing and the age of electronic mass com munications in the twentieth century, *played a pivotal role* i n the social, economic, and religious upheavals that occurr ed during the fifteenth and sixteenth centuries. The modern nation developed as a result of the vigorous spirit of nation alism that swept over Europe and led to the American and French revolutions of the late eighteenth century. In additi on to being a powerful vehicle for spreading ideas about h uman rights and the sovereignty of the people, typographic printing stabilized and unified languages. Illiteracy, the ina

---

12/13

Typography, the major communications advance between the invention of writing and the age of el ectronic mass communications in the twentieth ce ntury, *played a pivotal role* in the social, economi c, and religious upheavals that occurred during the fifteenth and sixteenth centuries. The modern nation developed as a result of the vigorous spirit of nationalism that swept over Europe and led to the American and French revolutions of the late e

---

10/12

Typography, the major communications advance between t he invention of writing and the age of electronic mass com munications in the twentieth century, *played a pivotal role* i n the social, economic, and religious upheavals that occurr ed during the fifteenth and sixteenth centuries. The modern nation developed as a result of the vigorous spirit of nation alism that swept over Europe and led to the American and French revolutions of the late eighteenth century. In additi on to being a powerful vehicle for spreading ideas about h uman rights and the sovereignty of the people, typographic

---

12/14

Typography, the major communications advance between the invention of writing and the age of el ectronic mass communications in the twentieth ce ntury, *played a pivotal role* in the social, economi c, and religious upheavals that occurred during the fifteenth and sixteenth centuries. The modern nation developed as a result of the vigorous spirit of nationalism that swept over Europe and led to the American and French revolutions of the late e

---

10/13

Typography, the major communications advance between t he invention of writing and the age of electronic mass com munications in the twentieth century, *played a pivotal role* i n the social, economic, and religious upheavals that occurr ed during the fifteenth and sixteenth centuries. The modern nation developed as a result of the vigorous spirit of nation alism that swept over Europe and led to the American and French revolutions of the late eighteenth century. In additi on to being a powerful vehicle for spreading ideas about h

---

12/15

Typography, the major communications advance between the invention of writing and the age of el ectronic mass communications in the twentieth ce ntury, *played a pivotal role* in the social, economi c, and religious upheavals that occurred during the fifteenth and sixteenth centuries. The modern nation developed as a result of the vigorous spirit of nationalism that swept over Europe and led to

insignificant

(ELEMeNT) *thing*

unexplored

find

" In everything there is an *unexplored element* because we are prone by habit to use our eyes in combination with the memory of what others before us have thought about the thing we are looking at. The most insignificant thing contains some little unknown element.

We must *find* it. "

Design: **Richard Woollacott**

Specimens are set in
Linotype Trump Mediaeval

Trump Mediaeval is a German type family designed in 1954 by Georg Trump, released in hand-set metal by the Weber foundry, and adopted for keyboard typesetting by the German Linotype Company. The term Venetian is often used in England and the United States for typefaces based on Nicolas Jenson's 15th century fonts designed in Venice, while typefaces based on Jenson's designs are called Mediaeval in Germany. Yet, Trump Mediaeval is not a true Venetian or Mediaeval design; it is a hybrid showing the influences of both Venetian and Old Style typefaces.

Trump Mediaeval projects its own unique feeling. The roundness of a typical old-style font is offset by a subtle squareness and sharpness; these attributes can be seen by examining the **a** and **c**. The **M** is splayed, and the **G** has a small foot serif. Serifs are pronounced and somewhat angular. The capitals are much shorter than the ascenders. This blends the capitals within lowercase settings, a quality that is important in the German language, for it uses far more capitals than most languages. The italic is a "modified slope roman." An italic often shows calligraphic origins; a sloped roman is essentially the roman face with its vertical strokes inclined. Trump Mediaeval has a sloped roman with a few cursive changes; for example, *a* and *f*.

Trump Mediaeval has been widely used in Europe for its vigorous elegance. It lends a distinctive textural energy to a typographic column, for it possesses just enough eccentricity to achieve a uniqueness without departing so far from the norm to be disruptive to the reader.

ABCDEF
GHIJKLM
NOPQRS
TUVWX
YZ&(.,''''";:)

abcdefghij
klmnopqr
stuvwxyz
$1234567
890!?

abcdefghijklmnopqrstuvwxyz
ABCDEFGHIJKLMNOPQRSTU
VWXYZ$&1234567890(.,"";:!?)

72

abcdefghijklmno
pqrstuvwxyz
ABCDEFGHIJK
LMNOPQRSTU
VWXYZ$&1234
567890(.,"";:!?)

36

abcdefghijklmnopqrstuvwxyz
ABCDEFGHIJKLMNOPQRSTU
VWXYZ$&1234567890(.,"";:!?)

abcdefghijklmnopqrstuvwxyz
ABCDEFGHIJKLMNOPQRSTU
VWXYZ$&1234567890(.,""";:!?)

72

abcdefghijklmn
opqrstuvwxyz
ABCDEFGHIJK
LMNOPQRSTU
VWXYZ$&1234
567890(.,"";:!?)

36

abcdefghijklmnopqrstuvwxyz
ABCDEFGHIJKLMNOPQRSTU
VWXYZ$&1234567890(.,"";:!?)

abcdefghijklmnopqrstuvwxyz
ABCDEFGHIJKLMNOPQRSTU
VWXYZ$&1234567890(.,""“”;:!?)

abcdefghijklmn
opqrstuvwxyz
ABCDEFGHIJK
LMNOPQRSTU
VWXYZ$&1234
567890(.,""“”;:!?)

abcdefghijklmnopqrstuvwxyz
ABCDEFGHIJKLMNOPQRSTU
VWXYZ$&1234567890(.,""“”;:!?)

abcdefghijklmnopqrstuvwxyz
ABCDEFGHIJKLMNOPQRSTU
VWXYZ$&1234567890(.,""";:!?)

18

72

abcdefghijklmn

opqrstuvwxyz

ABCDEFGHIJK

LMNOPQRSTU

VWXYZ$&1234

567890(.,""";:!?)

36

abcdefghijklmnopqrstuvwxyz
ABCDEFGHIJKLMNOPQRSTU
VWXYZ$&1234567890(.,""";:!?)

Trump Mediaeval

abcdefghijklmnopqrstuvwxyz
ABCDEFGHIJKLMNOPQRSTUVWXYZ
$1234567890&(.,""¡!?)

abcdefghijklmnopqrstuvwxyz
ABCDEFGHIJKLMNOPQRSTUVWXYZ
$1234567890&(.,""¡!?)

8/8

Typography, the major communications advance between the inven
tion of writing and the age of electronic mass communications in
the twentieth century, *played a pivotal role* in the social, econ
omic, and religious upheavals that occurred during the fifteenth and
sixteenth centuries. The modern nation developed as a result of the
vigorous spirit of nationalism that swept over Europe and led to the
American and French revolutions of the late eighteenth century. In
addition to being a powerful vehicle for spreading ideas about hum
an rights and the sovereignty of the people, typographic printing sta
bilized and unified languages. Illiteracy, the inability to read and
write, began a long, steady decline. Typography radically altered edu
cation. The medieval classroom had been a scriptorium of sorts,
where each student penned his own book. Learning became an incre
asingly private, rather than communal, process. Human dialog, exte

9/9

Typography, the major communications advance between
the invention of writing and the age of electronic mass com
munications in the twentieth century, *played a pivotal role*
in the social, economic, and religious upheavals that occur
red during the fifteenth and sixteenth centuries. The modern
nation developed as a result of the vigorous spirit of nation
alism that swept over Europe and led to the American and
French revolutions of the late eighteenth century. In addition
to being a powerful vehicle for spreading ideas about human
rights and the sovereignty of the people, typographic printing
stabilized and unified languages. Illiteracy, the inability to
read and write, began a long, steady decline. Typography radi
cally altered education. The medieval classroom had been a
scriptorium of sorts, where each student penned his own

8/9

Typography, the major communications advance between the inven
tion of writing and the age of electronic mass communications in
the twentieth century, *played a pivotal role* in the social, econ
omic, and religious upheavals that occurred during the fifteenth and
sixteenth centuries. The modern nation developed as a result of the
vigorous spirit of nationalism that swept over Europe and led to the
American and French revolutions of the late eighteenth century. In
addition to being a powerful vehicle for spreading ideas about hum
an rights and the sovereignty of the people, typographic printing sta
bilized and unified languages. Illiteracy, the inability to read and
write, began a long, steady decline. Typography radically altered edu
cation. The medieval classroom had been a scriptorium of sorts,
where each student penned his own book. Learning became an incre

9/10

Typography, the major communications advance between
the invention of writing and the age of electronic mass com
munications in the twentieth century, *played a pivotal role*
in the social, economic, and religious upheavals that occur
red during the fifteenth and sixteenth centuries. The modern
nation developed as a result of the vigorous spirit of nation
alism that swept over Europe and led to the American and
French revolutions of the late eighteenth century. In addition
to being a powerful vehicle for spreading ideas about human
rights and the sovereignty of the people, typographic printing
stabilized and unified languages. Illiteracy, the inability to
read and write, began a long, steady decline. Typography radi

8/10

Typography, the major communications advance between the inven
tion of writing and the age of electronic mass communications in
the twentieth century, *played a pivotal role* in the social, econ
omic, and religious upheavals that occurred during the fifteenth and
sixteenth centuries. The modern nation developed as a result of the
vigorous spirit of nationalism that swept over Europe and led to the
American and French revolutions of the late eighteenth century. In
addition to being a powerful vehicle for spreading ideas about hum
an rights and the sovereignty of the people, typographic printing sta
bilized and unified languages. Illiteracy, the inability to read and
write, began a long, steady decline. Typography radically altered edu
cation. The medieval classroom had been a scriptorium of sorts,

9/11

Typography, the major communications advance between
the invention of writing and the age of electronic mass com
munications in the twentieth century, *played a pivotal role*
in the social, economic, and religious upheavals that occur
red during the fifteenth and sixteenth centuries. The modern
nation developed as a result of the vigorous spirit of nation
alism that swept over Europe and led to the American and
French revolutions of the late eighteenth century. In addition
to being a powerful vehicle for spreading ideas about human
rights and the sovereignty of the people, typographic printing
stabilized and unified languages. Illiteracy, the inability to

8/11

Typography, the major communications advance between the inven
tion of writing and the age of electronic mass communications in
the twentieth century, *played a pivotal role* in the social, econ
omic, and religious upheavals that occurred during the fifteenth and
sixteenth centuries. The modern nation developed as a result of the
vigorous spirit of nationalism that swept over Europe and led to the
American and French revolutions of the late eighteenth century. In
addition to being a powerful vehicle for spreading ideas about hum
an rights and the sovereignty of the people, typographic printing sta
bilized and unified languages. Illiteracy, the inability to read and
write, began a long, steady decline. Typography radically altered edu

9/12

Typography, the major communications advance between
the invention of writing and the age of electronic mass com
munications in the twentieth century, *played a pivotal role*
in the social, economic, and religious upheavals that occur
red during the fifteenth and sixteenth centuries. The modern
nation developed as a result of the vigorous spirit of nation
alism that swept over Europe and led to the American and
French revolutions of the late eighteenth century. In addition
to being a powerful vehicle for spreading ideas about human
rights and the sovereignty of the people, typographic printing

abcdefghijklmnopqrstuvwxyz
ABCDEFGHIJKLMNOPQRSTUVWXYZ
$1234567890&(.,"";:!?)

abcdefghijklmnopqrstuvwxyz
ABCDEFGHIJKLMNOPQRSTUVWXYZ
$1234567890&(.,"";:!?)

10/10

Typography, the major communications advance betwe en the invention of writing and the age of electronic mass communications in the twentieth century, *played a pivotal role* in the social, economic, and religious upheavals that occurred during the fifteenth and sixteenth centuries. The modern nation developed as a result of the vigorous spirit of nationalism that swept over Europe and led to the American and French revol utions of the late eighteenth century. In addition to being a powerful vehicle for spreading ideas about hum an rights and the sovereignty of the people, typographic

10/11

Typography, the major communications advance betwe en the invention of writing and the age of electronic mass communications in the twentieth century, *played a pivotal role* in the social, economic, and religious upheavals that occurred during the fifteenth and sixteenth centuries. The modern nation developed as a result of the vigorous spirit of nationalism that swept over Europe and led to the American and French revol utions of the late eighteenth century. In addition to being a powerful vehicle for spreading ideas about hum

10/12

Typography, the major communications advance betwe en the invention of writing and the age of electronic mass communications in the twentieth century, *played a pivotal role* in the social, economic, and religious upheavals that occurred during the fifteenth and sixteenth centuries. The modern nation developed as a result of the vigorous spirit of nationalism that swept over Europe and led to the American and French revol utions of the late eighteenth century. In addition to

10/13

Typography, the major communications advance betwe en the invention of writing and the age of electronic mass communications in the twentieth century, *played a pivotal role* in the social, economic, and religious upheavals that occurred during the fifteenth and sixteenth centuries. The modern nation developed as a result of the vigorous spirit of nationalism that swept over Europe and led to the American and French revol utions of the late eighteenth century. In addition to

12/12

Typography, the major communications advan ce between the invention of writing and the age of electronic mass communications in the twe ntieth century, *played a pivotal role* in the so cial, economic, and religious upheavals that oc curred during the fifteenth and sixteenth centuries. The modern nation developed as a result of the vigorous spirit of nationalism that swept over Europe and led to the American

12/13

Typography, the major communications advan ce between the invention of writing and the age of electronic mass communications in the twe ntieth century, *played a pivotal role* in the so cial, economic, and religious upheavals that oc curred during the fifteenth and sixteenth centuries. The modern nation developed as a result of the vigorous spirit of nationalism that swept over Europe and led to the American

12/14

Typography, the major communications advan ce between the invention of writing and the age of electronic mass communications in the twe ntieth century, *played a pivotal role* in the so cial, economic, and religious upheavals that oc curred during the fifteenth and sixteenth centuries. The modern nation developed as a result of the vigorous spirit of nationalism that

12/15

Typography, the major communications advan ce between the invention of writing and the age of electronic mass communications in the twe ntieth century, *played a pivotal role* in the so cial, economic, and religious upheavals that oc curred during the fifteenth and sixteenth centuries. The modern nation developed as a result of the vigorous spirit of nationalism that

Design: **John T. Drew**

Specimens are set in
Linotype Univers

Univers was designed in 1957 by Adrian Frutiger. Relying upon Swiss objectivity, he used a numerical coding system for the twenty-one-member Univers family as a means to clearly distinguish one variation from another and to avoid the confusing descriptions normally found in the industry, such as light, regular, demi, bold, etc. The first digit in each font's number refers to stroke weight, three being the lightest and eight the heaviest. The second digit refers to the width of the letters, revealing expanded and condensed forms. Roman fonts are assigned odd numbers and italics are assigned even numbers. Univers 55 is the book weight and the source from which all other designs were developed. Frutiger intended the variations within the family to be used interchangeably; he carefully balanced the need for unity as well as diversity within the system.

With the design of Univers, Frutiger initiated a trend toward larger x-heights. All strokes within each letter contrast in width only slightly, but the severe geometry of the modern sans serif was replaced with optical subtlety. Other distinguishing characteristics include flat terminals in letters such as **a**, **c**, and **e**; slightly squared appearance as seen in the letter **O**; square dots on the **i** and **j**; and an angled ascender on the **t**. The arm and leg of the **K** join at a single junction, and the **G** does not have a spur.

Frutiger removed from Univers most of the quirky features of the traditional grotesque face and came up with a very legible text and display face. Univers continues to be widely used in signage because of its simplicity and clarity. As a sans-serif text face, it rivals some of the most frequently used serif faces for readability.

ABCDEF
GHIJKM
NOPQRS
TUVWX
YZ&(.,""";:)

abcdefgh
ijklmnop
qrstuvwx
yz$12345
67890!?

abcdefghijklmnopqrstuvwxyz
ABCDEFGHIJKLMNOPQRSTUVWXYZ
$&1234567890(.,""'';:!?)

72

abcdefghijklmnop
qrstuvwxyzABC
DEFGHIJKLMNO
PQRSTUVWXYZ
$&1234567890
(.,""'';:!?)

36

abcdefghijklmnopqrstuvwxyz
ABCDEFGHIJKLMNOPQRSTUVW
XYZ$&1234567890(.,""'';:!?)

abcdefghijklmnopqrstuvwxyz
ABCDEFGHIJKLMNOPQRSTUVWXYZ
$&1234567890(.,""";:!?)

18

72

abcdefghijklmnop
qrstuvwxyzABC
DEFGHIJKLMNO
PQRSTUVWXY
Z$&1234567890
(.,""";:!?)

36

abcdefghijklmnopqrstuvwxyz
ABCDEFGHIJKLMNOPQRSTUVW
XYZ$&1234567890(.,""";:!?)

abcdefghijklmnopqrstuvwxyz
ABCDEFGHIJKLMNOPQRSTUVWXYZ
$&1234567890(.,"";:!?)

72

abcdefghijklmno
pqrstuvwxyzAB
CDEFGHIJKLMN
OPQRSTUVWX
YZ$&123456789
0(.,"";:!?)

36

abcdefghijklmnopqrstuvwxyz
ABCDEFGHIJKLMNOPQRSTUV
WXYZ$&1234567890(.,"";:!?)

abcdefghijklmnopqrstuvwxyz
ABCDEFGHIJKLMNOPQRSTUVWXYZ
$&1234567890(.,"";:!?)

18

72

abcdefghijklmno
pqrstuvwxyzAB
CDEFGHIJKLMN
OPQRSTUVWX
YZ$&123456789
0(.,"";:!?)

36

abcdefghijklmnopqrstuvwxyz
ABCDEFGHIJKLMNOPQRSTUVW
XYZ$&1234567890(.,"";:!?)

abcdefghijklmnopqrstuvwxyz
ABCDEFGHIJKLMNOPQRSTUVWXYZ
$&1234567890(.,"";:!?)

72

abcdefghijklmn
opqrstuvwxyz
ABCDEFGHIJK
LMNOPQRSTU
VWXYZ$&1234
567890(.,"";:!?)

36

abcdefghijklmnopqrstuvwxyz
ABCDEFGHIJKLMNOPQRSTU
VWXYZ$&1234567890(.,"";:!?)

abcdefghijklmnopqrstuvwxyz
ABCDEFGHIJKLMNOPQRSTUVWXYZ
$&1234567890(.,"";:!?)

abcdefghijklmn
opqrstuvwxyz
ABCDEFGHIJK
LMNOPQRSTU
VWXYZ$&1234
567890(.,"";:!?)

abcdefghijklmnopqrstuvwxyz
ABCDEFGHIJKLMNOPQRSTU
VWXYZ$&1234567890(.,"";:!?)

abcdefghijklmnopqrstuvwxyz
ABCDEFGHIJKLMNOPQRSTUVWX
YZ$&1234567890(.,"";:!?)

65

abcdefghijklm
nopqrstuvwxyz
ABCDEFGHIJK
LMNOPQRSTU
VWXYZ$&1234
567890(.,"";:!?)

32

abcdefghijklmnopqrstuvwxyz
ABCDEFGHIJKLMNOPQRSTUV
WXYZ$&1234567890(.,"";:!?)

abcdefghijklmnopqrstuvwxyz
ABCDEFGHIJKLMNOPQRSTUVWX
YZ$&1234567890(.,"";:!?)

18

65

abcdefghijklm
nopqrstuvwxyz
ABCDEFGHIJK
LMNOPQRSTU
VWXYZ$&1234
567890(.,"";:!?)

32

abcdefghijklmnopqrstuvwxyz
ABCDEFGHIJKLMNOPQRSTUV
WXYZ$&1234567890(.,"";:!?)

abcdefghijklmnopqrstuvwxyz
ABCDEFGHIJKLMNOPQRSTUVWXYZ
$&1234567890(.,"";:!?)

72

abcdefghijklmnopqrstuvwxyz
ABCDEFGHIJKLMNOPQRSTUVWXY
Z$&1234567890(.,"";:!?)

36

abcdefghijklmnopqrstuvwxyz
ABCDEFGHIJKLMNOPQRSTUVWXYZ
$&1234567890(.,"";:!?)

abcdefghijklmnopqrstuvwxyz
ABCDEFGHIJKLMNOPQRSTUVWXYZ
$&1234567890(.,"";:!?)

18

72

abcdefghijklmnopqrst
uvwxyzABCDEFGHIJ
KLMNOPQRSTUVWXYZ
$&1234567890(.,"";:!?)

36

abcdefghijklmnopqrstuvwxyz
ABCDEFGHIJKLMNOPQRSTUVWXYZ
$&1234567890(.,"";:!?)

Univers 55

abcdefghijklmnopqrstuvwxyz
ABCDEFGHIJKLMNOPQRSTUVWXYZ
$1234567890&(.,"";:!?)

abcdefghijklmnopqrstuvwxyz
ABCDEFGHIJKLMNOPQRSTUVWXYZ
$1234567890&(.,"";:!?)

8/8

Typography, the major communications advance between the invention of writing and the age of electronic mass communications in the twentieth century, *played a pivotal role* in the social, economic, and religious upheavals that occurred during the fifteenth and sixteenth centuries. The modern nation developed as a result of the vigorous spirit of nationalism that swept over Europe and led to the American and French revolutions of the late eighteenth century. In addition to being a powerful vehicle for spreading ideas about human rights and the sovereignty of the people, typographic printing stabilized and unified languages. Illiteracy, the inability to read and write, began a long, steady decline. Typography radically altered education. The medieval classroom had been a scriptorium of sorts, where each student penned his own book. Learning became an increasingly private, rather than communal, process. Human dialog, extended by type, began to take place on a global scale that

9/9

Typography, the major communications advance between the invention of writing and the age of electronic mass communications in the twentieth century, *played a pivotal role* in the social, economic, and religious upheavals that occurred during the fifteenth and sixteenth centuries. The modern nation developed as a result of the vigorous spirit of nationalism that swept over Europe and led to the American and French revolutions of the late eighteenth century. In addition to being a powerful vehicle for spreading ideas about human rights and the sovereignty of the people, typographic printing stabilized and unified languages. Illiteracy, the inability to read and write, began a long, steady decline. Typography radically altered education. The medieval classro

8/9

Typography, the major communications advance between the invention of writing and the age of electronic mass communications in the twentieth century, *played a pivotal role* in the social, economic, and religious upheavals that occurred during the fifteenth and sixteenth centuries. The modern nation developed as a result of the vigorous spirit of nationalism that swept over Europe and led to the American and French revolutions of the late eighteenth century. In addition to being a powerful vehicle for spreading ideas about human rights and the sovereignty of the people, typographic printing stabilized and unified languages. Illiteracy, the inability to read and write, began a long, steady decline. Typography radically altered education. The medieval classroom had been a scriptorium of sorts, where each student penned his own book. Learning became

9/10

Typography, the major communications advance between the invention of writing and the age of electronic mass communications in the twentieth century, *played a pivotal role* in the social, economic, and religious upheavals that occurred during the fifteenth and sixteenth centuries. The modern nation developed as a result of the vigorous spirit of nationalism that swept over Europe and led to the American and French revolutions of the late eighteenth century. In addition to being a powerful vehicle for spreading ideas about human rights and the sovereignty of the people, typographic printing stabilized and unified languages. Illiteracy, the inability to read and write, began a long, steady decline. Ty

8/10

Typography, the major communications advance between the invention of writing and the age of electronic mass communications in the twentieth century, *played a pivotal role* in the social, economic, and religious upheavals that occurred during the fifteenth and sixteenth centuries. The modern nation developed as a result of the vigorous spirit of nationalism that swept over Europe and led to the American and French revolutions of the late eighteenth century. In addition to being a powerful vehicle for spreading ideas about human rights and the sovereignty of the people, typographic printing stabilized and unified languages. Illiteracy, the inability to read and write, began a long, steady decline. Typography radically altered education. The medieval classroom had been a scriptorium of s

9/11

Typography, the major communications advance between the invention of writing and the age of electronic mass communications in the twentieth century, *played a pivotal role* in the social, economic, and religious upheavals that occurred during the fifteenth and sixteenth centuries. The modern nation developed as a result of the vigorous spirit of nationalism that swept over Europe and led to the American and French revolutions of the late eighteenth century. In addition to being a powerful vehicle for spreading ideas about human rights and the sovereignty of the people, typographic printing stabilized and unified languages. Illiteracy, the

8/11

Typography, the major communications advance between the invention of writing and the age of electronic mass communications in the twentieth century, *played a pivotal role* in the social, economic, and religious upheavals that occurred during the fifteenth and sixteenth centuries. The modern nation developed as a result of the vigorous spirit of nationalism that swept over Europe and led to the American and French revolutions of the late eighteenth century. In addition to being a powerful vehicle for spreading ideas about human rights and the sovereignty of the people, typographic printing stabilized and unified languages. Illiteracy, the inability to read and write, began a long, steady decline. Typography radically alter

9/12

Typography, the major communications advance between the invention of writing and the age of electronic mass communications in the twentieth century, *played a pivotal role* in the social, economic, and religious upheavals that occurred during the fifteenth and sixteenth centuries. The modern nation developed as a result of the vigorous spirit of nationalism that swept over Europe and led to the American and French revolutions of the late eighteenth century. In addition to being a powerful vehicle for spreading ideas about human rights and the sovereignty of the people, typograp

abcdefghijklmnopqrstuvwxyz
ABCDEFGHIJKLMNOPQRSTUVWXYZ
$1234567890&(.,"";:!?)

abcdefghijklmnopqrstuvwxyz
ABCDEFGHIJKLMNOPQRSTUVWXYZ
$1234567890&(.,"";:!?)

10/10

Typography, the major communications advance bet
ween the invention of writing and the age of electron
ic mass communications in the twentieth century, *pl
ayed a pivotal role* in the social, economic, and religi
ous upheavals that occurred during the fifteenth and
sixteenth centuries. The modern nation developed as
a result of the vigorous spirit of nationalism that swe
pt over Europe and led to the American and French r
evolutions of the late eighteenth century. In addition
to being a powerful vehicle for spreading ideas abou
t human rights and the sovereignty of the people, ty
pographic printing stabilized and unified languages. I

12/12

Typography, the major communications adv
ance between the invention of writing and t
he age of electronic mass communications i
n the twentieth century, *played a pivotal rol
e* in the social, economic, and religious uph
eavals that occurred during the fifteenth and
sixteenth centuries. The modern nation dev
eloped as a result of the vigorous spirit of n
ationalism that swept over Europe and led t
o the American and French revolutions of th

10/11

Typography, the major communications advance bet
ween the invention of writing and the age of electron
ic mass communications in the twentieth century, *pl
ayed a pivotal role* in the social, economic, and religi
ous upheavals that occurred during the fifteenth and
sixteenth centuries. The modern nation developed as
a result of the vigorous spirit of nationalism that swe
pt over Europe and led to the American and French r
evolutions of the late eighteenth century. In addition
to being a powerful vehicle for spreading ideas abou
t human rights and the sovereignty of the people, ty

12/13

Typography, the major communications adv
ance between the invention of writing and t
he age of electronic mass communications i
n the twentieth century, *played a pivotal rol
e* in the social, economic, and religious uph
eavals that occurred during the fifteenth and
sixteenth centuries. The modern nation dev
eloped as a result of the vigorous spirit of n
ationalism that swept over Europe and led t

10/12

Typography, the major communications advance bet
ween the invention of writing and the age of electron
ic mass communications in the twentieth century, *pl
ayed a pivotal role* in the social, economic, and religi
ous upheavals that occurred during the fifteenth and
sixteenth centuries. The modern nation developed as
a result of the vigorous spirit of nationalism that swe
pt over Europe and led to the American and French r
evolutions of the late eighteenth century. In addition
to being a powerful vehicle for spreading ideas abou

12/14

Typography, the major communications adv
ance between the invention of writing and t
he age of electronic mass communications i
n the twentieth century, *played a pivotal rol
e* in the social, economic, and religious uph
eavals that occurred during the fifteenth and
sixteenth centuries. The modern nation dev
eloped as a result of the vigorous spirit of n
ationalism that swept over Europe and led t

10/13

Typography, the major communications advance bet
ween the invention of writing and the age of electron
ic mass communications in the twentieth century, *pl
ayed a pivotal role* in the social, economic, and religi
ous upheavals that occurred during the fifteenth and
sixteenth centuries. The modern nation developed as
a result of the vigorous spirit of nationalism that swe
pt over Europe and led to the American and French r
evolutions of the late eighteenth century. In addition

12/15

Typography, the major communications adv
ance between the invention of writing and t
he age of electronic mass communications i
n the twentieth century, *played a pivotal rol
e* in the social, economic, and religious uph
eavals that occurred during the fifteenth and
sixteenth centuries. The modern nation dev
eloped as a result of the vigorous spirit of n

abcdefghijklmnopqrstuvwxyz
ABCDEFGHIJKLMNOPQRSTUVWXYZ
$1234567890&(.,"";:!?)

abcdefghijklmnopqrstuvwxyz
ABCDEFGHIJKLMNOPQRSTUVWXYZ
$1234567890&(.,"";:!?)

8/8

Typography, **the major communications advance between the inve ntion of writing and the age of electronic mass communications i n the twentieth century,** *played a pivotal role* in the social, econo mic, and religious upheavals that occurred during the fifteenth an d sixteenth centuries. The modern nation developed as a result of the vigorous spirit of nationalism that swept over Europe and led to the American and French revolutions of the late eighteenth cen tury. In addition to being a powerful vehicle for spreading ideas a bout human rights and the sovereignty of the people, typographi c printing stabilized and unified languages. Illiteracy, the inability to read and write, began a long, steady decline. Typography radic ally altered education. The medieval classroom had been a scripto rium of sorts, where each student penned his own book. Learning became an increasingly private, rather than communal, process. Human dialog, extended by type, began to take place on a global

9/9

Typography, **the major communications advance between t he invention of writing and the age of electronic mass co mmunications in the twentieth century,** *played a pivotal r ole* in the social, economic, and religious upheavals that o ccurred during the fifteenth and sixteenth centuries. The modern nation developed as a result of the vigorous spirit of nationalism that swept over Europe and led to the Ame rican and French revolutions of the late eighteenth centur y. In addition to being a powerful vehicle for spreading ide as about human rights and the sovereignty of the people, typographic printing stabilized and unified languages. Illite racy, the inability to read and write, began a long, steady decline. Typography radically altered education. The medi

8/9

Typography, **the major communications advance between the inve ntion of writing and the age of electronic mass communications i n the twentieth century,** *played a pivotal role* in the social, econo mic, and religious upheavals that occurred during the fifteenth an d sixteenth centuries. The modern nation developed as a result of the vigorous spirit of nationalism that swept over Europe and led to the American and French revolutions of the late eighteenth cen tury. In addition to being a powerful vehicle for spreading ideas a bout human rights and the sovereignty of the people, typographi c printing stabilized and unified languages. Illiteracy, the inability to read and write, began a long, steady decline. Typography radic ally altered education. The medieval classroom had been a scripto rium of sorts, where each student penned his own book. Learning

9/10

Typography, **the major communications advance between t he invention of writing and the age of electronic mass co mmunications in the twentieth century,** *played a pivotal r ole* in the social, economic, and religious upheavals that o ccurred during the fifteenth and sixteenth centuries. The modern nation developed as a result of the vigorous spirit of nationalism that swept over Europe and led to the Ame rican and French revolutions of the late eighteenth centur y. In addition to being a powerful vehicle for spreading ide as about human rights and the sovereignty of the people, typographic printing stabilized and unified languages. Illite racy, the inability to read and write, began a long, steady

8/10

Typography, **the major communications advance between the inve ntion of writing and the age of electronic mass communications i n the twentieth century,** *played a pivotal role* in the social, econo mic, and religious upheavals that occurred during the fifteenth an d sixteenth centuries. The modern nation developed as a result of the vigorous spirit of nationalism that swept over Europe and led to the American and French revolutions of the late eighteenth cen tury. In addition to being a powerful vehicle for spreading ideas a bout human rights and the sovereignty of the people, typographi c printing stabilized and unified languages. Illiteracy, the inability to read and write, began a long, steady decline. Typography radic ally altered education. The medieval classroom had been a scripto

9/11

Typography, **the major communications advance between t he invention of writing and the age of electronic mass co mmunications in the twentieth century,** *played a pivotal r ole* in the social, economic, and religious upheavals that o ccurred during the fifteenth and sixteenth centuries. The modern nation developed as a result of the vigorous spirit of nationalism that swept over Europe and led to the Ame rican and French revolutions of the late eighteenth centur y. In addition to being a powerful vehicle for spreading ide as about human rights and the sovereignty of the people, typographic printing stabilized and unified languages. Illite

8/11

Typography, **the major communications advance between the inve ntion of writing and the age of electronic mass communications i n the twentieth century,** *played a pivotal role* in the social, econo mic, and religious upheavals that occurred during the fifteenth an d sixteenth centuries. The modern nation developed as a result of the vigorous spirit of nationalism that swept over Europe and led to the American and French revolutions of the late eighteenth cen tury. In addition to being a powerful vehicle for spreading ideas a bout human rights and the sovereignty of the people, typographi c printing stabilized and unified languages. Illiteracy, the inability to read and write, began a long, steady decline. Typography radic

9/12

Typography, **the major communications advance between t he invention of writing and the age of electronic mass co mmunications in the twentieth century,** *played a pivotal r ole* in the social, economic, and religious upheavals that o ccurred during the fifteenth and sixteenth centuries. The modern nation developed as a result of the vigorous spirit of nationalism that swept over Europe and led to the Ame rican and French revolutions of the late eighteenth centur y. In addition to being a powerful vehicle for spreading ide as about human rights and the sovereignty of the people,

abcdefghijklmnopqrstuvwxyz
ABCDEFGHIJKLMNOPQRSTUVWXYZ
$1234567890&(.,"";:!?)

abcdefghijklmnopqrstuvwxyz
ABCDEFGHIJKLMNOPQRSTUVWXYZ
$1234567890&(.,"";:!?)

10/10

Typography, **the major communications advance bet ween the invention of writing and the age of electro nic mass communications in the twentieth century,** *played a pivotal role* **in the social, economic, and reli gious upheavals that occurred during the fifteenth a nd sixteenth centuries. The modern nation develope d as a result of the vigorous spirit of nationalism tha t swept over Europe and led to the American and Fr ench revolutions of the late eighteenth century. In a ddition to being a powerful vehicle for spreading ide as about human rights and the sovereignty of the p eople, typographic printing stabilized and unified lan**

10/11

Typography, **the major communications advance bet ween the invention of writing and the age of electro nic mass communications in the twentieth century,** *played a pivotal role* **in the social, economic, and reli gious upheavals that occurred during the fifteenth a nd sixteenth centuries. The modern nation develope d as a result of the vigorous spirit of nationalism tha t swept over Europe and led to the American and Fr ench revolutions of the late eighteenth century. In a ddition to being a powerful vehicle for spreading ide as about human rights and the sovereignty of the p**

10/12

Typography, **the major communications advance bet ween the invention of writing and the age of electro nic mass communications in the twentieth century,** *played a pivotal role* **in the social, economic, and reli gious upheavals that occurred during the fifteenth a nd sixteenth centuries. The modern nation develope d as a result of the vigorous spirit of nationalism tha t swept over Europe and led to the American and Fr ench revolutions of the late eighteenth century. In a ddition to being a powerful vehicle for spreading ide**

10/13

Typography, **the major communications advance bet ween the invention of writing and the age of electro nic mass communications in the twentieth century,** *played a pivotal role* **in the social, economic, and reli gious upheavals that occurred during the fifteenth a nd sixteenth centuries. The modern nation develope d as a result of the vigorous spirit of nationalism tha t swept over Europe and led to the American and Fr ench revolutions of the late eighteenth century. In a**

12/12

Typography, **the major communications adva nce between the invention of writing and th e age of electronic mass communications in the twentieth century,** *played a pivotal role* **in the social, economic, and religious uphea vals that occurred during the fifteenth and s ixteenth centuries. The modern nation deve loped as a result of the vigorous spirit of na tionalism that swept over Europe and led to the American and French revolutions of the**

12/13

Typography, **the major communications adva nce between the invention of writing and th e age of electronic mass communications in the twentieth century,** *played a pivotal role* **in the social, economic, and religious uphea vals that occurred during the fifteenth and s ixteenth centuries. The modern nation deve loped as a result of the vigorous spirit of na tionalism that swept over Europe and led to**

12/14

Typography, **the major communications adva nce between the invention of writing and th e age of electronic mass communications in the twentieth century,** *played a pivotal role* **in the social, economic, and religious uphea vals that occurred during the fifteenth and s ixteenth centuries. The modern nation deve loped as a result of the vigorous spirit of na tionalism that swept over Europe and led to**

12/15

Typography, **the major communications adva nce between the invention of writing and th e age of electronic mass communications in the twentieth century,** *played a pivotal role* **in the social, economic, and religious uphea vals that occurred during the fifteenth and s ixteenth centuries. The modern nation deve loped as a result of the vigorous spirit of na**

hnkb
dpgrt

abcdefghijklmnopqrstuvwxyz
ABCDEFGHIJKLMNOPQRSTUVWXYZ
& 1234567890   ITC Zapf Book Light

The *quick* **brown** fox
jumps over the *lazy* dog.

abcdefghijklmnopqrstuvwxyz
ABCDEFGHIJKLMNOPQRSTUVWXYZ
& 1234567890   ITC Zapf Book Light Italic

Design: **Hermann Zapf**

Specimens are set in
ITC Zapf Book

Zapf Book was designed by Hermann Zapf, one of this century's most revered type designers and calligraphers. It was released in 1976 by the International Typeface Corporation and has since been licensed to a great many type manufacturers. The Zapf Book family, which consists of light, medium, demi, and heavy variations and accompanying italics, is a blend of three typefaces: Walbaum, Bodoni, and Melior. The latter typeface was also designed by Zapf in 1952. Zapf's primary design objective was to combine the spirit of Modern styles with a calligraphic flair.

The proportions of Zapf Book letters provide an even texture and pleasing color that encourage readability. The vertical stress of the letters echoes the formal qualities of Walbaum and Bodoni, yet the squarishness of the rounded characters point to the calligraphic features of Melior. Other calligraphic references are seen in the tail of the **Q** and the ear of the lowercase **g**. The face has a comfortable x-height, and the unbracketed serifs are horizontal and thin. Zapf Book Italic is cursive in form, with a swashlike lowercase *g* and *x*. The stroke terminals of the italic are anchored to the baseline rather that swinging up as in a traditional cursive.

Zapf Book invites readers with openness and spontaneity, and it is suitable for applications that require a sophisticated yet friendly presence. It is not an overbearing typeface, but it does command respect and attention. Used in combination, the variants of Zapf Book provide designers with enough contrast to achieve an effective typographic hierarchy. Zapf Book is a versatile typeface that is currently used as text type for everything from books and magazines to advertising.

ABCDEF
GHIJKL
MNOPQR
STUVWX
YZ&(,""";:)

abcdefgh
ijklmnop
qrstuvwx
yz$12345
67890!?

abcdefghijklmnopqrstuvwxyz
ABCDEFGHIJKLMNOPQRSTUVWXYZ
$&1234567890(.,"";:!?)

72

abcdefghijklmno
pqrstuvwxyzAB
CDEFGHIJKLM
NOPQRSTUVWX
YZ$&123456780
(.,"";:!?)

36

abcdefghijklmnopqrstuvwxyz
ABCDEFGHIJKLMNOPQRSTUWX
YZ$&1234567890(.,"";:!?)

abcdefghijklmnopqrstuvwxyz
ABCDEFGHIJKLMNOPQRSTUVWXYZ
$&1234567890(.,""::!?)

18

72

abcdefghijklmno
pqrstuvwxyzAB
CDEFGHIJKLMN
OPQRSTUVWX
YZ$&1234567890
(.,"";::!?)

36

abcdefghijklmnopqrstuvwxyz
ABCDEFGHIJKLMNOPQRSTUVW
XYZ$&1234567890(.,"";::!?)

abcdefghijklmnopqrstuvwxyz
ABCDEFGHIJKLMNOPQRSTUVWXYZ
$&1234567890(.,"";:!?)

72

abcdefghijklmno
pqrstuvwxyzAB
CDEFGHIJKLM
NOPQRSTUVWX
YZ$&123456780
(.,"";:!?)

36

abcdefghijklmnopqrstuvwxyz
ABCDEFGHIJKLMNOPQRSTUWX
YZ$&1234567890(.,"";:!?)

Zapf Book Medium Italic

abcdefghijklmnopqrstuvwxyz
ABCDEFGHIJKLMNOPQRSTUVWXYZ
$&1234567890(.,"";:!?)

18

72

abcdefghijklmn
opqrstuvwxyzAB
CDEFGHIJKLM
NOPQRSTUVWX
YZ$&1234567890
(.,"";:!?)

36

abcdefghijklmnopqrstuvwxyz
ABCDEFGHIJKLMNOPQRSTUVW
XYZ$&1234567890(.,"";:!?)

abcdefghijklmnopqrstuvwxyz
ABCDEFGHIJKLMNOPQRSTUVWXYZ
$&1234567890(.,“”;:!?)

70

abcdefghijklmn
opqrstuvwxyzA
BCDEFGHIJKL
MNOPQRSTUV
WXYZ$&123456
7890(.,“ ”;:!?)

36

abcdefghijklmnopqrstuvwxyz
ABCDEFGHIJKLMNOPQRSTU
VWXYZ$&1234567890(.,“”;:!?)

abcdefghijklmnopqrstuvwxyz
ABCDEFGHIJKLMNOPQRSTUVWXYZ
$&1234567890(.,"";::!?)

18

70

abcdefghijklmn
opqrstuvwxyzA
BCDEFGHIJKL
MNOPQRSTUV
WXYZ$&123456
7890(.,"";::!?)

36

abcdefghijklmnopqrstuvwxyz
ABCDEFGHIJKLMNOPQRSTUV
WXYZ$&1234567890(.,"";::!?)

abcdefghijklmnopqrstuvwxyz
ABCDEFGHIJKLMNOPQRSTUVWXYZ
$&1234567890(.,"";:!?)

65

abcdefghijklmn
opqrstuvwxyz
ABCDEFGHIJKL
MNOPQRSTUV
WXYZ$&123456
7890(.,"";:!?)

32

abcdefghijklmnopqrstuvwxyz
ABCDEFGHIJKLMNOPQRSTUVW
XYZ$&1234567890(.,"";:!?)

abcdefghijklmnopqrstuvwxyz
ABCDEFGHIJKLMNOPQRSTUVWXYZ
$&1234567890(.,"";:!?)

18

65

abcdefghijklmno
pqrstuvwxyz
ABCDEFGHIJKL
MNOPQRSTUV
WXYZ$&123456
7890(.,"";:!?)

32

abcdefghijklmnopqrstuvwxyz
ABCDEFGHIJKLMNOPQRSTUVW
XYZ$&1234567890(.,"";:!?)

Zapf Book Medium

abcdefghijklmnopqrstuvwxyz
ABCDEFGHIJKLMNOPQRSTUVWXYZ
$1234567890&(.,"";:!?)

abcdefghijklmnopqrstuvwxyz
ABCDEFGHIJKLMNOPQRSTUVWXYZ
$1234567890&(.,"";:!?)

8/8

Typography, the major communications advance between the inventi on of writing and the age of electronic mass communications in the tw entieth century, *played a pivotal role* in the social, economic, and religi ous upheavals that occurred during the fifteenth and sixteenth centuri es. The modern nation developed as a result of the vigorous spirit of n ationalism that swept over Europe and led to the American and Frenc h revolutions of the late eighteenth century. In addition to being a pow erful vehicle for spreading ideas about human rights and the sovereign ty of the people, typographic printing stabilized and unified languages. Illiteracy, the inability to read and write, began a long, steady decline. T ypography radically altered education. The medieval classroom had be en a scriptorium of sorts, where each student penned his own book. L earning became an increasingly private, rather than communal, proce ss. Human dialog, extended by type, began to take place on a global sca le that bridged time and space. Gutenber g's invention was the first me

9/9

Typography, the major communications advance between th e invention of writing and the age of electronic mass communi cations in the twentieth century, *played a pivotal role* in the soc ial, economic, and religious upheavals that occurred during th e fifteenth and sixteenth centuries. The modern nation develo ped as a result of the vigorous spirit of nationalism that swept over Europe and led to the American and French revolutions o f the late eighteenth century. In addition to being a powerful ve hicle for spreading ideas about human rights and the sovereig nty of the people, typographic printing stabilized and unified la nguages. Illiteracy, the inability to read and write, began a long, steady decline. Typography radically altered education. The m edieval classroom had been a scriptori um of sorts, where eac

8/9

Typography, the major communications advance between the inventi on of writing and the age of electronic mass communications in the tw entieth century, *played a pivotal role* in the social, economic, and religi ous upheavals that occurred during the fifteenth and sixteenth centuri es. The modern nation developed as a result of the vigorous spirit of n ationalism that swept over Europe and led to the American and Frenc h revolutions of the late eighteenth century. In addition to being a pow erful vehicle for spreading ideas about human rights and the sovereign ty of the people, typographic printing stabilized and unified languages. Illiteracy, the inability to read and write, began a long, steady decline. T ypography radically altered education. The medieval classroom had be en a scriptorium of sorts, where each student penned his own book. L earning became an increasingly private, rather than communal, proce

9/10

Typography, the major communications advance between th e invention of writing and the age of electronic mass communi cations in the twentieth century, *played a pivotal role* in the soc ial, economic, and religious upheavals that occurred during th e fifteenth and sixteenth centuries. The modern nation develo ped as a result of the vigorous spirit of nationalism that swept over Europe and led to the American and French revolutions o f the late eighteenth century. In addition to being a powerful ve hicle for spreading ideas about human rights and the sovereig nty of the people, typographic printing stabilized and unified la nguages. Illiteracy, the inability to read and write, began a long, steady decline. Typography radically altered education. The m

8/10

Typography, the major communications advance between the inventi on of writing and the age of electronic mass communications in the tw entieth century, *played a pivotal role* in the social, economic, and religi ous upheavals that occurred during the fifteenth and sixteenth centuri es. The modern nation developed as a result of the vigorous spirit of n ationalism that swept over Europe and led to the American and Frenc h revolutions of the late eighteenth century. In addition to being a pow erful vehicle for spreading ideas about human rights and the sovereign ty of the people, typographic printing stabilized and unified languages. Illiteracy, the inability to read and write, began a long, steady decline. T ypography radically altered education. The medieval classroom had be en a scriptorium of sorts, where each student penned his own book. L

9/11

Typography, the major communications advance between th e invention of writing and the age of electronic mass communi cations in the twentieth century, *played a pivotal role* in the soc ial, economic, and religious upheavals that occurred during th e fifteenth and sixteenth centuries. The modern nation develo ped as a result of the vigorous spirit of nationalism that swept over Europe and led to the American and French revolutions o f the late eighteenth century. In addition to being a powerful ve hicle for spreading ideas about human rights and the sovereig nty of the people, typographic printing stabilized and unified la nguages. Illiteracy, the inability to read and write, began a long,

8/11

Typography, the major communications advance between the inventi on of writing and the age of electronic mass communications in the tw entieth century, *played a pivotal role* in the social, economic, and religi ous upheavals that occurred during the fifteenth and sixteenth centuri es. The modern nation developed as a result of the vigorous spirit of n ationalism that swept over Europe and led to the American and Frenc h revolutions of the late eighteenth century. In addition to being a pow erful vehicle for spreading ideas about human rights and the sovereign ty of the people, typographic printing stabilized and unified languages. Illiteracy, the inability to read and write, began a long, steady decline. T ypography radically altered education. The medieval classroom had be

9/12

Typography, the major communications advance between th e invention of writing and the age of electronic mass communi cations in the twentieth century, *played a pivotal role* in the soc ial, economic, and religious upheavals that occurred during th e fifteenth and sixteenth centuries. The modern nation develo ped as a result of the vigorous spirit of nationalism that swept over Europe and led to the American and French revolutions o f the late eighteenth century. In addition to being a powerful ve hicle for spreading ideas about human rights and the sovereig nty of the people, typographic printing stabilized and unified la

abcdefghijklmnopqrstuvwxyz
ABCDEFGHIJKLMNOPQRSTUVWXYZ
$1234567890&(.,""%;:!?)

abcdefghijklmnopqrstuvwxyz
ABCDEFGHIJKLMNOPQRSTUVWXYZ
$1234567890&(.,""%;:!?)

10/10

Typography, the major communications advance betw een the invention of writing and the age of electronic ma ss communications in the twentieth century, *played a piv otal role* in the social, economic, and religious upheavals that occurred during the fifteenth and sixteenth centurie s. The modern nation developed as a result of the vigoro us spirit of nationalism that swept over Europe and led t o the American and French revolutions of the late eighte enth century. In addition to being a powerful vehicle for spreading ideas about human rights and the sovereignty of the people, typographic printing stabilized and unifie d languages. Illiteracy, the inability to read and write, be

---

12/12

Typography, the major communications adva nce between the invention of writing and the a ge of electronic mass communications in the t wentieth century, *played a pivotal role* in the so cial, economic, and religious upheavals that oc curred during the fifteenth and sixteenth centu ries. The modern nation developed as a result of the vigorous spirit of nationalism that swept over Europe and led to the American and Fren ch revolutions of the late eighteenth century. I

10/11

Typography, the major communications advance betw een the invention of writing and the age of electronic ma ss communications in the twentieth century, *played a piv otal role* in the social, economic, and religious upheavals that occurred during the fifteenth and sixteenth centurie s. The modern nation developed as a result of the vigoro us spirit of nationalism that swept over Europe and led t o the American and French revolutions of the late eighte enth century. In addition to being a powerful vehicle for spreading ideas about human rights and the sovereignty of the people, typographic printing stabilized and unifie

---

12/13

Typography, the major communications adva nce between the invention of writing and the a ge of electronic mass communications in the t wentieth century, *played a pivotal role* in the so cial, economic, and religious upheavals that oc curred during the fifteenth and sixteenth centu ries. The modern nation developed as a result of the vigorous spirit of nationalism that swept over Europe and led to the American and Fren

---

10/12

Typography, the major communications advance betw een the invention of writing and the age of electronic ma ss communications in the twentieth century, *played a piv otal role* in the social, economic, and religious upheavals that occurred during the fifteenth and sixteenth centurie s. The modern nation developed as a result of the vigoro us spirit of nationalism that swept over Europe and led t o the American and French revolutions of the late eighte enth century. In addition to being a powerful vehicle for spreading ideas about human rights and the sovereignty

---

12/14

Typography, the major communications adva nce between the invention of writing and the a ge of electronic mass communications in the t wentieth century, *played a pivotal role* in the so cial, economic, and religious upheavals that oc curred during the fifteenth and sixteenth centu ries. The modern nation developed as a result of the vigorous spirit of nationalism that swept over Europe and led to the American and Fren

---

10/13

Typography, the major communications advance betw een the invention of writing and the age of electronic ma ss communications in the twentieth century, *played a piv otal role* in the social, economic, and religious upheavals that occurred during the fifteenth and sixteenth centurie s. The modern nation developed as a result of the vigoro us spirit of nationalism that swept over Europe and led t o the American and French revolutions of the late eighte enth century. In addition to being a powerful vehicle for

---

12/15

Typography, the major communications adva nce between the invention of writing and the a ge of electronic mass communications in the t wentieth century, *played a pivotal role* in the so cial, economic, and religious upheavals that oc curred during the fifteenth and sixteenth centu ries. The modern nation developed as a result of the vigorous spirit of nationalism that swept

Sources for quotations and images

The quotation used for the text type specimens is from page 73 of *A History of Graphic Design,* Second Edition, by Philip B. Meggs, used by courtesy of the publisher, Van Nostrand Reinhold, New York.

The John Baskerville quotation on page 30 is from the preface of his 1768 edition of *Milton.*

On page 70 the main body text is from "Steps in the Development of Caledonia, An Account by the Designer," the original promotional brochure published by Mergenthaler Linotype Company circa 1941.

The brief biography of W.A. Dwiggins on page 70 is from "The Work of W.A. Dwiggins" by Philip Hofer, published in *The Dolphin,* No. 2, 1935. The brief quotation at the bottom of page 70 is by Rudolph Ruzicka, reprinted in *Twentieth Century Type Designers* by Sebastian Carter, Taplinger Publishing Company, 1987.

The 1933 title page from *Fra Luca de Pacioli of Borgo S. Sepolcro* – designed by Bruce Rogers and reproduced on page 90 – is used by permission of the publisher, The Grolier Club, New York.

The 1958 graphic design by Bradbury Thompson on page 118 from *Westvaco Inspirations No. 210,* page 4198, is reproduced by permission of Westvaco.

The sample page and text on page 218 are from *The Elements of Lettering* by Frederic W. Goudy, 1922.

The quotation on page 302 is from *An Account of Calligraphy and Printing in the Sixteenth Century, from dialogues attributed to Christophe Plantin* and published by him at Antwerp in 1567. This English translation by Ray Nash was published by the Liturgical Arts Society, New York, 1949.

The quotation on page 372 is from *Pierre and Jean* by Guy de Maupassant, from the English translation by Leonard Tancock for Penguin Books, 1979.

The initial *N* with fish image reproduced on page 292 was drawn by Eric Gill for *The Four Gospels.* The quotation from *The Passion of Perpetua* reprinted on page 292 was translated by W.H. Shewring and is from *The Fleuron,* Vol. 7, The Cambridge University Press, 1930. The quotation about Eric Gill by Beatrice Warde on page 292 is from *The Fleuron,* Vol. 7, The Cambridge University Press, 1930.

Music and lyrics for "Let's Call the Whole Thing Off", page 60, are by George Gershwin and Ira Gershwin. © 1936 (renewed) George Gershwin Music & Ira Gershwin Music. All rights on behalf of George Gershwin Music & Ira Gershwin Music. Administered by WB Music Corporation. All rights reserved.

Adobe Systems, Incorporated
P.O. Box 6458
Salinas, CA 93912-6458

1 800 64-ADOBE

Bitstream Inc.
215 First Street
Cambridge, MA 02142

1 800 237-3335

Carter & Cone Type Inc.
2155 Massachusetts Avenue
Cambridge, MA 02140

1 617 876-5447

Linotype-Hell Company
425 Oser Avenue
Hauppauge, NY 11788

1 800 633-1900

Monotype Typography, Inc.
Suite 504
53 West Jackson Boulevard
Chicago, Il 60604

1 800 MONOTYPE